"This is a stimulating and accessible approach to the Viking Age. Focusing on Vikings as Christian rulers and their followers opens up the question of just what we mean when we think of 'Vikings'. Violent barbarians of legend have their place in this book but the authors look deeper at what it meant to live and prosper in early medieval societies, taking the 'end' of the Viking Age beyond where it is often assumed to be and ensuring that the story is told in terms which make it a truly international one."

Dr Ryan Lavelle, Reader in Early Medieval History, University of Winchester

Also by Martyn Whittock and Hannah Whittock
The Viking Blitzkrieg, 789–1098 AD
The Anglo-Saxon Avon Valley Frontier
1016 & 1066: Why the Vikings caused the Norman Conquest
Norse Myths and Legends

THE Vikings

From Odin to Christ

MARTYN WHITTOCK
& HANNAH WHITTOCK

LION

In memory of the, often-forgotten, Christian Vikings:

"Fram kristmenn, krossmenn, kongsmenn alle!"
("Onward, Christ's men, cross men, king's men all!"
The battle cry of the army of Olaf Haraldson, 1030.)

And to Enrico. From a time when Western
Christendom was united.

Published by

Lion Hudson Limited

Wilkinson House, Jordan Hill Business Park

Banbury Road, Oxford OX2 8DR, England

www.lionhudson.com

Hardback ISBN 978 0 74598 020 1
Paperback ISBN 978 0 74598 018 8
e-ISBN 978 0 74598 019 5

First edition 2018

Acknowledgements

Scripture quotations taken from *The Holy Bible, New Revised Standard Version
(Anglicised Edition)*, Oxford: Oxford University Press, 1995.

Extracts from D. Whitelock (ed.), *English Historical Documents*, Volume I, c.500–1042,
London: Routledge, 2nd edn, 1996, reprinted with permission from
Taylor & Francis Group.

A catalogue record for this book is available from the British Library.

Printed and bound in the UK, May 2018, LH26.

Contents

Western Settlement

Greenland

Middle
Settlement

Skrælingjar

Eastern
Settlement

NORWEGIAN
SEA

Vinland
(North America)

Iceland

Faroes

Shetland

ATLANTIC
OCEAN

Hebrides

Orkneys

NORTH
SEA

Ireland

Wales   England

Frisia

Normandy

France

**Scandinavian
Settlement**

eighth century

ninth century

tenth century

eleventh century

denotes areas subjected to
frequent Viking raids but
with little or no Scandinavian
settlement

Iberian
Kingdoms

al Andalus

Saami (Lapps)

Permia (Bjarmland)

Norway

Finns

Sweden

Chuds

Rus'
States

Volga
Bulgars

Skane

Letts

Lithuanians

Denmark

Prus

Wends

East Slavs

West Slavs

Khazar
Khaganate

CASPIAN
SEA

Bulgars

South Slavs

BLACK SEA

Shirvia

Daylam

Italy

Byzantine Empire

Africa

Sicily

Abbasid
Caliphate

MEDITERRANEAN SEA

Timeline of Key Events

650 Scandinavian merchants present in eastern Baltic settlements of the Slavs and Balts

750 By this date, Scandinavians had settled in the Finnish trading settlement of Staraja Ladoga on the River Volkhov

789 First recorded Viking raid on England, at Portland, Dorset

792 Offa of Mercia upgrades coastal defences

793 Viking attack on Lindisfarne

795 Vikings burn the Irish monastery at Rathlin and the church on Lambey Island

826 Harald Klak of Denmark baptized in Mainz, but driven out by pagan Danes in 827

829 Missionary, Anskar, preaches and converts a number of Swedes in Birka

830 Civil war in Frankish Empire attracts Viking raiders

Viking explorers from Sweden establish direct contact with Arab traders on the Volga and with the Byzantine Empire at Constantinople

834 Vikings raid Dorestad, Netherlands (raided again in 846)

836 Vikings sack the Irish monastery of Clonmacnoise

841 Grant of Island of Walcheren, Netherlands, to Viking settlers

Vikings establish a port and base at Dublin

842 Vikings devastate London, Rochester and Quentovic (France)

845 Swedish pagan reaction to Christianity leads to expulsion of Bishop Gautbert

847 Vikings face defeats in Ireland

849 Irish army sacks Viking base of Dublin and many Vikings shift their operations to Francia and then to England

851 Norwegian Viking, Olaf the White, declares himself king of Dublin

862 Traditional date for establishment of Viking rule in the east at Novgorod, Beloozero and Izborsk – the *Rus*

866 The *micel hæðen here* arrives in East Anglia

867 Vikings seize York

870 Martyrdom of King Edmund of East Anglia

Start of significant Norse migration to settle Iceland (started piecemeal in the 860s)

872 Harald Finehair unites Norway under his rule, after the Battle of Hafrsfjord

874 Vikings occupy Mercian royal centre at Repton

875 Final abandonment of the monastery on Lindisfarne

878 Alfred the Great almost captured, but fights back and defeats Vikings under Guthrum

880 Guthrum returns to East Anglia and shares out the land

882 Viking Rus seize control of Kiev in the Ukraine

886 Vikings besiege Paris

896 Viking raiders withdraw from England in the face of Alfred's defences

902 Vikings temporarily expelled from Dublin

911 Viking raider, Rollo, granted land in Normandy

914 End of the Forty Years Rest in Ireland, as Viking raids escalate once more

917 Norwegian Vikings back in control of Dublin

918 Death of Æthelflæd, the Lady of the Mercians, who had led the fight back against theVikings in the Midlands in alliance with her brother, King Edward the Elder

936 Vikings driven out of Brittany

937 Athelstan decisively defeats Viking, Scots, Welsh alliance at Battle of Brunanburh

Viking Olaf Guthfrithson of Dublin defeats the fleet of the Limerick Vikings

941 Irish king of the Northern *Úi Néill* attacks Viking settlements in the Hebrides

954 Death of Erik Bloodaxe, Viking king of York

960 Start of Silver Famine

963 Harald Bluetooth of Denmark converts to Christianity

980 Start of Christian missionary activity in Iceland

983 Erik the Red first visits Greenland, from Iceland

987 Norman, Count Richard I, the Fearless, becomes virtually independent of Frankish king

989 Sihtric II, Olafson, also known as Silkenbeard, becomes king of Dublin

Vladimir of Kiev Rus converts to Christianity

994 Conversion of Olaf Tryggvason of Norway, while in England

995 Olaf Tryggvason converts Orkney, then Norway, to Christianity

Olof *Skötkonung* of Sweden begins minting coins carrying Christian symbols

996 Completion of the Church of the Tithe in Kiev

1034–41 Harald Hardrada of Norway serves in the Byzantine Varangian Guard

1035 Death of Cnut the Great

William becomes duke of Normandy

1042 Edward the Confessor becomes king of England

End of the Anglo-Danish North Sea Empire

1048 Bishop established at Birsay, Orkney, by Jarl Thorfinn Sigurdarson, the Mighty

1050 Bishops once again established in Sweden

1052 Diarmait, Irish king of Leinster, seizes Dublin from the Norse

1066 Harald Hardrada of Norway invades England, and is killed at the Battle of Stamford Bridge

William of Normandy invades England, and is victorious at the Battle of Hastings

1080 End of royal involvement in pagan cults at Swedish cult centre at Uppsala

1086 Dublin becomes the capital of the Irish ruler Muirchertach, king of Munster and overlord of Ireland

1098 Magnus Barelegs, king of Norway, campaigns down the Irish Sea

1107 Norwegian king Sigurd *Jorsalafari* leads crusade to the Holy Land

1123 Sigurd *Jorsalafari* of Norway leads a crusade into southern Sweden against pagans in Småland

1124 First bishop of Garðar ordained for Greenland

1136 Novgorod breaks free from rule of Kiev

1147 Danes cooperate with German Saxons against the pagan Wends

1153 Eystein of Norway leads the last recorded Viking raid from Norway against England

1156 Somerled seizes the Kingdom of the Isles

1158 Somerled devastates the Isle of Man

1160–1220 Danes campaign across the southern Baltic as far as Estonia

1164 Following the death of Somerled, his extended sea-king empire disintegrates

1171 Dublin falls to the Anglo-Normans

1172 Official union of the *Svear* and *Götar* in Sweden

1240 Kiev Rus falls to the Mongols

1261 Norway takes control of Greenland

1263 Norway takes control of Iceland

1266 The Norse Western Isles become part of the kingdom of Scots

1292 Swedish expansion into north-west Russia blocked by Novgorod

1293 Final Swedish crusade to convert Finland

Key People

Ælfgifu of Northampton: one of the two wives of **Cnut the Great** (the other being **Emma of Normandy**), mother of **Harald Harefoot** and **Svein Cnutson** (died 1040)

Ælle: king of Northumbria, killed by Vikings (a later legend claimed he was subject to the "blood eagle") (died 867)

Æthelflæd: the Lady of the Mercians, sister of **Alfred the Great**, led the fight back against the Vikings in the Midlands (died 918)

Æthelred II: (also known as Æthelred *unræd* or Æthelred the unready) king of Anglo-Saxon England, married **Emma of Normandy** (the sister of Duke **Richard II, the Good**) (died 1016)

Æthelweard: compiler of the tenth-century English source *Æthelweard's Chronicle*

Adam of Bremen: German chronicler who wrote about the conversion of Scandinavia, compiler of the *Gesta Hammaburgensis ecclesiae pontificum* (*Deeds of Bishops of the Hamburg Church*), written c. 1070 (died in the 1080s)

Alcuin of York: Northumbrian churchman, and scholar, living at the court of the Frankish ruler when Lindisfarne was sacked (died 804)

Alexander II: pope who granted a papal banner to **William of Normandy** (died 1073)

Alfred the Great: king of Wessex (died 899)

Anskar: often called the Apostle of Scandinavia, first archbishop of Hamburg (died 865)

Ari Thorgilson: early-twelfth-century compiler of *Íslendingabók* (*Book of Icelanders*)

Asser: Welsh bishop and biographer of **Alfred the Great** (died c. 909)

Athelstan: king of England, overlord of Welsh, Scots and Norse (died 939)

Brian Boru: Irish king of Munster and victor at the Battle of Clontarf, 1014 (died 1014)

Charlemagne: Frankish emperor (died 814)

Charles III: (also known as Charles the Simple) king of West Francia, granted Normandy to **Rollo the Viking** in 911 (died 929)

Charles the Bald: Frankish emperor (died 877)

Cnut the Great: king of Denmark and England, also ruled in Norway (died 1035)

Edmund: king of East Anglia, martyred by Vikings (died 870)

Edward the Confessor: king of England after exile in Normandy (died 1066)

Emma of Normandy: sister of the Norman duke **Richard II, the Good**, wife and queen of **Æthelred II** and **Cnut** (died 1052)

Erik IX: (also known as St Erik) king of Sweden, leader of a mid-twelfth-century Christian crusade into Finland (died 1160)

Erik Bloodaxe: king of York, son of **Harald Finehair** (died 954)

Erik the Red: Viking adventurer and founder of the Norse settlements on Greenland (died c. 1003)

Eystein: king of Norway, led the last ever recorded Viking raid from Norway against England in 1153 (died 1157)

Freydis Eriksdottir: daughter of **Erik the Red**, wife of Thorvard, responsible for murders in Vinland (born: c. 970)

Gorm: king of Denmark and father of **Harald Bluetooth** (died c. 958)

Gudrid Thorbjornsdottir: journeyed to Vinland, mother of first Christian born in North America (Snorri Thorfinnson), went on pilgrimage to Rome, died as an anchoress on Iceland (born: c. 980)

Gunnhildr *konungamóðir*: (mother of kings) wife of **Erik Bloodaxe** (died 980)

Guthrum: Viking leader defeated by **Alfred the Great** in 878. He took the Anglo-Saxon name of Athelstan after his baptism, as part of his new treaty relationship with King Alfred (died 890)

Hakon Sigurdarson: earl of Lade in Norway, son of **Sigurd Hakonson**, a pagan, he was forced to flee after an uprising and killed by his own slave and friend while hiding in a pig sty (died 995)

Hakon the Good: (also known as Hakon *Athalstein's fóstri*) king of Norway, son of **Harald Finehair** and half-brother of **Erik Bloodaxe**, tried to convert Norway to Christianity but gave up in the face of pagan resistance (died 961)

Harald II, Sveinson: king of Denmark, son of **Svein Forkbeard** and brother of **Cnut the Great** (died 1018)

Harald and **Rorik:** Viking brothers granted land in the Netherlands in 841

Harald Bluetooth: king of Denmark, converted to Christianity in the 960s (died 986)

Harald Finehair: united Norway after the Battle of Hafrsfjord in 872, father of **Erik Bloodaxe** (died c. 930)

Harald Hardrada: adventurer in Kiev Rus and the Byzantine Empire, king of Norway, killed at the Battle of Stamford Bridge (died 1066)

Harald Harefoot: son of **Cnut the Great** and **Ælfgifu of Northampton**, king of England (died 1040)

Harald Klak: king of Denmark, baptized in Mainz (Germany) in 826 (died 852)

Harold II, Godwinson: earl of Wessex and king of England, killed at the Battle of Hastings (died 1066)

Harthacnut: son of **Cnut the Great** and **Emma of Normandy**, king of Denmark and then of England (died 1042)

Ingvar the Far-Travelled: Swedish Viking adventurer who died in the east (Rus) (died c. 1042)

Ivar the Boneless and **Halfdan:** traditionally named as leaders of the *micel hæðen here* (great heathen army), which invaded England in 866, sons of **Ragnar** *Lothbrok*

Lanfranc: prominent intellectual, influential in Normandy and, later, in England, where he became archbishop of Canterbury in 1070 (died 1089)

Leif Erikson: (also known as Leif the Lucky) son of **Erik the Red**, responsible for the Christian conversion of Greenland, explorer of Vinland (died c. 1020)

Louis the Pious: Frankish emperor (died 840)

Magnus III, Barelegs: (also known as Magnus Olafson) king of Norway (died 1103)

Magnus Erlendson: (also known as St Magnus and Magnus the Martyr) Christian jarl of Orkney who refused to engage in warfare, and was executed by his cousin and rival for power, Hakon (died 1115)

Magnus the Good: king of Norway, son of **Olaf II, Haraldson** (died 1047)

Olaf II, Haraldson: (also known as St Olaf) king of Norway, drove forward the Christian conversion of Norway, killed at the Battle of Stiklestad (died 1030)

Olaf Guthfrithson: king of Dublin, king of York (died 941)

Olaf Sihtricson: (also known as *Amlaíb Cuarán* in Ireland) grandson of **Sihtric** *Cáech* of the Norse dynasty of the *Uí Ímair*, baptized a Christian in 943, died a monk on Iona (died 980)

Olaf the White: Norwegian Viking who became the first king of Dublin in 853 (born c. 820)

Olaf Tryggvason: king of Norway, drove forward the Christian conversion of Orkney and then of Norway, killed at the Battle of Svolder (died 1000)

Olof *Skötkonung*: king of Sweden, Christian king who faced significant pagan opposition (died 1022)

Ragnar *Lothbrok* or *Lodbrok*: (leather or hairy breeches) legendary father of **Ivar the Boneless** and **Halfdan** who were leaders of the *micel hæðen here* which invaded England in 866. He was allegedly king of Sweden and Denmark, and according to legend was killed by King **Ælle** of Northumbria by being thrown into a snake pit. As a result, the Viking army which eventually seized York was led by Ragnar's sons, with the aim of avenging his death (died before 866)

Richard I, the Fearless: count of Normandy (died 996)

Richard II, the Good: duke of Normandy, brother of **Emma of Normandy** (died 1026)

Robert of Jumièges: bishop of London and then briefly the archbishop of Canterbury under King **Edward the Confessor** (died 1070)

Robert the Magnificent: (also known as Robert I) duke of Normandy, father of **William the Conqueror** (died 1035)

Rognvald Eysteinson: jarl of Møre (western Norway), allegedly made first jarl of Orkney but granted the islands to his brother (died c. 890)

Rollo: (or Rolf) founder of Normandy, granted land there in 911 by the Frankish king **Charles III**, probably to be identified with the Viking known as *Ganger-Hrolf* (died c. 930)

Rurik: (or Riurik) legendary Rus ruler in Novgorod, accompanied by his brothers, Sineus in Beloozero, and Truvor in Izborsk (arrived c. 862)

Sigurd Hakonson: jarl of Lade, a pagan during the Christian conversion of Norway led by **Hakon the Good**, father of **Hakon Sigurdarson** (died 962)

Sigurd Hlodvison, the Stout: jarl of Orkney, forced to convert to Christianity in 995 by **Olaf Tryggvason**, married the daughter of the Scottish king Malcolm II (died 1014)

Sigurd *Jorsalafari*: (Jerusalem-farer) (also known as Sigurd the Crusader) king of Norway, went on crusade to the Holy Land in 1107, then launched a crusade into southern Sweden against pagans in Småland in 1123 (died 1130)

Sihtric *Cáech*: (squint) king of Dublin, king of York, member of the Norse dynasty – the *Uí Ímair* – who dominated the Irish Sea region and northern England (died 927)

Sihtric II Olafson: (also known as Sihtric Silkenbeard) consolidated Christian rule in Viking Dublin, main Norse leader at the Battle of Clontarf, 1014 (died 1042)

Snorri Sturluson: Icelander responsible for the recording of much Viking tradition and mythology, assassinated on the orders of King Hakon IV of Norway (died 1241)

Somerled: lord of the Isles, of mixed Norse and Scots ancestry from one of the side-branches of the mighty Norse dynasty of the *Uí Ímair* (died 1164)

Svein Cnutson: son of **Cnut the Great** and **Ælfgifu of Northampton**, king of Norway until expelled by the Norwegians in 1034 (died 1035)

Svein Forkbeard: king of Denmark, king of England (died 1014)

Svyatoslav: first ruler of Kiev Rus with a Slavic name, father of Vladimir (died 972)

Thorfinn Karlsefni: one of the husbands of **Gudrid Thorbjornsdottir**, Vinland explorer, father of first Christian born in North America c. 1010

Thorfinn Sigurdarson, the Mighty: jarl of Orkney and founder of the first bishopric there (died 1065)

Thorgeir Thorkelson: law speaker of Iceland's *Althing* responsible for the final decision to convert to Christianity in 1000

Thorstein Erikson: son of **Erik the Red**, one of the husbands of **Gudrid Thorbjornsdottir**, and associated in the sagas with attempts to sail to Vinland in the early eleventh century

Thorvald Erikson: son of **Erik the Red**, brother of **Leif the Lucky,** first person buried as a Christian in North America in the early eleventh century

Thyra: tenth-century queen of Denmark, mother of **Harald Bluetooth**

Vladimir: ruler of Kiev Rus, son of **Svyatoslav**, converted to Christianity in 989 (died 1015)

William Longsword: count of Normandy, son of **Rollo** (died 942)

William of Normandy/William the Conqueror: duke of Normandy and king of England (died 1087)

Wulfstan: (also known as Wulfstan I) archbishop of York, arrested and imprisoned by the king of Wessex, because he was felt to be politically unreliable and an ally of pagan Viking rulers in Northumbria (died 956)

Wulfstan: (also known as Wulfstan II) archbishop of York, author of *Sermo Lupi ad Anglos* (*The Sermon of the Wolf to the English*) (died 1023)

Yaroslav the Wise: ruler of Kiev Rus and active promoter of Christian government and culture (died 1054)

Glossary

Æsir: one of the two main families of Norse gods and goddesses

Ætheling: Old English (Anglo-Saxon) word, meaning "prince"

Airer Goidel: Gaelic term meaning "coastline of the Gaels" and referring to south-western Scotland, in contrast to *Innse Gall* ("Islands of the foreigners/Scandinavians")

Althing: the national assembly of Iceland

Asgard: home of the gods and goddesses in the **pagan** religion of the **Norse**

Blood-eagle: legendary rite supposed to have been used to sacrifice a human victim

Byzantine Empire: alternative name for the Eastern Roman Empire, ruled from Constantinople

Caliphate: name of an Islamic state. The ones in the Viking Age were the Umayyad Caliphate (661–750) with its political centre in Damascus, and the Abbasid Caliphate (750–1258) with its political centre in Baghdad

Chronicle: historical record of events, often year by year. Some annals were recorded contemporaneously with events; many were compiled later, often from earlier sources

Comes: (count) as in counts of Normandy

Crusade: military campaign conducted for religious reasons

Danegeld: (Dane tax) Old English term used to describe payments in England to Vikings. However, this term was not coined until decades later and, at the time, these would have been described using the Old English word *gafol* (tribute)

Dirham: a coin produced within the Islamic states

Drápa: a long poem with a refrain

Dubh-gaill: (black foreigners) a Gaelic (Irish) term used to describe some Vikings, usually considered to be Danish

Dux: (duke) as in dukes of Normandy

Ealdorman: regional representative of an Anglo-Saxon king

Eastern Orthodox Church: Christian church in Greece, the eastern Mediterranean, Russia and the Balkans

Eddas: collections of Norse mythological material. Two versions exist: the *Poetic Edda* and the *Prose Edda*, both compiled in Iceland

Eddic poetry: a form of Old Norse poetry that is looser and less complex than **skaldic** verse. As found in the *Poetic Edda* and drawing on mythological and legendary themes

Fenrir the wolf: mythological creature destined to devour the Norse god Odin at **Ragnarok**

Finn-gaill: (white foreigners) Gaelic (Irish) term used to describe some Vikings, usually considered to be Norwegians

Francia: the western lands of the **Frankish Empire**, in modern-day France and the Low Countries. The empire itself extended into Germany and northern Italy

Frankish Empire: large and complex collection of states stretching from France and the Low Countries into Germany and northern Italy

Gafol and **geld:** terms describing Anglo-Saxon tribute/taxes

Gall-Gaedhil: (foreign Gaels) Gaelic term for the mixed Norse-Gael population of south-western Scotland and the Western Isles

Garðaríki: (kingdom of the towns) or *Garðar* (the towns): a Scandinavian name for the mixed Slavic/Norse settlements of northern Russia

Götar: tribal group in Sweden, one of the component parts of the later kingdom of Sweden

Goði: (plural *goðar*) an Icelandic chieftain, who also acted as a pagan priest

Goðorð: area in Iceland overseen by a *goði*

Grave goods: items buried with a dead person

Heathen: term used to describe a religion that does not accept the God of the Bible and, instead, has a number of gods and goddesses. An Old English term, with the same meaning as **pagan**

Hogback: a form of carved stone monument found in Viking areas of England, resembling stylized houses (bow-sided with a ridged roof) often decorated on their ends with carved beasts

Hólmgarðr: Scandinavian name for the trading settlement of Novgorod in Russia

Innse Gall: Gaelic term meaning "Islands of the foreigners/ Scandinavians", in contrast to *Airer Goidel* ("coastline of the Gaels")

Jarl: (earl) a Scandinavian nobleman, as in jarls of Lade, in Norway

Jormungand: the mythical Midgard Serpent (also known as *Miðgarðsormr*). It was believed that at **Ragnarok** the Norse god Thor would kill it but would himself be killed by its poisonous breath

Kennings: complex metaphors found within **skaldic** poetry

Kiev Rus: the mixed Norse/Slav state in Russia

Kingdom of the Isles: comprising the Inner and Outer Hebrides, the islands in the Firth of Clyde and the Isle of Man. Called the *Suðreyjar* (southern isles) to differentiate them from the *Norðreyjar* (Northern Isles) of Orkney and Shetland, it was also known as "the Kingdom of Man and the Isles"

Legends: stories which attempt to explain historical events but told in a non-historical way; they often include supernatural events

Longphort: (fortified base) term used to describe Viking bases in Ireland

Micel hæðen here: (great heathen army), a Viking army that invaded England in 866

Miklagarðr (or *Miklagard*): the Scandinavian name for Constantinople

Minster: an important Anglo-Saxon church serving a local area

Miollnir: the hammer carried in Norse mythology by the god Thor

Myths/mythology: non-historical stories of a religious nature that explain origins and the nature of the spiritual

Norse: a general term used to describe those of related Scandinavian culture during the **Viking Age**

North Germanic: family of languages, including Danish, Icelandic, Norwegian, and Swedish

Numismatics: the study of coins

Old English: the language of the Anglo-Saxons

Old Norse: the language spoken between the eighth and thirteenth centuries across Scandinavia and the areas of Viking settlement. There were western and eastern dialects of Old Norse, and a third form was spoken on the island of Gotland in the Baltic. From this Old Norse language modern Danish, Faroese, Icelandic, Norwegian and Swedish eventually developed. There were also once the Norn languages of Orkney and Shetland but these have died out

Pagan: term used for a religion that does not accept the God of the Bible and, instead, has a number of gods and goddesses. A Latin term with the same meaning as **heathen**

Pallium: symbol of office of an archbishop

Papar: Norse term for priests

Picts: a people of northern Britain (large parts of modern-day Scotland) and the Northern and Western Isles

Prima signatio: (first-signing) Christian priest making the sign of the cross on the forehead of a person, as a preliminary step towards baptism

Ragnarok: the end of the world in Norse mythology, involving the destruction of the gods

Realpolitik: beliefs and actions based on practical considerations rather than ideology

Reeve: local representative of an Anglo-Saxon king

Reliquary: a box, often adorned with costly metalwork, to hold a holy relic

Romance language: family of languages including Italian, French, and Spanish

Runes/runic: form of alphabet used in the Germanic world

Runestone: a memorial stone carrying a commemorative inscription in **runes**

Rurikids: ruling dynasty of **Kiev Rus**

Rus: name for the Viking settlers in Russia, as in **Kiev Rus**

Sagas: prose stories about ancient Norse and Germanic history and heroic deeds, which may also include mythological material. Compiled after the events they claim to describe (often several centuries later), they mix some historical events with literary developments of their themes. Written in Old Norse and mostly compiled in Iceland, some contain poetry. As historical evidence, they need to be used with caution

Serkland: the name used by Scandinavians for the Islamic Abbasid Caliphate and other Muslim areas of the east

Skaldic poetry: a form of Norse poetry characterized by a complex metrical structure and syntax, and metaphors called *kennings*. Often attributed to named poets or skalds

Skraeling: derogatory term used by Vikings to describe indigenous North Americans (including those on Greenland)

Svear: tribal group in Sweden, one of the component parts of the later kingdom of Sweden

Thing: an assembly

Thingmenn: those entitled to attend a *thing*

Uí Ímair: Norse dynasty of the Irish Sea region

Unræd: Old English term meaning "no counsel/wisdom", or perhaps "badly advised" and applied to the Anglo-Saxon ruler King Æthelred II

Valkyries: mythological warrior-women tasked with choosing the best of slain warriors to join the war band of the god Odin

Varangians: name used for Viking warriors serving in the bodyguard of the emperor of the **Byzantine Empire** in Constantinople

Viking: term used to describe Scandinavian raiders and adventurers, of the period c.750–1150. Often now commonly used to describe Norse communities (including traders and settlers) generally during this period

Viking Age: historical period in Scandinavia and across the geographical range of Norse expansion, c.750–1150

Introduction

There are few groups in history who have had more of an impact on the modern imagination than the Vikings. They have been explored in academic history books, popular history books, novels, comic-books, documentaries, films purporting to "show it like it was", advertising images and slogans, fantasy novels and films loosely based on Norse (i.e. Viking) mythology, sites to visit, and the work of re-enactors! Where this book stands out from a great many of these is in its focus. While placing the Vikings in their pagan context, our main aim is to explore what happened to "Vikings" when they converted to Christianity. This may come as a surprise to some readers since their overriding image of Vikings is of pagan warriors worshipping gods such as Odin and Thor and pillaging Christian monasteries. There is much truth underlying this image, as we shall see, but "Viking history" and the "Viking Age" were much more complex.

It is true that Scandinavia and its far-flung settlements were some of the last Western European communities to convert to Christianity; Iceland did not convert until the year 1000 and Norway and Sweden contained significant numbers of pagans for even longer. By "pagans", in these cases, we mean followers of the pre-Christian Norse pantheon of gods and goddesses; although in northern Norway and Sweden, as well as along the Baltic and in Russia, Vikings interacted with other non-Christian religious beliefs, from Sami shamanism to the gods of the Balts and Slavs. The eventual kingdoms of Denmark, Norway and Sweden did not establish their own independent church archdioceses (mirroring the situations in kingdoms further south in Europe) until 1104, 1154 and 1164 respectively. King Sigurd the Crusader of Norway led a crusade against Småland, in the south-east of the Swedish kingdom, in the early twelfth century in order to forcibly convert the locals from paganism to Christianity.

Even after these dates, many Scandinavian communities took centuries to become as fully Christian in their culture and practice as communities in more established Christian kingdoms, such as in the British Isles, France or among the Germans. Runic inscriptions from Bergen, Norway, show lingering pagan beliefs as late as the thirteenth century. In Iceland the thirteenth-century sagas (purporting to record the events of the not-so-distant past) reveal that farming communities with mixed Christian and pagan beliefs continued for many generations after the official conversion. And even that official conversion only stopped the open and officially sanctioned practice of pagan beliefs and sacrifices. Back home on the isolated farmsteads many families continued much as before but in a lower-key way, with a less visible profile. In the far north of Scandinavia the Sami (though, it is fair to say, not part of the Norse culture of the Viking Age) did not convert to Christianity until the eighteenth century.

To complicate things further, there were different contemporary views on what actually constituted conversion. The German chronicler Adam of Bremen only viewed the Icelanders as truly converted once Isleif, the first Icelander to be elected bishop (in 1055), had been consecrated (in 1056) by the archbishop of Hamburg-Bremen who claimed authority over Scandinavian Christians. For others, conversion involved embracing new habits and rejecting old ones. So, for Rimbert (archbishop of Hamburg-Bremen until his death in 888), generosity towards Christians was a step to conversion; whereas for Pope Nicholas I (pope 858–867) official baptism was required. Furthermore, the conversion was not a single event but a long, drawn out process and, although there are certain features which characterize the conversion in all of the continental Scandinavian countries, each conversion took place in different circumstances and is therefore unique to the individual country and even to areas within those countries. So although the conversion of Iceland is inextricably linked to the rise of Christianity in Norway, the process of conversion in both countries was profoundly different. Away from Scandinavia, the experience of conversion gave rise to even more variety. Nevertheless, all of Scandinavia and the scattered Viking diaspora were officially Christian by the twelfth century.

However, many Viking communities had converted generations before this and had a history of being "Christian Vikings" that was several centuries old by the early twelfth century. The focus of this book ends in about the year 1150, when the Viking Age was effectively over, the extended raiding and settlement ended and the settled kingdoms of Scandinavia had emerged. At this point, many Viking communities in England had been Christian for almost 300 years, some in Denmark had been Christian for 150 years, and some in Normandy for about 200 years. Even in Iceland, many farming families had been Christian for 150 years. And that is before one considers the Scandinavians who had settled among the Orthodox Christians of southern Russia or the Byzantine Empire of the eastern Mediterranean.

We are seeking in this book to correct the over-emphasis in popular culture on the Odin-worshipping warriors of film and fiction. That is why it is entitled *The Vikings: From Odin to Christ*. While rape and pillaging dominate the popular image, rulers such as Harald Bluetooth of Denmark, Olaf Tryggvason of Norway, Cnut the Great (of Denmark and England), William of Normandy, Olof *Skötkonung* of Sweden and Sigurd the Crusader of Norway (to name just a few) would all have seen themselves as part of mainstream European civilization. In contrast to twenty-first-century pluralism, they saw only one way to achieve that: Christianity. This book looks at why they felt this way and how it impacted on their rule and the lives of their subjects – alongside the experiences of countless nameless individuals who converted to Christianity. Having made their choices, they were clearly often enthusiastic supporters of the new order and all it entailed. They had become, in their own eyes at least, pillars of civilization. Consequently (and controversially), the pope turned to a descendant of the Vikings in 1066 in order to sort out the inadequacies (as he saw it) of the Anglo-Saxon church. That is not how we tend to view 1066 but that was the outlook from the heart of Western Christendom.

SOME THOUGHTS ABOUT LANGUAGE

We have used the term "Viking" as a group name to describe the Scandinavians in this period because it is so established in the popular consciousness. Most people know what is meant by it and so it is useful. We will explore more of its meaning – and its complexity – in Chapter 1. It is less used in some academic circles than it once was, but it is still seen in recent academic papers and books.[1] When the British Museum put on an exhibition of artefacts and art from the areas and the period in question in 2014, it was called "Vikings: life and legend". Clearly, the term "Viking" is alive and well, even if it has been under a bit of pressure.

However, where "Vikings" were clearly from a particular area of Scandinavia (Danes, Norwegians, Swedes) we will indicate this because the Vikings never were a uniform and homogenous group. Nevertheless, we have retained the group name as a general term to describe those involved in the extraordinary events of the "Viking Age". However, we need to remember that the term "Viking", when it was originally used, was done so to describe the warrior adventurers, rather than the lower class farmers, craftspeople and merchants who lived in Scandinavia and settled in the lands that the warriors conquered; or who travelled there independently of any warrior adventurers. Many other terms were also used to describe them in the original sources from the period and we will make this clear when appropriate to do so. That brings us to the evidence...

As well as the evidence from archaeological discoveries (which are very varied), we also have available a wide range of written sources for the Vikings and the Viking Age. The sources explored in this book were largely written in Old English, Old Norse and Latin but we will also find references in other languages such as the Old Slavonic of Russia and the Greek of the Byzantine Empire. To engage with these sources, we have used accessible modern translations. If at any time we have referred to an event in the original language this will only be in the form of a short phrase, always accompanied by its translation.

Sometimes we have continued to use a phrase in the original language because it has become so well known to those exploring the Viking Age. An obvious example is the *micel hæðen here* (the great heathen army) which devastated Anglo-Saxon England in the 860s and 870s. At times these words in the original language are very revealing and worth exploring. For example the Anglo-Scandinavian word *lið* (seaborne military) was used in the *Anglo-Saxon Chronicle* to describe both the forces of the Anglo-Saxon Harold Godwinson's sons and those of Svein Estrithson of Denmark after 1066. It seems that it was hard to tell who was the Viking and who the Anglo-Saxon at this point. However, these examples are relatively few in number, and all other descriptions/phrases that we use are in modern English.

When it comes to the title of medieval written sources, on the first occasion of use we have also given their titles in translation in order to explain the meaning. Examples are: *Jómsvíkinga saga* (*Saga of the Jómsvíkings*); the *Vita Ædwardi Regis* (*Life of King Edward*); the *Encomium Emmae Reginae* (*In Praise of Queen Emma*); *Heimskringla* (*Circle of the world*), the great saga history of Norwegian Viking kings; *Eiríksmál* (*Erik's story*), the anonymous elegy for King Erik Bloodaxe and *Orkneyinga saga* (*Saga of the Orcadians*), the history of the earls of Orkney. However, when a source has a modern name, such as the *Anglo-Saxon Chronicle*, we use that modern form throughout.

The evidence was originally written in a number of languages. The official language of the Christian Church and of many documents was Latin. In Anglo-Saxon England the language spoken is today described as Old English. Among the Scandinavians themselves various forms of Old Norse were spoken. Consequently, some people prefer the term "Norse" to that of "Viking" because the former term is more encompassing of a whole culture, whereas the latter term originally described an activity (warrior raiding). But, for reasons already explained, we will use "Viking" as the general label, "Norse" to describe the general culture, and "Old Norse" to describe the language. In addition, Old Slavonic, Greek and Arabic were used by some of those who encountered Vikings. The Normans spoke Norman French.

Although Old Norse was spoken in various forms and dialects across the Viking world, it has left few early written examples. This is because literacy (brought by the Christian Church) came much later to Scandinavia than to other areas of Western Europe. Strangely enough, it does not always seem like this because a number of very famous and dramatic Old Norse written sources survive; the most famous being the sagas. At first reading these appear to shed light on the Viking Age. However, many of these sources date from a century or more after the events they describe and most were written in Iceland. As a result, their evidence needs to be used with caution. This does not make them valueless; it simply means they are a rather complex "witness", and one with quite a lot of attitude!

The ancient languages of Old English and Old Norse used letters that are no longer current in modern English. The most commonly used ones were: Æ or lower case æ (ash), Ð or lower case ð (eth) and Þ or lower case þ (thorn). The last two basically approximated to the "th" sound in modern English. In most cases we have translated these letters into modern English ones. So, to give an example, we have anglicized the name of the Norse god Oðinn to the more familiar form of Odin. However, these letters will occasionally appear when referring to a word, written source or place name that employs them, along with modern Scandinavian letters not used in English when these appear in modern place names. We have only used Ð/ð and Þ/þ occasionally, when a word or phrase quoted in the original language uses them, as in *micel hæðen here*.

However, the letter we have frequently employed when referring to personal names is Æ/æ because it was so commonly used and does not have a direct parallel in modern English. So we refer to Æthelred and Æthelflæd, not Ethelred and Ethelfled. But where a name has become more familiar in a modernized form, we have used the modern appearance; so we refer to Alfred not Ælfred, Athelstan not Æthelstan.

THE USE OF PERSONAL NAMES

Many of the personal names of the Viking Age can be spelled in more than one way. So, for example, Harold is the same name as Harald; Svein is the same name as Swein and Swayne. To complicate things further, fashions change in how later writers represent these ancient names. So, the Danish personal name Knutr is today usually spelled Cnut but in the past it was written as Canute. To simplify things we have followed a consistent pattern so that Cnut is used of all rulers with that name; Svein is used of the various men with that name. An exception to this rule is when we refer to Harold Godwinson (also known as Harold II) – the noble who became king of England in 1066 and died at Hastings – but Harald Hardrada of Norway who was killed by him in 1066. This makes it easier to differentiate them. But all the other Scandinavians with this name we just refer to as Harald, plus any additional title or nickname that helps to differentiate them. The same reasoning lies behind our referring to Olaf Tryggvason but Olof *Skötkonung*. While on this subject, where there is such an additional name we will use it in order to avoid confusion. So, Cnut I of Denmark and England is "Cnut the Great", whereas Cnut IV of Denmark is "Cnut the Holy". It doesn't matter that these differentiating titles/descriptions were invented later. They clarify things and avoid confusion.

We are grateful to our agent, Robert Dudley, and to all at Lion Hudson (especially to Ali Hull for the original commissioning of the book and Jessica Tinker and Joy Tibbs in the editorial stages) for their help and support in the writing of this book. We are also indebted to the historians whose explorations of events and interpretations regarding their significance we have consulted. Hannah's studies in the department of Anglo-Saxon, Norse and Celtic (ASNC) at Cambridge University (both as an undergraduate and then in an MPhil year) provided a great many insights (including her ability to read Old Norse), which assisted in the exploration of the evidence and its interpretation. All errors, of course, are our own.

Martyn and Hannah Whittock

CHAPTER 1

The Pagan Vikings

W ho and what were the Vikings? Where did they come from? What did they believe before conversion to Christianity? What are our modern images of the Vikings and how do they affect our outlook regarding them? We need to answer these questions before we explore the Vikings of the Viking Age, those who experienced their impact and how the Vikings eventually converted to Christianity. As we explore the final question, it will become obvious that the "Christian Vikings" do not get a look in when it comes to the popular image of marauders in horned helmets. The pagan Vikings totally dominate the headlines.

WHO AND WHAT WERE THE VIKINGS?

Those at the receiving end of attacks from the north used various names for those responsible.

In Anglo-Saxon written sources, the terms "Danes", "Northmen", "pagans" or "heathens" were most often used. What is intriguing is that the term "Danes" did not carry much geographical accuracy. Consequently, when we read "Danes" in the accounts of a particular raid we cannot be certain that

8

those responsible actually came from Denmark. For example, in one report of a raid on Portland, Dorset, in 789, the same entry says they were Danes – yet they came from Norway. The Franks (in what is now France and western Germany) called them the *Nordmanni* (Northmen) and so an area ceded to them in the tenth century would become Normandy (land of the Northmen).

Slavs knew them from their ruddy complexions as the *Rus* (red) and a related word, *Rhos*, was used by the Byzantines, who employed them as mercenaries and met Scandinavians who had travelled down the rivers leading into the Black Sea and on into the eastern Mediterranean and the Byzantine Empire. This latter word (in the form *Rus*) would eventually give rise to the name of Russia: what started as a mixed Viking/Slav state centred on Kiev was at the core of the early Russian nation. The Byzantines also called them *Varangians* (those who swear loyalty) and the mercenaries of the Varangian Guard served the Byzantine emperor in Constantinople. Then in Ireland they were the *Lochlannach* (Northmen), a designation similar to the one used by the Franks. The Irish went on to differentiate between the Norwegians as *Finn-gaill* (white foreigners) and the Danes as *Dubh-gaill* (black foreigners), which will be explained in Chapter 5. Far from Scandinavia, Islamic writers called them *al-madjus* (heathens) in a religiously derived label similar to that used by Anglo-Saxons. What is surprising to the modern reader is the fact that we hardly ever hear them called *Vikings* outside of Scandinavia.

So where does the familiar term *Viking* come from? There is no definite answer as the term may have had a number of possible origins. In Old Icelandic (a variant of the Old Norse language) the word *vík* (bay, creek) may have been used to describe seamen hiding in, or sailing from, these coastal inlets, so a geographical term may have become a group name. In addition, an area of southern Norway was called Vik, so this may have become attached to those sailing from this area. Then again, the Old Icelandic verb *víkja* (moving, turning aside) may have come to describe seafarers who were always "on the move". Old Norse Scandinavian written sources (which appear very late in Scandinavia) call a raider a *víkingr*, and a raiding expedition of such men a *víking*. This reminds us that "the word 'Viking' is something you *did* rather than what you *were*".[1]

For many so described, this would have been a part-time occupation.[2] At other times of the year or during other phases of their lives, they would not have gone out "viking" or been considered as "Vikings". And this did not necessarily carry a negative connotation. In Old Norse sources, if you were not on the receiving end of one of these raids, then going out viking was an adventure; taking part in a spot of muscular free enterprise. It is not surprising, therefore, that the victims of the Vikings coined their own terms – and these were often not positive ones. Even the red-faced foreigners of the Byzantine accounts suggest a sense of an alien other. However, as we have seen, it must be admitted that sometimes more neutral geographical terms were used ("Danes", "Northmen") but even these were usually used in the context of a negative account. There was certainly no romance of the Vikings for those on the receiving end of their attentions.

So, we might ask, when did the term "Viking" get into English usage? There was an Old English term derived from the Old Norse word – in Old English, *wicing* or *wicingas* – but this does not appear as a label for Scandinavian pirates until the tenth century. More surprisingly, it is only used very rarely, and (not surprisingly) had a negative connotation. In contrast, some English east coast place names contain the word and, in these cases, it may have been derived from a Scandinavian personal name. In which case, we are back to a more positive spin on the term since the person in question almost certainly carried the name with pride: "I am an adventurer", rather than "My employment is smash and grab... and worse". But that is not surprising, given that the person in question was almost certainly a Scandinavian settler. Examples include Wickenby (Lincolnshire) which means "Viking's by" (village); Wiganthorpe (Yorkshire) which means "Viking's thorp" (dependent farm); Wigston (Leicestershire) which means "Viking's tun" (village).[3] The last example couples a Scandinavian personal name with an Old English place-name term.

After this infrequent use in Old English, the word did not surface again until almost a millennium later, when it finally became the standard term for Scandinavian invaders during the nineteenth century. It is not known in its modern spelling Viking before 1840. After that, it was used to describe both those involved in raiding expeditions (as Scandinavians originally used the term) and also Scandinavians generally during the Viking Age (as it was never used in the past). It is now so popular that it is the label of choice for most people and it would confuse many if we insisted on using something else. However, we just have to remember that few of those meeting the original Vikings would have recognized the term and most Scandinavian merchants and settlers would not have thought that it applied to them since it was not what they did. But "Vikings" it now is.

What is less contentious is the conclusion that (for all their differences) they shared many common cultural characteristics and this included their mutually understood dialects of what we now call "Old Norse". This term describes a Scandinavian language spoken between the eighth and thirteenth centuries AD, and generally mutually understood across the range of areas within which it was spoken. There were, though, western and eastern dialects of Old Norse and a third form was spoken on the island of Gotland in the Baltic. From this Old Norse language, modern Danish, Faroese, Icelandic, Norwegian and Swedish eventually developed. There were also once the Norn languages of Orkney and Shetland but these have died out. This is why some scholars prefer the term "Norse" to that of "Vikings" as a group term, but we will use the former when describing language or general cultural features (as in "Norse mythology", which was basically the beliefs of Vikings) but the latter term we will generally use for the people.

Modern historians tend to use the term the "Viking Age" to describe a period which ran from the late eighth century until about 1100. During this period people from Scandinavia first of all raided and then later settled across a wide geographical area, from Russia in the east, to Greenland and the coast of North America in the west. They raided on both sides of the English Channel and then later settled in Normandy, in eastern and northern England, across the Northern and Western Isles of Scotland, and also established a Viking kingdom in Dublin. Vikings colonized

Iceland, the Faroe Islands and parts of Greenland. These North Atlantic colonists used both Norway and Ireland as springboards for these particular settlements and modern DNA testing shows that a large proportion of the female genetic heritage in modern-day Iceland is Irish-derived (clearly brought there as wives, slaves or both combined). Some Vikings took part in raids which reached Spain and North Africa, while Swedish Vikings explored the eastern Baltic and followed the river systems down into the eastern Mediterranean. This is a staggeringly diverse area and remarkable in its geographical range. In this book we will, at times, extend the final end date of the Viking Age beyond 1100, in order to see how Christianity influenced some Scandinavian Viking societies.

We are now sure that the Vikings made it to North America and so will include American Vikings. The later (mostly thirteenth-century) sagas refer to exploration of a region to the west of Greenland they call "Vinland". This was clearly North America but which part remains open to question. The word *vínber* (wine berries) from which Vinland was named can indicate both wild grapes and other plants. Depending on which plant is described we can guess different areas of the western North American coast that might have been reached, as there is a clear northern geographical limit to the growth of wild grapes. We will explore this later (Chapter 12) but suffice it to say that, since Greenland was so named as a PR ploy to encourage settlement, it may have been that Vinland (wineland) was similarly named in order to give a positive eleventh-century spin to reality. Impressively, Vikings could be found from North Africa to the North Cape and from Greece and Turkey to North America.

In the early part of this period, there were no recognizable nations in Scandinavia and, consequently, when we use the terms "Denmark", "Norway" and "Sweden" they describe geographical areas and then, a little later, loose political units, not distinct nation states. But things were changing during the Viking Age, as from the tenth century onwards we see the gradual emergence of kingdoms in Denmark, Norway and, finally, Sweden. Then we can start talking of kings of these kingdoms but, even then, nation building took time and the borders of these kingdoms were fluid for many generations. Alongside this, there were political rivalries for dominance, times when kings of Denmark ruled in Norway, and times when kings of Norway ruled an independent kingdom. We will see kings of Denmark ruling large parts of southern Sweden in what we might call Greater Denmark and a king of Norway operating against pagans in Sweden due to a political opportunity provided by a much weaker Swedish kingdom (where the local king exercised much less authority than in neighbouring kingdoms).

WHERE DID THE VARIOUS VIKING SETTLERS COME FROM?

As we have seen, most of the Vikings involved in attacking and settling in England – and Britain generally – came from what we now know as Denmark and Norway.

Norwegians (often today simply described as the "Norse" to differentiate them from the Danes) raided and then settled Shetland, Orkney, northern Scotland, the Western Isles and Ireland. They eventually set up a Viking kingdom in Dublin and from there became actively engaged in northern English politics, so at times kings of Dublin were also kings of York. Back home, Norway was – until the late ninth century when Harald Finehair unified much of the land – divided and dominated by Denmark and it was well into the tenth century before its future as an independent kingdom seemed secure. Even then it was often dominated by (or directly ruled by) Danish kings at various times until the early eleventh century. The richest area was Vestfold, with a trading centre at Kaupang.

In contrast, the Danes raided the coasts of eastern and southern England and France. They would have the greatest impact on Anglo-Saxon consciousness, hence the tendency to describe all raiders as "Danes" in some Anglo-Saxon sources. Things, though, could be more complex since Rollo (the founder of Normandy) is variously described as Danish *and* Norwegian in different medieval sources, both in Normandy and Britain. Denmark dominated the trade routes from the North Sea to the

Baltic, so it always had the potential to develop into a formidable threat to its southern neighbours. The Danes also controlled regions in southern Sweden and often acted as overlords of Norway. Denmark became increasingly centralized by the eighth century. After this, it was strong enough to threaten the coast of the Frankish Empire by the ninth century (by 814 this empire comprised what is now modern-day France, Belgium, the Netherlands, western Germany, northern Italy, Austria, Slovenia, and Croatia). Denmark then fragmented in the late ninth/early tenth centuries between dynasties competing for control of the kingdom, but was reunited later in the tenth century.

Swedish Vikings mostly sailed eastward into the Baltic and down the river systems of what would later become Russia. It is only from the late tenth/early eleventh century that we hear of Swedish Vikings joining the fleets sailing for England, 200 years after Danish and Norwegian Vikings had first impacted this region. Denmark ruled much of the south of what we now call Sweden and the rest of the country lacked political unity. In the ninth century, petty kings are mentioned in the written sources; all of which were compiled outside of Sweden but which clearly reflect a divided reality, as is clear from other evidence.[4] There seem to have been two main political units in Sweden: the *Svear* (centred on Uppsala) and the *Götar* (centred on the plains of Östergötland and Västergötland, near Lake Vättern).[5]

There is much debate over what triggered the explosion of movement out of Scandinavia in the later eighth century. Overall, it seems that changes occurring within Scandinavia combined with events outside of the region to trigger the start of raids and later settlement. In the eighth century, an increased population in Norway may have sparked competition for scarce resources. Internal power struggles in a gradually more unified state meant that warriors on the losing side looked elsewhere for a means of gaining wealth and prestige. This led to raids on foreign territories. This may have been accelerated by increased political unity in the ninth century. Again, the losers had to look elsewhere. Within Denmark, there were both internal and external triggers. The southern Danish frontier was threatened by the expansion of the Christian Frankish Empire.

This external trigger encouraged greater Danish political unity as a defence against the Franks. Those Danes who lost out in this process of internal unification had to look outside Denmark for a future. In addition, the Danish nobles who did well in this power struggle financed their new political power by launching raiding expeditions abroad and could now do so from a stronger power base. Soon the Franks found that their northward expansion had inadvertently kicked over a hornets' nest. It illustrates the law of unintended consequences.

All of this came on top of a long-established Scandinavian tradition of taking part in wars to the south which stretched back to mercenary employment in the Roman Empire. Scandinavia did not exist in a vacuum. Increased international trade from the seventh century onwards meant that Scandinavians were very familiar with the wealth of their neighbours to the south and south-west, with their developing towns and trading ports. Trading and raiding were not necessarily separate operations and one could turn into the other depending on the defences and preparedness of those being traded with. Alongside this, an established seafaring tradition led to improved oceangoing vessels that were suitable for long-range activities.[6]

There might also have been an ideological motivation, and the clash of civilizations described by Christian monastic chroniclers might not have just been the inevitable outlook of those who had seen their monastery trashed. Instead, the first century of raids may have had an extra ideological motive as an attack on the very ideology of the Franks and their Christian neighbours. The monks of north-western Europe certainly felt so. Such an aggressive paganism may well have been a response to the aggressive religious as well as political expansion of the Frankish Empire. Once more we are back to the law of unintended consequences. Under threat from the Christian south, pagan Denmark struck back.

There is also another factor that may have prompted the start of Viking raids. The late-eighth-century Danish attacks on the Frankish Empire and the British Isles coincided with changes occurring in the far off Middle Eastern Islamic Caliphate from the 740s onwards, as the Umayyad dynasty lost out to the new Abbasid dynasty and the centre of political power shifted from Damascus to Baghdad. These distant political and economic changes disrupted the flow of silver to Scandinavia. For some time Islamic merchants and their middle men had brought silver to northern Europe to trade it for the products of the north: slaves, furs, amber. However, the violently shifting politics within the Caliphate were followed by its fragmentation and a decline in central authority. As a result of this, in the late ninth century the Caliphate lost control of the silver mines in what is now Tajikistan. This precipitated a crisis in Scandinavia. Scandinavian economies began to falter as trade with the Islamic world declined. It was now harder for (suddenly silver poor) Scandinavian elites to engage in traditional gift-giving which cemented social bonds. Raiding offered an alternative method of obtaining both precious metals and slaves.[7] Changes in Baghdad rippled out to the western Baltic like a stone thrown into a pond. The Viking Age was about to explode…

WHAT DID THE VIKINGS BELIEVE BEFORE THEIR CONVERSION TO CHRISTIANITY?

The Vikings before their conversion to Christianity believed in a pantheon of northern gods, goddesses and mythical semi-divine heroes and supernatural beings. Male divinities included Odin, Thor, Freyr, Loki, Baldr, Hod, Niord and many others. Female divinities included Freyia, Frigg, Sif and Hel. Odin was often described as "All Father" and was the chief of the gods, ruling from his hall, Valhalla. Norse mythology envisaged two families or races of gods: the Æsir and the Vanir, who once fought each other but then made peace and intermarried. They lived in Asgard which was connected to other worlds by the bridge called Bifrost. In a complex cosmology, the different worlds (including Midgard or Middle Earth, the realm of people) were united by the ash tree known as Yggdrasil.

As well as the gods and goddesses, major players in the Norse mythology were the giants, often portrayed as the enemies of the gods, with Thor frequently described as the crusher of giants' skulls with his hammer, *Miollnir*. Giants often desired beautiful goddesses and many conflicts occurred in the mythology as the gods sought to deny the giants possession of a goddess. On the other hand, some gods were married to giantesses, such as the giantess Gerd, daughter of the mountain giant Gymir and the wife of Freyr of the Vanir; and the giantess Angrboda, with whom Loki had children: Fenrir the wolf, Jormungand the Midgard Serpent, and Hel. The mythology was complex and never subject to a unifying religious organization which controlled it. Alongside the beings already describeds were elves, dragons, dwarfs and valkyries who chose dead warriors to go to serve Odin in Valhalla. It was also believed that this series of worlds would eventually come to a cataclysmic end on the Day of Ragnarok, when the forces of chaos would break loose (including the giants Fenrir-wolf and Jormungand the Midgard Serpent), Asgard would be stormed and the gods killed.[8]

Two later medieval sources, the thirteenth-century *Prose Edda* and the *Poetic Edda*, tell us most of what we now know about Norse mythology.[9] There are, though, also clues in *skaldic* poetry (a form of Norse poetry),[10] in the sagas and in place names. Norse legends that involve more human plots are found mostly in the sagas, most of which were written in thirteenth-century Iceland.

The *Prose Edda* is also known as the *Snorra Edda* or the *Younger Edda* and it is believed to have been written by Snorri Sturluson, an Icelandic chieftain, in the early thirteenth century. Snorri was also the author of *Heimskringla* (*Circle of the World*), a collection of sagas about the early Norwegian kings.

The *Poetic Edda* is a collection of anonymous Old Norse poems, focusing on Norse mythology and the Germanic heroic world. These are all *eddic* poems; the second main form of Old Norse poetry, generally looser and less complex than *skaldic* verse. Although the manuscript evidence for this source was not written until the 1270s in Iceland, it is generally accepted that the poems in it date from before the conversion to Christianity. However, it is difficult to identify where they were originally composed.[11]

Lastly, a rich source of Old Norse literature are the *sagas*.[12] These were written in Iceland, mainly in prose, although some of them contain poetry. They feature tales about the migration to

Iceland, the early Viking voyages and feuds in Iceland. Some also refer to the wider Viking diaspora. They appear historical but have to be used with caution as they are primarily works of literature which also contain traditional material.

It is important to remember that all these manuscripts were written by practising Christians, in a country (usually Iceland) which had been officially Christian for over 200 years. Consequently, none of the evidence for Norse mythology and Norse religion was written down by those who believed in it, who lived in the Viking Age.[13] We always view Norse mythology through a medieval Christian lens. The Vikings are not alone in having their beliefs later recorded by Christians who no longer subscribed to these earlier beliefs. The same is true of the evidence for Irish and Anglo-Saxon paganism. Some handling of the original material may have changed it, to make it more understandable to Christian audiences. This may have affected the way Odin is described as "All Father"; and the characterization of Loki (a complex trouble-making character) may have been influenced by Christian beliefs about the devil. It is now hard to be sure.

Another written source for pagan Viking practices comes from Adam of Bremen, a German chronicler and monk who wrote in the second half of the eleventh century. He records gods named Thor, Wotan (Odin) and Frikko (Freyr) being worshipped at the temple at Uppsala in Sweden,[14] and has Thor rather than Odin as the chief god. Odin is also depicted mainly as a god of war, rather than the god of poetry that we see in the later sources from Iceland. This is a reminder that Viking pagan beliefs may have changed over time and/or varied somewhat from place to place. We should beware of assuming that the surviving written sources represent how these beliefs were held, always and everywhere, among Scandinavian communities in the Viking Age.

Despite this, the names of the gods and goddesses are consistent across all the written sources, so we can be fairly certain these were the divinities the people of early medieval Scandinavia worshipped, even if we cannot be completely certain about the exact belief system surrounding them in the Viking Age.

The evidence from archaeology can also be used to test the

picture of Norse beliefs from the later written evidence. In a number of areas we find a general correlation. Thor's hammer was clearly used as a pendant across Scandinavia and also in Britain.[15] Birds accompany a mounted warrior on decorated Vendel-style helmets unearthed in Sweden, probably representing Odin with his two ravens, Hugin and Munin (thought and memory).[16] An amulet from Öland, Sweden, in the shape of a woman carrying a drinking horn, probably represented a valkyrie.[17] There is a carving of Odin's eight-legged horse, named Sleipnir, from Gotland.[18] Then there are ship burials from Norway, Sweden and the British Isles, as well as sacrifices of animals and occasionally of people. Runestones from Denmark, Sweden and Norway should also be considered. These are usually memorial stones but the images, and the words carved on them, give an insight into the belief system of at least some of those who produced them.

On the subject of runes, these were twig-like letters devised for carving on bone, metal or stone; hence the straight lines that form most runes. Vikings used them for a number of purposes: straightforward communication of ownership (e.g. "Thorfast made a good comb"); commemoration (e.g. "They bravely travelled far in search of gold, and in the east fed the eagle"); and for religious or magical purposes (e.g. the runes for the word "Protection" cut on a comb). The latter use of runes, in magic, evokes the story in *Egil's Saga* where the poet Egil used runes to cure a young girl previously cursed by the use of false runes. This echoes mythological traditions in the *Edda* that Odin sacrificed himself to gain the knowledge of rune-magic. It should also be noted that runes continued to be used for communication after the conversion to Christianity and were not just a feature of pagan belief and practice.

All of these pieces of evidence appear to corroborate themes and practices found in the later written myths. Consequently, archaeology suggests fairly widespread acceptance of the Norse beliefs (as known from literature) across a wide area during the Viking Age. On the other hand, while there is evidence for common beliefs across what we might call a wide "Norse culture area", we should not expect uniformity. As already stated, the beliefs were not codified or policed by a common religious authority.

Other clues fossilize Viking Age beliefs in some surprising contexts. Early Anglo-Saxon settlers in England also worshipped similar gods to the later Vikings and so religious beliefs that once stretched beyond the Scandinavian homelands into other Germanic areas can be compared with later Viking Age beliefs. Names of divinities differed slightly across related Germanic cultures but similarities are obvious: the Old Norse Odin and Thor were clearly the same gods as the Old English Woden and Thunor. And beliefs were clearly comparable, since the English word for "thunder" is derived from Thor and in the Viking Age he was also associated with weather in Scandinavian communities. The modern English Thursday (containing the Old English form of the Old Norse name Thor) and Wednesday (Woden/Odin's day) also show these deities were worshipped across a wide area.

Place names, too, record the worship of these Scandinavian deities in England. These include the Wansdyke (Woden/Odin's dyke) earthwork in Wiltshire and also south of Bath, and the many Grim's Ditches (formed from the word *grima*, "the masked one", another name for Woden/Odin) in a number of places. Further afield and less surprisingly, given the later conversion date, we can still find the names of Viking gods in the Icelandic landscape such as at Thórsmörk (Thor's valley) and there are many others. Across the lands settled by the Vikings – from Sweden to Iceland – the names of Norse gods and goddesses, dwarfs, dragons and elves still appear on the map and are linked to woods, rivers and other natural features. These can be compared with the documentary evidence from the *Eddas* and elsewhere to gain a wider understanding of Viking Age beliefs before the conversion.

In the ninth and tenth centuries, invading Vikings reintroduced their form of these gods to Christian England, prior to their later conversion to Christianity. This, as we shall see, was a terrible shock to Anglo-Saxon Christians. As a result, today there survive scenes illustrating Odin's fight with Fenrir-wolf at Ragnarok, carved on a cross from Kirk Andreas (Isle of Man). We can see Thor fishing for Jormungand the Midgard Serpent on a standing cross at Gosforth (Cumbria), and this cross also has a valkyrie carved on it. The legendary swordsmith Regin can be seen forging the hero Sigurd's sword on a stone cross from Halton (Lancashire) and the same cross has a carving which also shows Sigurd roasting a dragon's heart; all scenes from Norse legend.[19] The *Anglo-Saxon Chronicle* also refers to Viking armies carrying raven banners – which represented the companions of Odin – and which also appear in the Viking myths as recorded in the *Eddas*.[20]

WHAT ARE OUR MODERN IMAGES OF THE VIKINGS AND HOW DO THESE AFFECT OUR OUTLOOK REGARDING THEM?

In England it is clear that the Viking Wars gave rise to some of the greatest myths of English national history: slaughtered monks at Lindisfarne; Alfred burning the cakes; Erik Bloodaxe ruling at York; Æthelred the Unready vainly battling invaders; the Massacre of St Brice's Day and the skins of Danes nailed to church doors; Cnut ordering the waves on the seashore to halt – and getting his feet wet. Such core national myths are reflected across the areas affected by Viking raiding and settlement. Across Scandinavia and Iceland, this rugged independence and voyaging is celebrated as part of the national character. Even in the USA, we find attempts to connect modern communities with heroic ancestors from the Viking past. Even Marvel comics and resulting films make connections with mythical ideas about Thor and the Norse gods.

Some of these images and associations are negative, others positive. What is undeniable is that they remain vibrant and widespread. An interesting case in point occurs if one simply enters "Viking" as a Google Images search (on a safe search setting). On the first page the largest number of images are of warriors, in mail and with swords and axes. Some are half naked. A lot wear horned helmets despite the total absence of such items from archaeological excavations. The occasional helmet is winged. There are quite a lot of longships, and the occasional woman appears, dressed in "Viking costume" and armed with axe, sword, helmet, shield; one assumes they are valkyries? Some of these women might have been very cold if they went out in these costumes on a longship. There is the occasional logo for an American football team, a brand of beer or a computer game (all wearing horned helmets).

These are Vikings as many like to imagine them. There is romance, drama, ruggedness, courage and battle. There is a threat of violence but, on this safe setting, the emphasis is generally on adventure or manliness. All the images seem in keeping with the phase of raiding in the Viking Wars. It is safe to assume that all are probably pagan. None of the Vikings are in church, and one would not imagine that they ever would be – unless it was in the act of striking down a monk or lifting a silver reliquary as booty.

CHAPTER 2

Storm from the North

A KILLING ON PORTLAND, DORSET

The earliest recorded Viking raid was on England in about 789. The record of this shocking event is found in the *Anglo-Saxon Chronicle*, compiled in the 880s in Old English, in the southern kingdom of Wessex, from a range of earlier material. The simplest and oldest surviving record of the attack is found in *manuscript A* of the *Chronicle* now in the Parker Library at Corpus Christi College, Cambridge University. The annal in question reads:

And in his days [this refers to the rule of Brihtric, king of Wessex] *there came for the first time three ships of Northmen and then the reeve* [the king's local representative] *rode to them and wished to force them to the king's residence, for he did not know what they were; and they slew him. Those were the first ships of Danish men which came to the land of the English.*[1]

More information is provided by a later manuscript of the *Chronicle*, called *manuscript E*, written in East Anglia to replace an earlier version destroyed in a fire in 1116. The writer first identified the raiders as "from Hörthaland" (in Norway), before adding the raiders were "Danes". So their origin was a matter of debate.

Other clues expand what we know about this raid. *Æthelweard's*

Chronicle – written in Latin for a wealthy West Country landowner in the late tenth century – adds that the murdered royal official was named "Beaduheard" and he was based in the nearby town of Dorchester (Dorset). *Æthelweard's Chronicle* adds that the reeve thought the new arrivals were traders. This proved to be a fatal error. To this information the Latin *Annals of St Neots* – compiled at Bury St Edmunds (Suffolk) in the early twelfth century – adds that the violence erupted at Portland (Dorset).

So we can conclude an unknown ship from somewhere in Scandinavia docked at Portland. The local royal official rode down from Dorchester to establish who they were and to sort out the import tax situation; they killed him. Then they sailed away. Everyone in the area must have been shocked. It certainly made enough of an impact to be recorded somewhere, so a century later, the compiler of *manuscript A* of the *Anglo-Saxon Chronicle* referred to it. By then everyone knew all about Vikings, so a record that might otherwise have been lost stood out as if its significance had been recognized at the time. It seemed a pointer to worse things to come.

About the same time (in 792) Offa, the great king of the Midlands kingdom of Mercia, set about improving his kingdom's coastal defences. Mercia had a North Sea coast since it included Lincolnshire and the southern Humber estuary with the great navigable rivers radiating inland from it. We do not know why Offa did this. But, looking back from our current vantage point, we can guess.

THE DESTRUCTION OF LINDISFARNE, 793

The monastery of Lindisfarne, on Holy Island, lay at the end of a causeway off the coast of the northern Anglo-Saxon kingdom of Northumbria. It was a spiritual, cultural and intellectual powerhouse. Arriving in 635 from the equally famous monastery of Iona in what is now western Scotland, the monk Aidan chose the site because it was situated close to the royal centre on the nearby Rock of Bamburgh. It was made famous by Cuthbert, who later became abbot of the monastery, then a bishop, and after his death the patron saint of Northumbria. It was at Lindisfarne that the beautifully decorated *Lindisfarne Gospels* (now in the British Library) were produced in the early eighth century.

Then in 793 – less than a century after the *Lindisfarne Gospels* were produced – the place was devastated. If any event in the Viking Wars represented a clash of civilizations then it was the sack of Lindisfarne. The fact that Anglo-Saxon war bands in the eighth century were not above sacking monasteries loyal to rival neighbouring kingdoms within England did not diminish the shock of this attack from the sea, by pagans.

Far away, in distant Aachen (in what is now Germany), the Northumbrian churchman and scholar Alcuin was living at the court of the Frankish ruler Charlemagne. He provides us with the only significant contemporary account of the Lindisfarne attack (since the equally famous account in the *Anglo-Saxon Chronicle* was not written until the 880s). Alcuin recorded his profound shock in a letter in 793, to Æthelred, king of Northumbria:

> *It is nearly 350 years that we and our fathers have inhabited this most lovely land, and never before has such a terror appeared in Britain as we have now suffered from a pagan race, nor was it thought that such an inroad from the sea could be made. Behold, the church of St Cuthbert spattered with the blood of the priests of God, despoiled of all its ornaments; a place more venerable than all in Britain is given as a prey to pagan peoples.*[2]

For contemporary Christians, the event seemed to fulfil the Old Testament prophecy of Jeremiah chapter 1, verse 14: "Then the Lord said to me: 'Out of the north disaster shall break out on all the inhabitants of the land.'"[3] This verse may have inspired Alcuin's identification of a premonition of the attack taking the form of a bloody rain which had fallen from a clear sky on the north side of the church at York. Alcuin spelled out the implication, in case the recipient of his letter had missed it: "from the north there will come upon our nation retribution of blood".[4] But Alcuin did not stop there. He denounced the sins, as he saw it, which had led to God sending this "retribution". The first two offences seem quite out of proportion to the destruction of a national treasure, but not to Alcuin. He was particularly incensed by sinful hair fashion which imitated that of the northern pagans, and by the sin of wearing luxurious clothing. Perhaps more proportionately, from a modern perspective, he then focused on the impoverishment of the common people as a result of the wealth enjoyed by the elites of Anglo-Saxon England.

The matter of imitating Viking hairstyles would run and run. As late as the early eleventh century (after a fresh outbreak of Viking raids) another ecclesiastical letter writer also complained about Anglo-Saxons who "dress in Danish fashion with bared necks and blinded eyes".[5] Copying the hairstyles of the Vikings was clearly offending a number of church leaders. The inclusion of this sin within Alcuin's letter suggests that people in Western Europe were already sufficiently acquainted with Scandinavians to copy their hair styling, and the arrival of the Vikings might not have been quite the shock the contemporary written sources suggest. Clearly, traders and travellers with distinctive hairstyles had already become noticeable, even before similarly coiffured compatriots appeared in a more alarming context.

Alcuin was not finished in his campaign of identifying Viking-related sins. He wrote a second letter in 793, this time to Higbald, bishop of Lindisfarne. In it, he met head on the question of why "St Cuthbert, with so great a number of saints, defends not his own".[6] It was a question that must have crossed the minds of a number of Anglo-Saxons. In response, Alcuin concluded that "it has not happened by chance, but is a sign that it was well merited by someone".[7] Having blamed hairstyles, fashion and rich elites, Alcuin pondered whether it was something sinful in the lifestyle of the bishop. Or the monks. While the recipients of the second letter were reflecting on these questions, Alcuin promised to use his influence with the Frankish ruler, the emperor Charlemagne, to see if anything could be done to secure the release of the monks of Lindisfarne enslaved by the Vikings. This suggests that methods of communication (maybe even what we might today call "back channels") existed between the rulers of the suffering states and the perpetrators of the violence. Other clues (some Christian rulers colluding with Vikings, precious items ransomed back) suggest that this was, indeed, the case.

Alcuin's letters are not our only record of the raid on Lindisfarne. A later source – *manuscript E* of the *Anglo-Saxon Chronicle* – took up the theme dramatically in a very famous reflection:

> *In this year dire portents appeared over Northumbria and sorely frightened the people. They consisted of immense whirlwinds and flashes of lightning, and fiery dragons were seen flying in the air. A great famine immediately followed those signs, and a little after that in the same year, on 8 June, the ravages of heathen men miserably destroyed God's church in Lindisfarne, with plunder and slaughter.*[8]

Some other manuscripts of the *Chronicle* date the attack to January 793 but the monk who wrote *manuscript E* was better informed about northern English events, as a summer attack is more credible than one in the depth of winter. The latter was well outside the parameters of what we might call the Viking raiding season.

It is now difficult to decide just how terrible the raid on Lindisfarne was. Alcuin's second letter was written to both the bishop and also the community of monks on Lindisfarne. This indicates that monastic life had somehow survived the assault of 793. A later mid-tenth-century source (the *History of St Cuthbert*) explains that it was not until 830–845 that the relics of St Cuthbert were moved from Lindisfarne to Norham-on-Tweed (Northumberland), and the church building dismantled. By 875 the community had returned to Lindisfarne, only to move again that year.

There is the famous gravestone from Lindisfarne, often said to illustrate seven weapon-waving Viking marauders advancing from left to right across the stone slab.[9] But this actually complicates things because its existence shows that a Christian religious community continued to bury its dead there until the site finally became too dangerous maybe two generations later. Furthermore, the marauding Vikings on the stone slab might simply represent soldiers generally, in a scene from events leading up to the Day of Judgement as recorded in the gospels: "For nation will rise against nation, and kingdom against kingdom, and there will be famines and earthquakes in various places."[10] There is nothing definitely Viking about their weapons or appearance.

The Vikings did not hold a monopoly on violence against churches and monasteries. Of 113 attacks on monasteries in Ireland between 795 and 820, only twenty-six were carried out by the Vikings. The rest were mostly the work of Christian Irish kings attacking monasteries in rival Irish kingdoms. Some attacks were even the work of monks from rival monasteries.[11] In 684 Ecgfrith, the Anglo-Saxon king of Northumbria, launched an attack on Ireland which involved the destruction of Irish churches. Mercia and Wessex targeted each other's monasteries if they were vulnerably sited close to their borders.[12] It was not just the Vikings who trashed churches situated in enemy kingdoms. But they take the sole blame in our collective memory of this period of history.

Consequently, the jury is still out on the severity of the damage caused by Vikings to Lindisfarne in this early raid. But what is beyond debate is that it was bad enough to shock contemporary Christians. And as the raids escalated there is evidence that the damage was real enough.

COASTAL RAIDS ACROSS NORTH-WEST EUROPE

The British Isles bore the brunt of these early raids, perhaps because these first attacks were carried out by Norwegian Vikings from across the northern North Sea. Sometimes they sailed down the eastern coast of Britain (like the raid that hit Lindisfarne), round Scotland and south-westward into the Irish Sea (raiding Irish monasteries). In time the Norwegians would specialize in the latter area and the Danes in the former area, and down through the English Channel. However, at least one tradition (a view reflected in *manuscripts D, E* and *F* of the *Anglo-Saxon Chronicle*) claimed that the troublemakers at Portland were Norwegians, so there was clearly no hard and fast rule.

What is clear is that it was not just the British Isles in the firing line. The coastal areas of Frisia and the Frankish Empire in the Low Countries and north-western France also experienced attacks. Until about 834 these were mostly small-scale, uncoordinated raids by solitary ships or very small fleets. Furthermore, while they harmed coastal communities, they did not penetrate far up the river systems, so were easier to resist than what would come later. Even so, many raiders had come and gone (with their loot and slaves) before local forces arrived. This was particularly a problem in the politically divided context of Ireland where constant warfare between rival small Christian kingdoms meant any coordinated defence was out of the question.

Defence would soon become increasingly problematic in the Frankish lands as, in the 830s the window of opportunity was flung open to these opportunistic Scandinavians. Civil war in the Frankish Empire disrupted coastal defences on the eastern side of the southern North Sea and the English Channel. Disunity would soon be severely punished by Viking raiders, who often responded to openings provided by divisions among their victims. The Franks delivered many of these opportunities. At one point, in the second half of the 830s, one exiled member of the Frankish royal family (Lothair I) was actually encouraging Viking raids on the Frisian coast in order to economically disadvantage his father (Louis the Pious), who had exiled him. What would the coastal civilians have said if they had known that they were the victims of political in-fights among their own rulers?

As a consequence, the focus of Viking activities in the period 830–865 shifted to the Continent and away from Britain; although Ireland continued to be targeted since its political weaknesses mirrored those of the now-disunited Franks. The range of targets increased, as larger fleets sailed up navigable rivers such as the Rhine, Seine and Loire, to sack inland towns. In Ireland the River Shannon provided a similar route into the interior. In 841 the coastal island of Walcheren, at the mouth of the Scheldt estuary (today in the province of Zeeland in the Netherlands), was granted to a Danish Viking leader named Harald, probably the earliest example of the strategy of buying off a troublesome Viking leader who could not be evicted, in the hope that he would act as a buffer against further Viking incursions. Sometimes it worked, often it did not. Either way, it was a sign of weakness on the part of the grantor. In this case, Harald and his brother Rorik soon dominated large parts of what is now the Netherlands. When Frankish forces attempted to evict these Viking newcomers, they failed and the largest Frankish trading settlement in the area (Dorestad) soon came under their control. This Viking rule would last in Frisia until the 880s.

THE CHRISTIAN CHURCH UNDER ATTACK

The raid on Lindisfarne seemed to coincide with an escalation of raids across the British Isles, a disquieting aspect to these attacks not lost on those recording them. In 794 the Irish annals report "the plundering of all the islands of Britain by pagans". Again, in 795, the Irish records tell us that the monastery at Rathlin was burned, and those at Iona, Inishmurray and Inisbofin attacked.[13] Christian centres of worship and learning were suffering disproportionately.

Later, Alfred of Wessex would go on the record to claim that all centres of learning had been destroyed in England in Viking attacks. In support of Alfred's claim, very few pre-Viking land charters (written records of gifts of land and kept in monasteries) survive. This indicates both a great loss of church libraries and records and a decline in the standards of literacy.[14] The charters which do survive suggest that something catastrophic had occurred in the centres of learning, since their Latin is very poor. Something terrible was happening to the Christian church across the British Isles: Vikings were having an appalling impact on the established faith of these islands. And Britain was not alone...

THE ASSAULT ON THE ANGLO-SAXON KINGDOMS

Between the years 789 and 866 the Viking attacks on England escalated. In 794, just one year after the attack on the monastery at Lindisfarne, the "heathens ravaged in Northumbria and plundered Ecgfrith's monastery at Donemuthan".[15] The name has not survived as a modern place name. However, the early-twelfth-century work *Historia Dunelmensis ecclesiae* (*History of the Church of Durham*), written by Simeon of Durham, states that it was the monastery of Jarrow (Tyne and Wear), where the Anglo-Saxon scholar Bede had once been a monk.[16]

A lull in raids on England followed, while Ireland experienced heavy raiding in the first thirty years of the ninth century, followed by some settlement in the 840s. As a result, it seems that the raiders and settlers – mostly Danes – were occupied on the other side of the Irish Sea. But then things escalated in England: in 835 "heathen men ravaged Sheppey" (Kent);[17] and in 836, thirty-five Viking ships (a large fleet by previous standards) landed on the Somerset coast at Carhampton. The battle there ended in a Viking victory. It was again the scene of a battle in 843 and, again, the Vikings won. The defeat was bad enough to be noted on the other side of the Channel, where people knew all about Viking attacks. The Frankish *Annales Bertiniani* (*Annals of St Bertin*) noted, of the last English conflict:

> *After a battle lasting three days, the Northmen emerged the winners: plundering, looting, slaughtering everywhere, they wielded power over the land at will.*[18]

Then, in 840, Southampton (Hampshire) – then called *Hamwic* – was attacked. This attack on a major trading port would, if successful, have offered rich pickings and human cargo for ransom or enslavement. However, the *ealdorman* (the king's regional representative) Wulfheard defeated the Vikings attacking the port. Elsewhere the targeting of trading settlements was more successful and lucrative. Just two years later, in 842, three major international trading centres were devastated, according to the *Anglo-Saxon Chronicle*. Two were in England: London and Rochester (Kent); and one in the Frankish Empire, Quentovic (east of Étaples, in what is now France). These were seriously important places. London was the leading trading centre in England. Quentovic was the leading port in northern France, the most important of all the Frankish seaports. These were no ordinary raids, nor did resistance drive off the Vikings as it had at Southampton. The *Anglo-Saxon Chronicle* records "great slaughter"[19] in all three places.

Another major Frankish trading settlement, at Dorestad (in the modern-day province of Utrecht in the Netherlands), went into decline in the 840s. It had been raided twice, in 834 and in 846. Peaceful trade at poorly defended sites was proving hard to maintain. Like Quentovic, its economic decline meant that it was eventually abandoned. This fairly drawn out decline was not the smoking result of one or two violent Viking raids – as other economic, trading, political and even ecological factors played their parts – but there is no denying the role played by Vikings in its decline and decay.

From the mid-840s to the mid-850s, Anglo-Saxon forces in the core shires of the kingdom of Wessex managed to fend off a number of attacks. Elsewhere things went badly for the defenders: London (a Mercian city at this point) was stormed (again), along with Canterbury. These assaults were on an unprecedented scale, since 350 enemy ships are reported.

In the winter of 851–852 England experienced the kind of crisis that a decade earlier had led to the loss of Walcheren and its region to the Vikings. The *Anglo-Saxon Chronicle* records: "And for the first time, heathen men stayed through the winter on Thanet."[20] Now there would be little respite from attacks, for as soon as winter was past, the Vikings were at the door. The crisis was escalating sharply.

THE DAMAGE CAUSED BY VIKING ATTACKS

We have seen the damage caused to continental trading centres such as Dorestad and Quentovic, and to English centres such as London and Canterbury. Archaeology bears witness to the resulting stagnation in trade, and so we cannot dismiss as self-serving political spin later comments made by Alfred the Great about the situation he inherited and began to turn around.

When Alfred wrote his own preface to a translation of a document called the *Regula Pastoralis (Pastoral Care)*, somewhere between 890 and 895, he recounted the devastation caused by the Vikings. He "remembered how, before everything was ravaged and burnt, the churches throughout all England stood filled with treasures and books…". Again, but in a letter, he described how the Anglo-Saxon church had "fallen in ruins in many respects" due to "the frequent invasion and attack of pagans".[21] Other evidence supports his account. In the Royal Library in Stockholm, Sweden, is a magnificent gospel book, called the *Stockholm Codex Aureus*. Originally produced in Kent, a mid-ninth-century inscription was added to it explaining that the book was ransomed from "a heathen army" for a payment in gold, by the *ealdorman* of Surrey and his wife. It was then returned to Christian use by being presented to Christ Church, Canterbury (Kent).[22] Its modern-day location in Sweden, though, is due to its legitimate purchase much later, in 1690. By that time it was in Madrid, but there is no record of how it got to Spain. It was later donated to the Swedish royal collection in 1705.

Many less valuable objects than the *Stockholm Codex Aureus* passed from western Europe to Scandinavia in this way but were not returned. In the twenty-first century almost identical late-ninth-century bronze book mounts, bearing the head of Christ or a saint, sometimes appear at auction with general English and Scandinavian provenances, reminders of how these items that once adorned Frankish or Anglo-Saxon books or reliquaries were scattered by Viking raids. It is not surprising that Anglo-Saxon charters from this period included caveats, such as being for "as long as the Christian faith should last in Britain", which hint that some people thought its continuation was in doubt. By the time of the compilation of *Domesday Book* (1086) the church owned twenty to thirty-three per cent of the land in England as a whole but consistently less than ten per cent in the north and eastern Midlands. These areas had experienced the worst of the Viking attacks and settlement. The implication is clear: in these areas estates went out of church ownership and never made it back. Between 844 and 864, a Kentish noblewoman promised regular food supplies from her estate at Bradbourne (Kent) to the monks at St Augustine's Abbey, Canterbury. Facing up to the realities of present difficulties, she added a clause to the effect that the monks could have the entire estate if the promised supplies were not delivered for three successive years due to the *hæðen here* (heathen army).

THE FRANKS FIGHT BACK

In the mid-860s, Viking attentions switched from the Frankish territories back to Britain. The reorganization of the Frankish defences had made it more difficult to campaign there. For example, the Frankish king Charles the Bald ordered the construction of a number of fortified bridges which stopped Viking fleets from raiding far up rivers. The first constructed was at Pont-de-l'Arche, on the River Seine, in 862, to protect the royal centre at Pîtres. Other fortified bridges were erected on the Rivers Loire and Oise. In 865, after a final raid up the River Seine with Paris as its target, Viking attention shifted back across the English Channel.[23]

In addition to the building of these bridges, other factors were also at work. Charles the Bald paid off the Vikings with 4,000 pounds (1,814 kilograms) of silver and large quantities of wine, with the proviso that they left western Francia. This, plus the bridge construction, meant the Viking leaders decided that the benefits of operating in Francia were declining and England offered an easier target.

ALMOST THE END OF ANGLO-SAXON ENGLAND

In the 860s and 870s, Viking raids turned to settlement on a wide arc of territory. This new phase can be discerned from Iceland to England. In 866 a Viking army landed in East Anglia, which was described in the *Anglo-Saxon Chronicle* as the *micel hæðen here*. Outright conquest and settlement was now on the Viking agenda.

Later tradition stated that this force was commanded by Danish Vikings named Ivar the Boneless and Halfdan, the sons of Ragnar *Lothbrok* (leather or hairy breeches). The *Chronicle* entry for 866 gives no names of the leaders of the Danes but *Æthelweard's Chronicle* names one of them as "Igwar", a form of Ivar. This is apparently confirmed by the *Anglo-Saxon Chronicle* entry for 878. This annal records the defeat of an unnamed "brother of Ivar and Healfdene" (Halfdan) and the capture of the Vikings' "raven banner" (as ravens were associated with Odin in Norse mythology).[24] In the early twelfth century, the *Annals of St Neots* claimed that the banner was woven by the daughters of Ragnar *Lothbrok*.

From a base in East Anglia, and now mobile since the East Angles had been forced to give them horses, the Viking army went north to York in the autumn of 867, seizing this strategic northern city, the capital of the Anglo-Saxon kingdom of Northumbria. The

Vikings had sniffed out political weakness since the kingdom was in the middle of a civil war. Later, Alfred the Great's biographer, the Welsh bishop Asser, considered that the swift destruction of the kingdom signalled "a people which has incurred the wrath of God".[25] It was an attitude similar to that earlier expressed by Alcuin in response to the attack on Lindisfarne.

The date of the Viking attack on York is also very significant, as the later medieval historian Simeon of Durham noted that the seizure of the city took place on 1 November: All Saints' Day, a major event in the Christian calendar. The city's swollen population would have been preoccupied with the celebration, both an incentive for Viking slave-takers. Viking raids in Ireland similarly targeted monasteries during religious celebrations. In 868 the Viking force moved south to Nottingham. Mercia was in their sights, but Burgred, king of Mercia, called on the West Saxons for assistance. In response, Æthelred, king of Wessex, accompanied by his younger brother Alfred, responded with the army of Wessex and the Vikings were forced away – for now. As a result, they returned to East Anglia, and killed its king, Edmund, in 870. We do not know why but probably he was showing signs of resistance and paid the price. *Manuscript E* of the *Anglo-Saxon Chronicle* preserves an East Anglian tradition that the Vikings then destroyed all the monasteries they came to. At Peterborough they killed the abbot, the monks and everyone else, then burned down the monastery.

After 871 it was the turn of Wessex. Unable to gain a decisive military victory, the West Saxons also found that it was almost impossible to do any lasting deal with the invaders. As part of a peace deal at Wareham (Dorset), the Vikings gave Alfred members of their army as hostages and also swore on their holy ring that they would leave Wessex. Much later sagas from Iceland refer to such holy rings kept in pagan Viking sanctuaries and worn by a leader at assemblies. Alfred's later biographer, Asser, was clearly not comfortable with the idea of a pagan item being used in truce negotiations, and adapted the story to make it acceptable to Christians by saying that the Vikings "took an oath, on all the relics in which the king placed the greatest trust after God Himself".[26] This is not convincing, since these would not have impressed pagan Scandinavians. Despite the use of their holy ring, they still broke the deal, killed their West Saxon hostages and escaped from Wareham under cover of darkness. How was one to work with such people? We will see how later much effort was put into converting Vikings, partly to try to establish some kind of level playing field where everyone knew and abided by the same rules – at least in theory.

Then, in the winter of 877–878, the Vikings almost captured Alfred, led by a leader named Guthrum. This attack took place after Twelfth Night (5 January), so it probably occurred on 6 January. This is the Christian feast of the Epiphany celebrating the visit of the magi to the infant Jesus. As in the 867 attack on York, the royal hall would have been well stocked with provisions and Christian minds would have been focused away from warfare.

However, the Vikings failed, even though Alfred only survived by escaping into the Somerset marshes. Leading a fight back, he eventually defeated the Vikings and, in a peace treaty that they largely honoured, they withdrew from Wessex. But something very important accompanied this move: Guthrum converted to Christianity and was baptized, with King Alfred as his godfather. He was the first Viking leader to become a Christian, in Britain at least, and the trend would spread. The Christian Vikings had arrived.

Guthrum then moved his army to Cirencester (Gloucestershire). Although the *Anglo-Saxon Chronicle* records the arrival of a new Viking fleet on the River Thames, at Fulham in 879, this did not prompt a renewed attack on Wessex, despite the new arrivals joining Guthrum. Instead, in 880, Guthrum returned to East Anglia and shared out the land with his army; the other Vikings sailed for Ghent, in Belgium, to seek easier pickings among the Franks. A further treaty, sometime between 886 and 890, divided up England into different spheres of influence. The east and north of England would be under Viking control, an area later referred to as the "Danelaw".

Faced with increased resistance in England, many Viking raiders shifted their operations back to Francia. In the 890s they returned to England. But in the meantime Alfred had reorganized his defences, creating a network of defended towns (*burhs*) to give refuge to locals and their valuables and provide a base for resistance. Military reorganization on a rota system allowed him to keep an army constantly in the field: he even experimented (with mixed success) with improved warships. In 896, after being constantly harried by the English defenders, the latest Viking force withdrew. There was no repeat of the success of the *micel hæðen here*. During the tenth century there would be more Viking incursions into Britain generally and England in particular. North-west England, for example, would be settled by Norwegian settlers after 900. Norse rulers from Dublin would fish in the troubled waters of northern English politics, with varying degrees of success, until the death of the last Scandinavian king of York, Erik Bloodaxe, in 954. These later incursions affecting England would eventually all be defeated by the West Saxon kings, who would unify England (including the Danelaw) under their rule (see later chapters). This would last until the second run of Viking Wars kicked off with great intensity from the 980s. But in the meantime it looked as if the Vikings could be dealt with: disaster had been averted.

Even in disunited Ireland, defences improved and Viking opportunities correspondingly diminished. Here the Irish experienced what they referred to as the "Forty Years Rest". This lasted there until 914 when Vikings once more targeted the island (see Chapter 5). Elsewhere, too, there was a lull lasting for several generations. In Francia, Vikings were allowed to settle in Normandy (see Chapter 6) with the expectation that they would keep other marauders out. As the saying goes, "Set a thief to catch a thief." Between 914 and 936 other Vikings attempted a takeover in Brittany but were eventually driven out in 936 (with Anglo-Saxon assistance). Only Frisia continued to be successfully targeted by Viking raids. The first great wave of Viking activity in mainland Europe had ended.[27]

But what was happening in those areas that had been occupied by – or ceded to – the Vikings? This was particularly difficult: all the Western European communities that had been occupied were profoundly Christian but were now under the rule of those termed the pagans by the Christian chroniclers. In England, which had suffered particularly devastating attacks, only one Christian Anglo-

Saxon kingdom had survived the pagan onslaught. What was to be the fate of Christianity in the other conquered kingdoms of Anglo-Saxon England? To that and its rather surprising character we shall now turn.

CHAPTER 3

The Viking
Conversion in England

There were varied roads to conversion in England during the years between 880 and the return of Viking fleets a century later. But how and why were such violent marauders converted from paganism to Christianity? And this, despite the fact that their paganism was a defining feature of their culture. Much of Western Europe had generally been Christian since the seventh century at the latest. In what is today the Netherlands and north-west Germany, the northern Germanic tribes, such as the continental Saxons (as opposed to Saxons who settled in Britain as part of Anglo-Saxon England), had started to convert in the late seventh and early eighth centuries. The latter process was violently completed by the Frankish emperor Charlemagne, in his so-called Saxon Wars, fought between 772 and 804, crushing the last rebellion of Saxon tribesmen against Frankish rule and cultural imperialism. This straddled the start of the Viking Wars (the West Saxon king's reeve had been killed on Portland in 789) and Alcuin criticized the brutality used by the Franks in forcing Christian conversion on the conquered Saxons. In his opinion, with more kindness and less ruthless demanding of tithes and enforcement of the Frankish legal system, the Saxons might have taken more willingly to the new faith imposed on them along with Frankish rule.[1]

Scandinavians strongly defined themselves by their paganism, possibly, as we touched on in Chapter 1, encouraged by what was happening to recalcitrant pagans south of Denmark, and the muscular Christianity so lethally apparent in Charlemagne's Saxon Wars. The Vikings' projection of assertive paganism was almost certainly a declaration of their freedom from Frankish imperial control. Although no early Vikings left a manifesto to this effect, the nature of their actions suggests it was probably a significant factor.

This assertive paganism was certainly not lost on their opponents. The *Anglo-Saxon Chronicle* sometimes refers to the Vikings as the "heathen army"; however, for Alfred the Great's Welsh biographer, Bishop Asser, the Vikings were always portrayed as the "pagans". The words *heathen* and *pagan* both refer to religions that do not accept the God of the Bible and, instead, believe in many deities. The word *heathen* is derived from an Old English word, whereas *pagan* is derived from an original Latin term meaning "country-dweller". The words were originally interchangeable, depending on the language used by the writer in question. For Asser, the conflict was an epic battle between paganism and Christianity. To start with, at least, the events seemed to support his opinion.

The Viking warriors who operated in England from the late eighth century onwards certainly represented a new resurgence of paganism. To Anglo-Saxons, who had been Christian since the seventh century, this was a shocking throwback to a distant and unlamented past. Whatever may sometimes appear in print in the twenty-first century, by the late eighth century, England was profoundly Christian. Not so the new incomers. They had no reservations about their paganism. What resulted was a profound culture shock.

The Viking influx into Britain between 789 and 900 was clearly an invasion of pagans and this pagan influence reverberated well into the tenth century. We have already seen evidence of this in the destruction of Christian monasteries. But other forms of evidence can also be presented. There is evidence for animal sacrifices (such as has been excavated from Skerne, in Yorkshire, on the River Hull); there are possibly cases of human sacrifice on the Isle of Man, and the deliberate destruction of Christian graves there can be seen in the same way as the Viking boat burial at Balladoole, showing no respect for an earlier Christian cemetery. In short, in the east and north of England, Christianity lost the Viking Wars... Or did it?

EVIDENCE FOR THE DESTRUCTION OF CHRISTIANITY: A TRASHED CHURCH IN THE EAST MIDLANDS

Initially things did not look good for the continuation of the Christian church and Christianity generally in the areas now under Viking rule. A shocking example of this comes from the year 874, when the *micel hæðen here* occupied the Mercian royal centre at Repton (Derbyshire). The great burial mausoleum of the Mercian royal family was sited here, so it was hallowed by Christian faith and royal associations. In the crypt at Repton lay buried Æthelbald the powerful eighth-century Mercian overlord whose rule had overshadowed other Anglo-Saxon kingdoms. But then, in 874, this great monument became a pagan Viking camp. The occupation was accompanied by considerable devastation of the site. First, the church was incorporated into the defences dug around the camp, providing an easily fortified point. The Viking army constructed two deep ditches which curved round between the church and the river until they enclosed a D-shaped area of some 1.4 hectares (3.5 acres). Archaeological excavations here from 1974 to 1988 (directed by Martin Biddle, Birthe Kjølbye-Biddle and Harold Taylor) revealed a burial mound within this enclosure which contained the skeletons of 200 men and 49 women. The latter we may presume were wives or camp followers (servants, slaves or prostitutes).[2]

All the bodies in the cemetery at Repton were inhumed, that is they were buried unburnt. However, another contemporary Viking cemetery – excavated at nearby Heath Wood, Ingleby – followed cremation rather than inhumation in its disposal of the dead. Here the combined rites of human cremation, animal sacrifice and mound burial were even more explicit statements of paganism in a combination that would have shocked the average Anglo-Saxon.

The humiliation of the Christian Mercians was apparent for all to see. What had once been its royal centre had been occupied and its meaning and message subverted by Scandinavian pagans. We can only imagine the pagan rites which accompanied the great mass burial. And at this time the Mercian king Burgred, who had attempted to accommodate the invading Vikings in 872 and 873 in order to survive, was now driven from his throne.

The destruction of the church at Repton was probably repeated across large swathes of the eastern Midlands and the north of England. The loss of church land in this area (as recorded in *Domesday Book* in 1086), that we remarked on in Chapter 2, is evidence of this: by then the church owned less than ten per cent of land in the north and eastern Midlands, compared with a national average of twenty to thirty-three per cent of the land in England as a whole.

This loss of land could well have meant a disaster for the Christian church in these areas: ownership of land was integral to how Christianity functioned in Anglo-Saxon England and elsewhere. First, Christianity was, and is, a religion with an organized community, a hierarchy and structure of clergy. All of this requires resources. In the early Middle Ages (c. 500–1000), wealth and resources equalled land. This should not be interpreted as materialism replacing spirituality. Rather, it allowed a certain kind of spirituality to function: the resources of rural estates (and over ninety per cent of the population worked in agriculture) could be used to feed priests and monks and nuns. When sold, it paid for craftspeople to build churches, make vestments and all the accompanying features of church life. When lay people gifted land to the church, they were helping to make these things happen. They were doing it for God and the good of their souls, because they knew that in order for the church, as it was then constituted, to function these resources were necessary. Clergy (serving at local churches) or monks or nuns (in monastic communities) were not working on the land, so somebody else had to, in order to support them and free up their time. It was this that made possible the network of monasteries across the kingdoms and the local churches (*minsters*) from which clergy could minister to their local area. These places then became the centres of community life and, in time, where baptisms, weddings and burials took place. In short, the ownership of land underpinned the organized church.

Secondly, Christianity (like Judaism and Islam) is a religion of the book. Today we take for granted the mass production and dissemination of the written word and the communication of words generally (in print or electronically). But in the early Middle Ages (as for much of the time prior to the fifteenth-century development of printing) producing a book was massively expensive, both in terms of physical resources and time. The *Lindisfarne Gospels*, for example, are made up of 258 leaves of high quality vellum (calf skin). This would have required at least 127 unblemished calf skins.[3] Many skins must have been discarded in order to achieve the consistently high quality that we see in the finished product. This probably involved the use of yearling calves and it could have taken as long as ten years to amass such a large number of high quality skins.[4] The *Codex Amiatinus*, a complete Bible produced at Monkwearmouth and Jarrow, probably required over 500 calf skins.[5] Totalling these resources has not even begun to calculate the hundreds and hundreds of hours of skilful work necessary to write and decorate these amazing works of art. Now, certainly not every local church had a *Lindisfarne Gospels* or a *Codex Amiatinus* but the existence of books underpinned the functioning of the church, and every monastery would certainly have had a library of works, both biblical texts and scholarly commentaries. All of these required a huge investment of resources.

Consequently, the loss of so many agricultural estates must have crippled the traditional functioning of the Christian church in areas lost to Viking control, where Viking war band members were rewarded with land in the newly conquered territories. The destruction at Repton was the mere tip of the iceberg of catastrophic loss experienced by the church. In such circumstances, it is easy to envisage a situation developing in which the collapse of Christian preaching and teaching, the end of pastoral care and the loss of Christian community events at local churches could well have occasioned the collapse of Christian faith.

This could also have been compounded by the very nature of pagan belief. As we have seen, there was no unified or hierarchical organization of Norse pagan practices and no codified set of myths. The appearance of this in later Icelandic texts is misleading, as it was only then that an attempt was made to both record and organize it, and the result was complex and lacked consistency and clarity. The thirteenth-century Icelanders did their best.[6]

The impression one gets is of a mixture of local cult centres presided over by a chieftain acting as priest (in Iceland termed a *goði*); larger cult centres patronized by royalty and elites (such as at Gamla Uppsala in Sweden); and the heads of extended households (consisting of free and slave members) overseeing religious practices and sacrifices. This was loose-knit, localized, generally small-scale, usually family-based with some local community cooperation, and lacked an overall priesthood or organizational structure or set of scriptures. But it shared beliefs that had common characteristics over a wide area, while also having much local variation and layering of different traditions that were not consistent across the Viking world. Given the collapse of organized Christian religious structures and the humiliation of local Christian elites, one could envisage a situation in which such localized and organizationally simple pagan cults experienced a high measure of success and were more easily sustainable, since they did not rely on an economically sophisticated and demanding support structure. They could have moved into the vacuum left by the collapse of the organized church.

The statistics of estate ownership are far more important than simply providing an index of economic power. Rather, they point to the real possibility of ideological implosion and collapse. Yet this did not happen: Christianity survived and was soon resurgent in areas where it might have been considered under threat. A striking example of this comes from late-ninth-century East Anglia.

A CURIOUS ROUTE TO CONVERSION
IN EAST ANGLIA

King Edmund of East Anglia (see Chapter 2) was killed by the Vikings in the year 870. According to later sources, he met a terrible and violent death. His fame is remembered today in the name of the town of Bury St Edmunds, in Suffolk. Unfortunately, we know surprisingly little about him. There are just a few brief references in the *Anglo-Saxon Chronicle* and we know of coins that were minted bearing his name. That is about it from his lifetime.

However, his fame spread rapidly after his death. In these traditions he was described as a Christian martyr, killed by pagans, the heathen Vikings. The *manuscript C* of the *Anglo-Saxon Chronicle* simply describes him as "King Edmund" but the *manuscript E*, written in East Anglia itself, calls him "Saint Edmund", revealing the way his death was commemorated in East Anglia. The transition from little known monarch to celebrated martyr was clearly felt keenly by a local East Anglian chronicler, as he continued to copy and update his copy of the *Anglo-Saxon Chronicle*. From that foundation the story would expand.

In the later years of the tenth century, Abbo of Fleury (in France) became Edmund's earliest recorded biographer. He wrote a Latin work entitled *Passio Sancti Eadmundi (Passion of St Edmund)*, around 985–987. The book proved popular and was translated into Old English by Ælfric of Eynsham (Oxfordshire), later in the tenth century. Abbo claimed he had heard the story of Edmund's death from no lesser person than the Anglo-Saxon ecclesiastic Dunstan, archbishop of Canterbury. Dunstan claimed to have heard the story at the royal court, when it was told to Athelstan, king of a united Wessex and Mercia, by a very old man who claimed to have been Edmund's armour-bearer. If true, the chain of witnesses is intriguing. There may actually be some eyewitness evidence in some of what Abbo later recounted.

The traditional story is harrowing. According to Abbo's account (and the tradition that he received), Edmund was not killed in battle: he was captured by the Viking army that had returned from the conquest of Northumbria and then tortured to death. Abbo claimed that Edmund was scourged, tied to a tree and then had arrows fired at him. This continued until he resembled a hedgehog. Then his torturers beheaded him. The body was left where it fell but his head was thrown into a wood. Later, those searching for it were guided to the spot where it lay by an unidentified voice calling out to them, in Latin, "*Hic, hic, hic*" ("Here, here, here"). When they eventually located the head, they discovered that it was protected by an enormous wolf. One can see why the story caught people's imagination – and why today we find it hard to say exactly where the eyewitness account ends and the myth-making begins.

While Abbo's account was written (and clearly embellished) over a century after the events described, we may be confident in assuming that Edmund was executed.[7] There is no doubt that his reign ended abruptly and later chroniclers of the Viking Wars knew the king of East Anglia had met a shocking end, one engineered by pagan Vikings, who may well have had ritual sacrifice in mind when they slaughtered him. This is despite the fact that the similarity between Edmund's death and that of St Sebastian may mean that Abbo's passion book copied details from the more famous martyrdom, to enhance the fame of St Edmund. So, while the arrows, the voice and the wolf in Abbo's account conform to the expected characteristics of a martyr's death, the reference to the words of the armour-bearer and the swift rise to prominence of the king/saint – with an eventual shrine at Bury St Edmunds – may mean that some historical evidence lies behind his claimed martyrdom.

Yet it was not long before the descendants of Edmund's killers were enthusiastically promoting the man their Viking ancestors had clearly considered to be a Christian enemy. Edmund rapidly became an extremely popular saint in an East Anglia that, after 870, had Viking rulers who were initially pagans. In fact, the new Viking rulers of East Anglia minted coins, between 895 and 910, in honour of the martyred Christian king.[8] One form of these coins bears the statement "SCE EADMUNDE REX" on one side, meaning "O Saint Edmund the King!" Other features of the coins produced under the late King Edmund were copied by the new Viking rulers, including a large letter "A" on the obverse and a cross (simplified from the ones used under Edmund) on the reverse.[9] One version of this coinage even had the title SC EADMUND REX on both sides of the coin.[10] These types of coins may have continued to be minted for over twenty years, until as late as 917/918, when East Anglia was eventually conquered by Edward the Elder, the Christian king of Wessex.

This minting was despite the fact that Edmund had been martyred only one generation earlier. The coins' striking significance goes further. Never before in the history of Anglo-Saxon coinage of the ninth century had a king's name (on the obverse, head-side, of a coin) ever been replaced with that of a saint. Strangely enough, though, this was sometimes done among the Christian Franks.[11] And then it was followed in East Anglia by these Viking kings.

Clearly, the Vikings were keen to fit into the Christian expectations of how a king should rule and behave. Even before the St Edmund coins were produced, the new Viking king, Guthrum, had issued coins copying those of his Christian godfather, King Alfred. This was true of most of his coins. Some of his other coins were minted with his Scandinavian name but others were produced carrying the name he had adopted at his baptism, Athelstan. This revealed "how significantly he regarded that Christian ceremony, and the ties that it gave him to King Alfred who had stood sponsor as his godfather".[12] We do not know which of the later Viking kings of East Anglia produced the St Edmund coinage, but, whoever it was, he too took the signalling of Christian beliefs very seriously and to a new level. Whether this was due to a sincere conversion or because the cult of St Edmund was so popular that "it was politically astute for the local Danish king to associate his regime with it"[13] is now impossible to say. But Viking rulers were swiftly starting to behave like Christian ones. Why did this occur?

THE CONVERSION OF THE VIKINGS

As early as the 940s, a man named Oda is recorded as being the archbishop of Canterbury. This Oda was the son of a pagan Viking settler who had converted to Christianity. His life reveals the astonishing speed at which many Scandinavians assimilated in

England.[14] There is plenty of evidence to show that the assimilation of other Scandinavian immigrants, as measured by burial customs, was equally rapid.[15] Very few pagan Viking burials have been discovered in Britain, and those that have, on the Isle of Man and the occasional Scandinavian-style burial on the British mainland, stand out because they are so unusual. They attract the attention of the news media and the archaeological press because of their rarity. In the same way, while there are hundreds of examples of Scandinavian-style ornamentation on tombstones in England, all but thirty of these are within a Christian context.

Such examples show people behaving as Christians but using some of the artistic styles from the Scandinavian homelands. This is despite the fact that the discovery of artefacts by metal detectorists and their reporting to the highly successful Portable Antiquities Scheme in England reveals that in large areas of the Danelaw (northern Lincolnshire for example) there was a sizeable influx of lower class Scandinavian farmers and their families in the wake of elite seizures of the land. In other words, the Viking settlement of eastern England was not just a swapping of landlords. There was real ethnic change. This is not the same as ethnic replacement, since all the evidence shows the continuance of Anglo-Saxon rural settlements and population, but there were many new neighbours speaking Old Norse and many new landlords doing the same. This shows itself in the distinctive place name formations of East Anglia, the eastern Midlands and the north, with the use of *-beck*, *-by*, *-thorp*, *-toft*, and *-thwaite*, Scandinavian terms that differentiated rural settlements.[16] Modern names on the map such as Wetwang Slack, Fangfoss and Whipmawhopmagate stand out as dramatic examples of this from Yorkshire but less striking examples can be mapped across the Danelaw.

This clearly shows that very large numbers of people of Scandinavian identity settled in England but they were drawn from a community which rapidly decreased its ethnic signals and adapted itself to Anglo-Saxon Christian burial customs in place of its traditional pagan practices. The Vikings appear to have soon adopted the lifestyle and beliefs of the English. The Viking impact was certainly dramatic, but it lacked cultural depth. Within two generations, at most, Christian continuity won out over pagan change. The Vikings were "cultural chameleons", soon taking on the characteristics of any dominant social influence. We will meet more examples as we explore other areas of Viking settlement.

The assimilation tended to occur whenever the original locals made up the majority of the population. There were, we can suggest, a number of reasons for this. First, the Scandinavian newcomers never achieved a critical mass which otherwise would have made them dominant in an area, so the native population, though subjugated, could maintain cultural integrity. Secondly, the sophisticated nature of Anglo-Saxon England was a great attraction. This included its Christian character, which linked it to a Europe-wide culture with its roots in the Roman past. The coinage shows how Viking rulers were keen to live up to established expectations of what royal rule should look like and this may have been emulated right down the social hierarchy after the initial conquest. This encouraged the adoption of Christianity with its package of literacy, organization, stone buildings and international connections. Even the burials at Repton, discussed earlier, have been suggested as revealing a desire on behalf of those carrying out the burials to "legitimate their own succession by their association with the Mercian royal house" and may even indicate a conversion to Christianity.[17] Thirdly, Christianity was well established in Anglo-Saxon England and it is reasonable to assume there was a resilience to it (as represented by ordinary believers), even when the established church hierarchy was thrown into chaos. The conversion of the Viking settlers may be a testimony to the behaviour of their Christian neighbours, though we have no evidence for why individual settlers converted. Fourthly, the localized and small-scale nature of pagan religious practice may have been a weakness and not the potential strength we alluded to earlier. The very process of immigration will have dislocated communities, severed ties with familiar cult centres in the Scandinavian homelands and broken the cohesion of the pagan community. In the context of the other factors, this may well have accelerated its fragmentation and eventual demise and the adoption of the new faith. What is clear is that there is no evidence that a missionary enterprise was launched to evangelize the Danelaw pagan Viking communities. In fact, there are no contemporary sources that inform us about their conversion whatsoever. But in the absence of a formal campaign aimed at conversion, the impetus clearly came via other routes.

An historical contrast to this situation in the Danelaw can be provided from the Isle of Man. The earliest occupants of Man almost certainly spoke a British language but, from the fifth century AD, this was replaced by Gaelic. Then in the seventh century the island was conquered by the Anglo-Saxons of Northumbria, who introduced the Old English language. Finally, in the ninth century, it came under Norse domination, becoming part of the Viking Kingdom of the Isles. After this a combined Norse-Gaelic culture survived on the island, which saw a mixing of Celtic and Scandinavian culture. Rather surprisingly, given the widespread evidence for Viking impact, the Norse language failed to survive and it was Manx or Manx-Gaelic (derived from Primitive Irish) which finally reasserted itself. Nevertheless, Norse culture initially dominated the local population and this may suggest a high number of Scandinavian settlers. This seems to have encouraged a more confident and self-conscious signalling of pagan character than is seen in eastern England. While a number of Viking settlers (identified by characteristic Scandinavian artefacts) were buried in the Christian cemetery at St German's Cathedral, St Patrick's Isle, Peel, their style of burial contrasted with Christian practice. Possessions were buried with a number of the dead in a continuation of pagan traditions. In addition, finds of Viking-style weapons at a number of other church sites suggests that here too the dead (in these instances warriors) were buried with possessions. This weapon burial was a rite long abandoned in Christian communities. So the Vikings were choosing to "assert their dominance, regardless of the wishes of the Christian community".[18] Then, at Balladoole, a Viking ship burial was apparently deliberately placed so as to destroy earlier Christian graves, as we have seen.[19] A pagan rite had been imposed on the indigenous Christian community. It was cultural imperialism. Other burials, in prominent mounds, similarly signalled pagan identity alongside control of the landscape.

Examples include the burial mounds at Ballateare, Cronk Mooar and Knoc-y-Doonee. The same argument for an assertive pagan Viking population on the island can also be made from the evidence of some twenty-six surviving stones with runic inscriptions. This can be compared to thirty-three in the whole of Norway and few in England and Scotland.

Further north, the situation was even more extreme. On the Orkney Islands and the Shetland Islands, Pictish culture was obliterated by the Vikings by the end of the tenth century at the latest. Few pre-Norse place names survive and – unlike on the Isle of Man, and elsewhere in Scotland and the Western Isles – the Gaelic language did not revive or later colonize these northern islands. In contrast, a form of Norse, called Norn, was spoken until the eighteenth century. The indigenous language was replaced and the Pictish Christian culture seems to have been rapidly (perhaps brutally) brought into line with that of the Viking immigrants. There may even have been ethnic cleansing. The change seems to have been at its most extreme on Orkney. While it is a single example, the confidence of Norse culture can be demonstrated in the fact that the reused prehistoric chambered tomb at Maeshowe contains the largest collection of runic inscriptions to be found in the British Isles.

Something similar initially also happened on Caithness and in the Outer Hebrides. The latter was thoroughly Scandinavianized, with this decreasing as one goes south through the Western Isles. So, on Lewis about seventy-eight per cent of village names are Norse, on Skye about sixty per cent and on Islay about thirty per cent. However, unlike in the Northern Isles, Gaelic eventually succeeded in making a comeback from the twelfth century onwards. As a consequence, the impact of Viking settlement was not as severe as in the Northern Isles but was still extensive.[20]

In all these examples we are probably seeing what *could* happen when an indigenous community lacked sufficient numbers, a cultural package that was thought worth emulating by the Scandinavian conquerors or useful trade opportunities that encouraged assimilation in order to allow access to it. These examples (from the Isle of Man, Orkney, Shetland and the Outer Hebrides) show what could have happened in East Anglia and the eastern Midlands if demography and cultural features there had been different. But there was also one other major factor that undermined confidence in paganism in eastern England – the subject Christians could look elsewhere for assistance. In some cases this may have been done reluctantly, since Wessex was the traditional rival of Mercia and East Anglia, but less so than it once would have been. The experiences of the Viking Wars had forced old rivals to cooperate to ward off disaster. This had certainly been the case with Mercia and Wessex, even if it was not emulated among the Christian communities of Northumbria, who never quite shook off their traditional distrust of their southern co-religionists (as we shall see in Chapter 4). But pagan settlers living in the East Midlands always had to look over their shoulders because Christian Wessex was not subjugated and threatened the independence of the newly established Norse communities. Wessex was coming...

WESSEX CONQUERS THE DANELAW

The survival of Wessex clearly meant that the Viking conquest was incomplete. Alfred the Great succeeded in creating a kingdom that withstood Viking attacks and then, in the reigns of his son (Edward the Elder) and grandson (Athelstan), conquered the eastern and northern regions of England that had been lost to Danish Viking rule and settlement. The West Saxons always liked to portray this as a "liberation" of English co-religionists but, in reality, it was also the creation of a "Greater Wessex".

As a result of this process, Viking confidence declined in the face of the victories of Edward the Elder (ruled 899–924) as he successfully set out to extend the areas under his control, assisted by his sister Æthelflæd, the Lady of the Mercians, and her Mercian husband Æthelred. The latter is not to be confused with a later king of England by the same name: Æthelred II, often known as "Æthelred *unræd*" or "Æthelred the unready". Together this brother and sister alliance conquered the East Midlands and East Anglia and brought it under the control of Wessex. This combination of the old kingdoms of the West Saxons and Mercians created a newly styled "kingdom of the Anglo-Saxons" and eventually a united England. Both would be Christian.

Resurgent Viking assaults challenged Edward the Elder's successor, Athelstan (ruled 924–939), but these were decisively defeated at the battle of Brunanburh in 937. After Athelstan's death, new arrivals of Vikings (originally from Norway), who had become the rulers of the Viking kingdom of Dublin, once again challenged southern Anglo-Saxon kings for control of the lands north of the River Humber. There the Viking kingdom of York continued as a focus for resistance, to the kings from the south, by local Northumbrians and Danish and Norwegian settlers. This was an alliance of those who preferred a Viking king based in York (even a pagan one) to a southern Anglo-Saxon king from the traditional rival kingdom of Wessex (even a Christian). So there was no simple ethnic divide between Scandinavian Vikings on one side and Anglo-Saxons on the other. This continued until the death of Erik Bloodaxe, the last Viking king of York, in 954.

It has been argued that many Danelaw Viking pagans "might not have been brought into the Christian fold until after they had lost their political independence",[21] in the mid-to-late tenth century. In which case, the conquest of the area by Christians from the newly united Wessex/Mercia was crucial for conversion. But there is a problem with this suggestion. It envisages somewhere in the region of two generations of Scandinavian paganism in East Anglia and the East Midlands, between the initial settlement and the final conversion to Christianity. The almost complete absence of pagan burial practices (with a tiny number of notable exceptions), pagan cult centres, and animal sacrifices argues strongly against this and in favour of a much earlier and decisive Christianization of the newcomers.

But what kind of relationship was there between Christians and pagans in the area where Viking rule lasted longest in England, until as late as the year 954? What was the interaction between the cross and the hammer in Northumbria? It is this question that we will now address...

CHAPTER 4

The Cross and
the Hammer

CHRISTIANS AND PAGANS
IN THE
NORTH OF ENGLAND

As late as the year 954, the Viking kingdom of York – which had morphed out of the old Anglo-Saxon kingdom of Northumbria – was ruled by Scandinavian kings. There had been times when kings from the south had asserted themselves but then the pendulum of power had swung back in favour of Viking rulers. At first these were Danish warriors who had arrived with the *micel hæðen here* and later they were Norwegians from the kingdom of Dublin. What stood out was they were pagans; either actively or in their immediate cultural background, representatives of the northern world with its beliefs in Odin and Thor. Yet now they had become the heirs to one of the premier Christian kingdoms of Anglo-Saxon England, where the kings had first become Christian in 627. How did Christianity fare in such a context?

A TOUGH TIME FOR
CHRISTIANITY IN THE NORTH

In 867, the political rulers of Northumbria were wiped out by the invading Vikings. The remaining members of the Northumbrian elite had been left with no choice. They had to make peace with the leaders of the Viking army, a peace as dictated by the winners. Years later, in the thirteenth century, the chronicler Roger of Wendover was probably drawing on authentic northern traditions (now lost to us) when he outlined the bitter consequences of the victory of the Vikings at York in 867: "Then these most abominable victors, the Danes, ravaged the whole province of Northumbria as far as the mouth of the Tyne."[1] It was a hard time to be living in the north and no amount of modern revisionism should cause us to ignore this.

The destruction caused by Viking conquest was accompanied by new political arrangements, because the invaders were no longer content to merely plunder and be gone. Roger recounted how an otherwise unknown Anglo-Saxon named Egbert was set up as a client king, to rule under the victorious Vikings. The relative powers were made clear by Simeon of Durham (died 1129) who, like Roger, had access to records that we can no longer consult. Simeon explained that Egbert was king "under their own domination". His authority was restricted to a rump state, the northern – the Bernician – component of the kingdom of Northumbria, beyond the River Tyne.[2] The new Viking rulers kept York under their direct control. This was not surprising as it was the wealthier part of Northumbria. It consisted of the area (once its own kingdom) called Deira, with the agricultural land of the rolling wolds and the control of the trade routes operating out of the Humber estuary. The *micel hæðen here* had done well since landing in East Anglia in 866: it now directly ruled the richest region of Northumbria and was overlord of the northern part, still nominally under Anglo-Saxon authority.

This left Northumbrians with the dilemma of whether or not to accept the new status quo. It is clear that, while some were reluctant to do so, other important sections of the northern elites fell into line with the new state of things. In 872, according to Roger of Wendover, some Northumbrians rebelled against their Viking overlords. These rebels (no doubt thinking themselves the true northern patriots) expelled the puppet-king Egbert and also Wulfhere, archbishop of York. The revolt failed and Wulfhere returned to York in 873. What is striking about this episode is that the Christian archbishop and the Christian puppet-ruler were both considered to be members of the Viking party.

The archbishop was clearly actively cooperating with the new Viking-dominated regime. How should we view this? It sounds opportunistic and treasonable but the cleric would have argued it differently. By forging a working relationship with the new rulers, he almost certainly thought that he could reduce the damage to individual churches and church administration generally. Times had changed and he had to decide how best to operate in a situation in which Viking rulers looked set to stay. In this, at least, Wulfhere was correct, for while there was much upheaval yet to come, Viking rule was no passing phase. Anglo-Saxon kings would not rule securely in Northumbria until the fall of Erik Bloodaxe and the collapse of the Viking kingdom of York in 954, a long time ahead.

As we have seen, when that did eventually occur, many in the north did not welcome it. They resented what they regarded as the imposition of rule from a southern dynasty – despite its Christian and Anglo-Saxon character. Far better a local king ruling from York (albeit a Scandinavian ruler), who was close to northern elites and their interests, than accepting a marginal place on the edge of a kingdom whose centre of political gravity lay far to the south. For such people (as for many at the time) their local politics and regional identity were stronger than any sense of a national English identity. We are in danger of reading back too much of later sensibilities when assessing what looks like treasonable behaviour, and prone to looking at it through the lens of the southern rulers. In the north, things looked a little different. From a northern perspective, Wulfhere's apparent cultural treason might have looked more like northern *Realpolitik* (beliefs and actions based on practical considerations rather than ideology). However, in 872 the matter was made more complex and sensitive from a Christian perspective, because the new Viking rulers were still pagan. Wulfhere's decision was not an easy one to make.

THE SHOCK OF PAGAN RULE
IN THE NORTH

The pagan nature of the new rulers is revealed in later – legendary – stories about how Vikings behaved in the aftermath of their initial victory. These are later traditions and not contemporary reflections but the impression we get is still telling. The story in question is found in a Scandinavian source entitled *Tháttr af Ragnars sonum (Tale of Ragnar's Sons)*, compiled in the thirteenth century, in Iceland. There is no evidence to suggest it draws on authentic ninth-century traditions. Despite this, it is very famous and clearly shows what later Icelanders thought to be the reason for the Viking invasion of Northumbria. It also, incidentally, provides the narrative underpinning of the TV series *Vikings*, which premiered in 2013.

The Viking leader in question was Ragnar *Lothbrok* or *Lodbrok*, king of Sweden and Denmark, who appears in several sources written long after his life and adventures. Most are from the twelfth or thirteenth century. These include: *Ragnars saga Loðbróka (Tale of Ragnar Lodbrok)*, which was a sequel to the legendary *Völsunga Saga (Saga of the Volsungs)*; the saga entitled *Tháttr af Ragnars sonum (Tale of Ragnar's Sons)*; a poem called *Ragnarsdrápa (Ragnar's poem)*, of which only fragments remain; the *Krákumál (Lay of Kraka)*, purporting to contain Ragnar's death-song; Book IX of the *Gesta Danorum (Deeds of the Danes)*; and the poem *Háttalykill*, which is found in late manuscripts of *Orkneyinga Saga (Saga of the Orcadians)*, which is also called *History of the Earls of Orkney*. These later traditions claim that it was Ragnar's sons who led the *micel hæðen here*.

The *Tháttr af Ragnars sonum (Tale of Ragnar's Sons)* recounts the story of Ragnar and his sons, who were named Björn Ironside, Hvitserk, Ivar the Boneless, Sigurd Snake-in-the-Eye and Ubbe. According to this legendary saga, Ragnar was captured after leading a raid on England. He was killed by King Ælle of Northumbria by being thrown to his death in a snake pit. As a result, the Viking army which eventually seized York was led by Ragnar's sons with the aim of avenging his death. The saga says that they did this by subjecting Ælle to the pagan rite of the "blood-eagle". This involved (in various traditions) either carving an eagle on the back of the victim or cutting the ribs away from the spine, then pulling out the lungs of the dying man before draping them over the victim. This, it was claimed, resembled an eagle's wings. The saga then tells how Ivar became king over Northumbria. The saga also claims that it was Ivar's two sons, Yngvar and Husto, who were responsible for the capture and torturing to death of King Edmund of East Anglia.

It is hard to tell how much truth there is in these atrocity stories. We have already seen that the details of the killing of King Edmund may have drawn on stock features of existing literature. Furthermore, the *Anglo-Saxon Chronicle* and other English sources maintain that Ælle died in battle. But what about the blood-eagle? There is no contemporary evidence that such an atrocity was ever committed, although its horror has gripped imaginations for centuries. Many modern historians believe that this mode of death was fictional and a product of later Norse literature, not actual events. According to this interpretation, it arose from a twelfth- and thirteenth-century fascination with Viking savagery. As one historian has memorably put it: "The ultimate begetter of the blood-eagle was not a sadistic bird-fancier but an antiquarian revival."[3] If correct, the Viking association with the rite was due to a much later generation of Icelandic and Scandinavian writers of Old Norse sagas who were fascinated by their fabled barbaric ancestors. Despite this, it remains an image of Viking savagery in the popular imagination and literature. And we in the twenty-first century may be too inclined to rehabilitate the first generation of Viking invaders: the world wars of the last century and then the genocidal horrors of Rwanda and Bosnia show what some human beings are capable of. Perhaps the impact of pagan invasion was less sanitized than it sometimes now appears and the blood-eagle could have occurred. Either way, pagan conquest had to be faced up to in the north and, in this situation, it prompted changes on both sides.

LEARNING TO LIVE WITH NEW
REALITIES IN NORTHUMBRIA

We have seen that it was not until 875 – some 80 years after the initial attack – that the monks of Lindisfarne finally left the island in order to protect themselves and their relics. This raises serious questions about the scale of destruction at other monastic sites in the north, where we do not have the same quantity of evidence to chart the scale of decline. The Irish annals, for example, reveal repeated attacks on the same six monasteries, which made up a quarter of all recorded ninth-century Viking raids. Clearly, these Irish communities both survived and prospered sufficiently to make them targets of further raids. The situation may well have been similar in England (at least to start with) and Lindisfarne points that way. Such communities continued to have some influence in their local areas and, no doubt, over the new Scandinavian settlers once things had settled down. This is not to deny the long-term decline of monasticism in the north, merely to assert that this did not happen overnight.

Lindisfarne, always the example of destructive conflict, may provide yet more evidence of this, and this evidence may signal a surprising change in the religious attitudes of the new Viking rulers. According to the anonymous *History of St Cuthbert* (written in the mid-tenth century), as early as the late ninth century, the Christian abbot of Carlisle was involved in the selection and public proclamation of a new Viking king.[4] This event seems to have taken place in the 880s and is very much in the great tradition of saints' lives. According to the account, St Cuthbert (whose relics were cared for by the Lindisfarne community) appeared to the abbot in a vision, in which it was claimed that the whole territory between the Rivers Tyne and Wear was placed under the special authority of St Cuthbert. This led to the abbot crossing the Tyne to meet with the Viking army. There he declared a slave named Guthfrith (presumably owned by members of the army) should be freed and proclaimed king. This is described in the source as "the reasonable command" of the saint. The abbot obeyed, the boy was made king and the relics of St Cuthbert were brought to the army, who "swore peace and fidelity".

This tale has all the trappings of legend and yet may contain a kernel of truth. It seems to suggest that a pagan royal inauguration rite was made legitimate by the presence of the relics of St Cuthbert. If so, it may indicate that the Viking rulers were seeking to legitimize their rule by reference to the famous saint. This is not the same as conversion but may suggest a step in that direction. This legend gives an unexpected insight into the new relationship between the church and the Viking army, one far removed from the image of the Vikings as despoilers of churches and enemies of Christianity. Despite its lack of historicity, it suggests that some intriguing political interaction occurred between the native Northumbrian Christian community and the Scandinavian pagan newcomers.[5]

The same source contains an equally legendary tale of the fate of a Viking leader named King Ragnald who swore opposition to the Christians: "by my mighty gods, Thor and Othin [Odin]" but was struck down by God.[6] Once again, it implies interaction between Christians and pagans, with Christians having a very obvious presence in a kingdom now dominated by pagans.

As we have already seen in the case of Wulfhere, these examples of the abbot of Carlisle and the monks of Lindisfarne reveal that many Christians in the north rapidly came to terms with the new realities. This continued well into the tenth century despite (perhaps because of) the likelihood of West Saxon expansion. When King Edmund of Wessex (not to be confused with the martyred Edmund of East Anglia) launched an attack on the Viking kingdom of York, he was contending with more than just Vikings. His enemy was Olaf Guthfrithson, who had invaded south as far as Leicester in the 940s, and in his company was Wulfstan, the archbishop of York. Once again northern support for a local king (i.e. in York) was more important than loyalty to a distant Christian king (i.e. from Wessex), especially when that king came from the south – the traditional rivals of northern Anglo-Saxon kingdoms. Wulfstan would later be arrested and imprisoned by his fellow Christian, the king of Wessex, because he was felt to be politically unreliable and an ally of pagan Viking rulers in Northumbria.

As these interactions occurred, so the Viking newcomers changed too. The relationship was no longer antagonistic and this eased the conversion process.

THE TRIUMPH OF CHRISTIANITY IN THE VIKING KINGDOM OF YORK

It is clear that Christianity continued to thrive at a grass roots level and there is little evidence for pagan activity in Northumbria. Despite extensive modern archaeological activity, very few overtly pagan Viking burials have been found in the north. With the exception of the burials on the Isle of Man, pagan burials from the Viking Age are very rare, as we have seen. There are, perhaps, fewer than thirty sites in the whole of England compared with over forty on the Isle of Man alone.[7] Apart from a scatter of individual burials (some with swords), ones such as that excavated in 2004 at Cumwhitton (Cumbria) – a cemetery of four men and two women and identified by characteristic Scandinavian brooches and weaponry – are extremely rare indeed. They stand out as "exceptional alien implants".[8] The greater number of such finds on the Isle of Man and in Cumbria may indicate that Norse (Norwegian) Vikings operating around the Irish Sea may have hung on to their paganism longer than the Danish Vikings settled to the east and south.[9]

This clearly points to both the vibrancy of native Christianity and the willingness of Scandinavian settlers to assimilate and become Christian. This does not fit the fire and sword image of wanton pagan destruction of Christian communities or rampant pagan practices. In contrast to pagan practices, there are many examples in the north of Scandinavians behaving in keeping with Christian traditions. At York Minster carved stone slabs decorated with Scandinavian-derived artwork probably represent the graves of the first generation of Viking Christians. The location is not surprising given that King Guthfrith, a Viking ruler of the kingdom of York, was buried at the minster as early as 895. The location was referred to in the late-tenth-century *Æthelweard's Chronicle*. Since this was compiled in the West Country, it seems that the burial place of this Viking king caught people's attention. This is the Guthfrith from the legendary royal acclamation in the *History of St Cuthbert*. Other burials accompanied by grave goods have been found at Carlisle Cathedral, and the occasional finding of Viking-related artefacts at a significant number of church sites (such as weapons at Kildale and Wensley in Yorkshire) suggests fairly widespread Viking Age burial at these church-based cemeteries.

One of the remarkable pieces of evidence for Viking Christianity in England and the Isle of Man lies in their adoption of the existing tradition of stone monuments. Back home in Scandinavia, none of the famous runestones (be they pagan or Christian) would appear until late in the tenth century. But in England and on the Isle of Man, Viking use of stone memorials had been developing in the century before this. Anglo-Saxon England had a long tradition of erecting memorials and other statements of faith in stone, and this tradition was embraced with enthusiasm by the new class of Viking Christians in Northumbria. This is a pointer to both their adoption of Christianity and the continuation of Christian traditions and available craftspeople (albeit in the service of a new clientele). This also included continuity of churches: some sixty per cent of churches with evidence of pre-Viking stone sculpture in Yorkshire go on to have Viking Age sculpture. In Cumbria this rises to eighty per cent.[10] These carvings – stone crosses and grave markers – carry a mixture of Scandinavian and Anglo-Saxon art styles.

These differ from earlier monuments in their location and social message. Despite what we have seen about the survival of some monastic communities, it is undeniable that, in the longer term, monasticism as a whole suffered massive decline in the north. The emerging "Viking Christianity" was now focused largely on local estates and their attendant churches. This was reflected in the nature of the carvings. Many appear to be as political as they are religious. So, on the Middleton Cross, from Middleton-in-Rydale (Yorkshire), is a helmeted Viking lord, with shield, sword and spear. Comparable depictions of Viking lords appear on carvings from Levisham (Yorkshire), Weston (Yorkshire) and Sockburn (County Durham). At Weston, the figures of a sword-wielding warrior and a female were re-cut over an existing Anglo-

Saxon stone cross. In this way both continuity and change are demonstrated on this one monument.

Clearly, as Scandinavian newcomers broke up large estates and established themselves in the northern countryside, they depicted their new status on these carved stones. The stones were a reflection of new political realities as well as of Christianization. A new class of secular Viking landowners had emerged as the major patrons of Christian artwork carved on stone. Examples of these monuments can be seen in a great many sites across Cumbria (c. 115 monuments) and Yorkshire (c. 400 monuments). The Isle of Man has forty-eight comparable crosses. The establishment of these local estate churches accelerated a process that had been occurring for some time in Anglo-Saxon England. They were often set up near a lord's hall and administered by the landowner, who also appointed the priest. This was already providing a focus for the local community under aristocratic control; and this trend increased under Viking influence in northern England, accompanied by the dissolution of monasteries and a huge increase (as we have seen) in carved personal stone monuments. The growth of these estate churches in the north reveals new Scandinavian lords who continued established practices, which allowed them to both give gifts to the church and still keep a close control over this land and its resources.[11]

A number of the crosses from the Isle of Man carry runic inscriptions, a practice we will explore further in later chapters focused on Scandinavia. The Manx examples (thirty-one, with most of them being crosses) stand out as uniquely dense within the Scandinavian diaspora outside of the homelands. None are found in Normandy or Iceland; two from the Faroes and a handful each from Ireland, Scotland, Orkney and Shetland. Only two runic memorials are known from England (a fragment at Winchester and a complete memorial from St Paul's churchyard in London). All other examples of Danish runic inscriptions in England are in the form of graffiti on objects such as animal bones or a comb-case. Norse (Norwegian) runes are found in graffiti at Carlisle Cathedral (Cumbria), Dearham (Cumbria) and Settle (Yorkshire); a sundial from Skelton-in-Cleveland (Yorkshire), a font at Bridekirk (Cumbria) and a record of the names of builders of the church at

Pennington (Cumbria). Why the style was so prevalent on Man is a mystery. This is especially puzzling given the island's connection with Norway, where erecting runestones was not common (it was much more prevalent in Denmark and hugely popular in Sweden). Almost all the Manx examples commemorate the dead. Inscriptions include: "Sandulfr the Black erected this cross in memory of Arinbjǫrg his wife", "Oddr raised this cross in memory of Frakki", "Grímr raised this cross in memory of Hróðmundr". But there are occasional mysteries such as the enigmatic "but Hrosketill betrayed the faith of his sworn confederate".[12]

This explosion of carvings stimulated the development of new local styles (such as wheel-head crosses) and must have provided work for many separate workshops. At Kirk Michael on Man the inscription records the name of one such Viking craftsman who was now employed in the new business of making monuments for fellow-Scandinavian patrons: "Gautr made this, and all in Man". For all the variety, the similarity in motifs found on the Isle of Man, in Cumbria, Lancashire and Yorkshire is testimony to the new culture of Christian Viking lords who were now dominating society.

A class of stone sculpture known as "hogbacks" also points to Viking Christians carrying Scandinavian art forms into their new faith in order to develop a new style of stone monument. These stone carvings of stylized houses (bow-sided with a ridged roof) are often decorated on their ends with carved beasts (usually bears but also including wolves) that are usually muzzled. Unlike carved stone crosses (see below), these decorations lack clearly recognizable Norse mythological scenes and may have been "personalised statements" and not intended for "didactic purposes".[13] Most date from the period 920–970.[14] While none appear on the Isle of Man, there are many examples from North Yorkshire and Cumbria. They seem to be associated with the culture of Norwegian Vikings since only around five are found in the areas of Danish Viking settlement south of the Humber. Their presence in Yorkshire is a reminder of how initial Danish control of land east of the Pennines eventually succumbed to Norwegian adventurers from the Irish Sea region. The absence of this type of monument on Man is probably due to the lack of suitable stone (that on Man being better suited for flat monuments).[15] Resembling earlier Anglo-Saxon house-shaped shrines marking saints' relics, the hogbacks were probably deployed as grave markers but this is uncertain.[16]

There are also other, more complex, glimpses of the way in which the pagan newcomers adapted to Christianity. As we have seen, there are scenes illustrating Odin being devoured by the wolf Fenrir on the Day of Ragnarok (the end of the world) carved on Thorwald's Cross from Kirk Andreas (Isle of Man). This is accompanied by a carving of Christ or a Christian (the figure holds a cross, a fish and a gospel book) trampling on the devil in the form of a serpent. Another cross at Kirk Andreas (Sigurd's Cross) has a scene depicting the legendary hero Sigurd, roasting the dragon's heart. In Norse mythology Sigurd burned his thumb on the roasted flesh and on putting it in his mouth gained the ability to understand the language of birds. Scenes from the legend of Sigurd also appear on other Manx crosses at Jurby, Malew and Maughold, and we have already seen the swordsmith Regin at work on a stone cross from Halton (Lancashire) and the same cross also has a carving that shows Sigurd roasting the dragon's heart. This latter scene also appears at Ripon (Yorkshire).

Further examples are Thor fishing for Jormungand the Midgard Serpent, and the god Vidar killing Fenrir the wolf (and so avenging Odin) can be seen on a standing cross at Gosforth (Cumbria). A crucifixion scene on one side of the cross is paired with these portrayals of scenes from the Day of Ragnarok depicted on the other side. The crucifixion scene includes a carving of the figure of Mary Magdalene depicted as a valkyrie with long dress and pigtail. The cross also shows the bound figure of the Norse trickster-god Loki being given a drink by Sigyn his wife. At Nunburnholme (Yorkshire), a scene depicting the Eucharist has been over-carved with the same Sigurd feast. And at Leeds (Yorkshire) the legendary hero smith Weland is depicted alongside Christian angels and the eagle symbol of St John the gospel writer.

These combinations of Christian and pagan motifs illustrate the use of familiar Norse images to illustrate new Christian beliefs. The contrasting scenes of Ragnarok and Christian triumph over the devil at Kirk Andreas can be read as signalling the end of one set of religious beliefs (illustrated by the death of Odin in the jaws of Fenrir) and the assertion of the new Christian beliefs (the figure trampling the serpent). This same message may underlie the contrasting scenes of the crucifixion and the Day of Ragnarok on the Gosforth cross. The popularity of the Sigurd legend (especially the feast scene) is more complex but may be using an existing myth of a transformative feast to point to the transformative power of the Christian Eucharist. In this regard, the over-cut Nunburnholme cross is particularly striking. The Mary Magdalene/valkyrie image may have been intended to emphasize Mary's role as an attendant of Christ on the cross, by the use of an already familiar concept of an attendant female in the form of the valkyries who attended to the warriors of Odin in Norse mythology. In these ways, the Norse myths were used to communicate Christian beliefs to the first generation of Viking Christians across northern England.

This assimilation to Christianity was almost certainly accelerated by the attitudes shown by Scandinavian rulers. The pagan Viking kings who ruled from York were clearly prepared to cooperate with local Christians. In the design of their coins there was a striking mixture of both Christian and pagan symbols which suggests that they considered this Christian community significant enough to appeal to. Under Sihtric (ruled 921–927) one coin issue carried a sword on the obverse with a reverse design of a cross. A similar coin issue carried a Thor's hammer in place of the cross, illustrating he had not yet abandoned paganism. Under Olaf Guthfrithson (died 941) the raven of Odin was displayed on the obverse, while on the reverse there was a small cross. Once again a ruler was hedging his bets and appealing to a mixed clientele. But this was not a strident paganism. Earlier in the tenth century, anonymous kings of York had issued coins without a ruler's name inscribed on them: instead these were issued in the name of St Peter. This was clearly meant to appeal to local York Christians, since there was a pronounced devotion to St Peter at York. Some related coins from this series even carried images of Thor's hammer on the reverse.[17] The rulers of York wanted to keep both local Christian and pagan elements happy.

A final example comes from the Silverdale Hoard (Lancashire), which was found in 2011. This dates from the late ninth or early tenth century (c. 900–910). In it one rare coin carried the otherwise unknown ruler's name, *AIRDECONUT* (possibly Harthacnut). On the reverse of this coin the letters *DNS* (*Dominus*) *REX* were arranged in the shape of a cross. This suggests that the Viking king had either converted to Christianity or, as with other examples, wished to appeal to Christian subjects.

Overall, an analysis of Viking coinage in England minted c. 900, comparing that of East Anglia (the St Edmund coinage) with that from York, has led leading numismatic experts to conclude:

> *The strong Christian element in the designs and inscriptions on the contemporary regal coinage of Scandinavian York have also been seen as a sign that the Scandinavian rulers chose to publicise their adoption of Christianity as part of a political agenda to gain acceptance and respect among other European states.*[18]

Even so, when the last independent Viking king of York – Erik Bloodaxe – was killed in 954, there was still an assumption among some Scandinavians that he had died a pagan. The Old Norse poem entitled '*Eiríksmál (Erik's Story)*' describes Erik's welcome into Valhalla, the Old Norse afterlife for dead warriors, where the bravest warriors were believed to feast with Odin until the Day of Ragnarok. It states he was welcome there:

> *'Because he has made many lands red*
> *with his sword', said Odin,*
> *'And carried a bloody blade.'*[19]

As a result, the poet explained that he was personally welcomed into Valhalla by Odin himself:

> *Hail to you, Erik,*
> *welcome here!*
> *Enter the hall, wise king;*

I must hear
what warriors follow you
fresh from the fight.[20]

This was almost certainly written soon after his death in battle. Despite the fact that he had been baptized, his wife Gunnhildr *konungamóðir* (mother of kings) had this panegyric composed in his honour in the old traditional style. The poem, which is incomplete, is preserved in only one manuscript, known as *Fagrskinna*. This name is derived from one of the manuscripts into which it was later copied and preserved and means "fair skin" or "parchment". This particular document was probably written in Norway or Iceland, and is one of the Viking kings' sagas, a compilation which dates from around 1220.

By the time it was composed we might question just how far Scandinavians in the kingdom of York believed in the pagan religion which is such a characteristic of this poem. Most were now well integrated into Christianity. Consequently, this poem, commissioned by Gunnhildr *konungamóðir*, was looking back to an old world, rather than reflecting the contemporary reality of the Christian Vikings of the north.

The Other Island...

In the history of the Viking Wars in Britain, the spotlight often stays firmly fixed on England. The sack of Lindisfarne, the wars of Alfred the Great, the conquest of the Danelaw by his descendants, conflicts in the kingdom of York and the campaigns of men like Erik Bloodaxe provide many of the headlines. But the island of Ireland also experienced the full impact of Viking raids, and their experiences deserve much more attention.

THE ARRIVAL OF THE VIKINGS IN IRELAND

An anonymous Irish poem, written (c. 845–850) in the upper margin of a manuscript now in the monastery of St Gall in Switzerland,[1] captures something of the impact of the first Viking attacks on Ireland.

> *Bitter is the wind tonight*
> *It tosses the ocean's white hair*
> *Tonight I fear not the fierce warriors of Norway*
> *Coursing on the Irish sea.*[2]

We do not know where in Ireland this poem was composed but the original manuscript may have been compiled in a northern Irish monastery, perhaps that at Nendrum or the religious community at Bangor (both in County Down). It is a poem of high drama. Its opening line, in Old Irish, grabs the reader's attention: "*Is acher in gaith in-nocht...*"[3] And it conveys something of the dread gripping coastal monasteries that they would find relief in a night of storms that closed the seas to the longships of the dreaded Vikings.

Those responsible, according to this poem, were "*dond láechraid lainn úa Lothlind*"[4] ("the fierce warriors of Lothlind").[5] The term *Lothlind* is a contraction of *Lochlann-aigh* (people from lake-land). In Modern Irish, the word *Lochlann* describes Scandinavia generally, but the geographical source of most of the raids prompted the modern translator to identify the land in question as Norway. In the context of mid-ninth-century Ireland, this almost certainly was the place in the mind of the original writer, since Ireland at this time was suffering at the hands of Norwegian Vikings. At some time the manuscript containing this poem was taken to St Gall: there was a strong connection between travelling Irish monks and this Swiss monastery. Or perhaps it was written there by an Irish monk who had experience of the Vikings in his homeland.

The first recorded Viking raid on Ireland took place in 795, two years after the attack on Lindisfarne in England, and the church on Lambey Island, near Dublin, was attacked. The monastery at Rathlin was also burnt that same year and three years later, in 798, the community on St Patrick's Island suffered attack. This phase of raiding lasted until about 830 and mirrored the experiences of England. Small and uncoordinated raiding parties struck at coastal monasteries and penetrated up rivers, threatening settlements up to twenty miles from the sea. But settlements further inland were safe.

Most of the Vikings involved in these early raids on Ireland – and indeed for much of the period of Viking involvement there – were, as we have already discussed, Norwegians. There is strong archaeological evidence for this: the highest concentration of Irish artefacts found by archaeologists outside Ireland comes from south-west Norway, in the vicinity of Stavanger. A wider survey, across Scandinavia, indicates that most finds of looted Irish metalwork in Viking graves come from western Norway generally, and most of these items were ecclesiastical in nature, stolen from churches and monasteries.[6]

In the Old Irish language the *Lochlannach* (Northmen) were more finely differentiated into *Finn-gaill* (white foreigners) if Norwegian and *Dubh-gaill* (black foreigners) if Danish. Why colour was used in this differentiation has prompted a great deal of debate. A longstanding suggestion was that it referred to something distinctive about the appearance of these two sets of warriors, hair colour or equipment. But this is unlikely, as it rests on a distinctive set of visible traits that are not feasible. Norwegians and Danes could not be identified by a particular ethnic look or colour of shield. A more persuasive interpretation is that, instead of "white" and "black", the meaning was actually "old" and "new". The seventeenth-century *Annals of Clonmacnoise* describe the tenth-century Viking leader Sihtric *Cáech* (one-eyed) as being "prince of the new and old Danes".[7] So perhaps the terms differentiated the origins of the first raiders (Norway) from that of later arrivals (Denmark).

The evidence supports this, with the proviso that Viking armies probably contained members drawn from a number of Scandinavian communities. That the terms ("white/old", "black/new") should be associated with Norwegians and Danes respectively has been part of Irish traditions since at least the twelfth century, when the compiler of the *Cogad Gáedel re Gallaib* (*The War of the Irish with the Foreigners*) described the Danes as *Duibgeinti Danarda* ("Danish black foreigners").

Another possibility is that the terms identified to whom these groups owed allegiance. In this interpretation the *Finn-gaill* were the original invaders, while the *Dubh-gaill* were those who later owed allegiance to the Viking dynasty (called the *Uí Ímair*) who ruled Dublin, the Hebrides and northern England from the middle of the ninth century.[8]

From the 830s – as in England – the attacks escalated and involved much larger fleets of ships which caused increasing damage to Irish communities. The land that they attacked was about to experience the end of something of a golden age of Christian civilization that had previously produced superb high crosses, illuminated manuscripts such as the *Book of Kells* and splendid metalwork such as the Ardagh Chalice.[9] Soon magnificent artworks such as these would be looted from Ireland and later found by archaeologists in Viking graves back in Scandinavia. A famous example is the "Copenhagen Shrine" or "Ranvaik's Casket". Now kept in the Danish National Museum, this reliquary of yew wood, copper alloy, tin and enamel was made in Ireland in the eighth century but unearthed in Norway. In the tenth century a runic inscription had been scratched into its base, reading *Ranvaick a kistu thasa* ("Ranvaik [a female name] owns this casket").[10] Other Irish-type reliquaries have also been found in Norway, at Melhus and Setnes.

The escalating new wave of Viking attacks brought destruction to large parts of the island, since by sailing far up major rivers such as the Shannon, they could reach large areas of inland Ireland. Though it is far from the sea, the monastery at Clonmacnoise was sacked in 836. In the 840s the major centre of the Irish church at Armagh was sacked no fewer than three times.

If divisions into small kingdoms hampered initial English defensive responses to the Viking attacks, the situation was much worse in Ireland, as we have seen. Not only were there five competing Irish high kingdoms (Connacht, Leinster, Meath, Munster, Ulster) but each was further sub-divided into petty sub-kingdoms that pursued their own ambitions with little control being exercised over them by a high king. This made a coordinated response impossible at first and gave a huge opportunity to the Scandinavians. It was also difficult for the Irish to unite because there was such a back story of violence between Irish communities and this included against churches built by rival Irish. For example, the fifteenth-century compilation known as *The Annals of Ulster* (drawing on earlier records) tells us that, in 807, the neighbouring Irish community of Cluain Ferta Brénainn slaughtered many of the church community at Corcach (later Cork, in the kingdom of Munster), and other eminent citizens. In 831 many died at Tailtiu (in the kingdom of Meath) in a dispute over holy relics.[11] None of this history of communal conflict assisted the creation of a united Irish response to the Vikings.

The situation was made more complex by the presence of *Gall-Gædhil* (foreigner Celts) among those creating mayhem. These were either Irish men who had allied themselves with the Vikings and adopted Scandinavian lifestyles, or the products of otherwise unrecorded Irish-Viking marriages. While not many in number, they added to the cocktail of violence. Then there were the straightforward cases of Irish rulers who allied themselves with Viking raiders against fellow Irish rivals, such as Cinaed, ruler of the North Brega, who joined the Viking raiders in 850 as part of his rebellion against his high king. This mixed army went on to wreak havoc in the territory of the Southern Úi Néill. Not that the alliance did Cinaed's political ambitions much good: he was eventually captured by his Irish opponents and drowned. But this was little consolation to those Irish communities he had devastated.

Generally, though, the main difference between Irish-on-Irish violence and Viking-on-Irish violence was that the former was fought within certain boundaries. In a number of cases we hear of Irish violence done "to the very door of the church". The implication seems clear that, although fellow Irishmen and Irishwomen might be killed and treasure looted, there was some respect shown to the institutions and buildings of the Christian church. Sanctuary sought in churches was respected or compensation was paid when it was violated.[12]

We should not go too far in this mitigation of Irish-on-Irish violence, since there were plenty of violations of traditional codes of expected conduct, and the close family connections of church leaders and royal families pulled the church into political conflicts.[13] But we can be sure that when it came to Viking violence, there was not even a pretence of restraint. Churches and monasteries were often burnt, people were enslaved, and sacred reliquaries (as we have seen) were emptied of the bones of revered Christian saints. The Vikings were only interested in the gold, silver and other finely worked metal of the shrines. In Ireland, as in England, the raiders also soon revealed an alarming familiarity with the Christian calendar: attacks timed to coincide with feast days could net a larger than usual haul of pilgrims to enslave, seized as captives and sold on the international slave market of the Viking world. For example, at Étar (later Howth, in the kingdom of Leinster) in 821, many Irish women were seized as slaves. When the church at Trevet (Meath) was attacked, 260 people who had taken refuge inside were burnt alive. Both occurred on Christian holy days. As in other areas that suffered Viking attacks, the Irish soon discovered that it was open season on anyone and everything. And the Scandinavians were soon making their presence felt on a permanent basis.

THE ESTABLISHMENT OF PERMANENT VIKING BASES IN IRELAND AND THE IRISH FIGHT-BACK

By the mid-ninth century, the Viking raiders had established a number of defended settlements in Ireland, referred to as a *longphort* (fortified base), where they could moor their ships, repair damage and rest between campaigns. The most famous of these was at Dublin, founded in 841 where the River Liffey meets the sea, and others were soon established at places such as Arklow, Cork, Mungrel, Waterford, and Youghal, to name some of the more prominent ones. These bases provided more than shelters for raiders. They were also springboards for conquest and the seizing of political control over Irish territories. Under leaders such as Turgeis, the Vikings now threatened the political integrity of Ireland.

As Vikings established permanent bases, they could launch more concerted attacks on the Irish kingdoms but, paradoxically, they also became vulnerable to counter-attacks. It was one thing to appear out of nowhere, loot, kill and enslave before vanishing; it was quite another to have bases, resources and non-combatants to defend. Suddenly invincible Vikings found themselves on the back foot. In 845, Turgeis was captured by the forces of Mael Seachlainn, the ruler of Meath. He was executed by drowning in Lough Owel.

In 847 the invaders suffered four major defeats: near Cork, near Castledermot, outside Dublin, and in northern Meath where some 700 Vikings were killed. In 849 the settlement at Dublin was sacked by an Irish army. The tide of war appeared to be turning. In the late 840s a number of Vikings shifted their operations to Francia and then to England, where richer pickings could be had at lower risk. However, this did not signal the end of Viking activity.

THE FOUNDING OF THE KINGDOM OF DUBLIN

Although the first Vikings to campaign in Ireland were Norwegians, Danes soon muscled in on the Norwegian operation. In 851 a group of Danish Vikings seized control of the Norwegian base at Dublin. It had clearly survived the Irish sack of 849, just as Irish settlements bounced back after apparently devastating raids. The Danes held it until 853 when they, in turn, were expelled by resurgent Norwegians under Olaf the White, a member of the Norwegian royal family. Olaf had ambitions: he declared himself king of Dublin in 853. Like the kingdom of York (with which it would become entangled in the tenth century) it soon became a significant player in local politics.

The slave trade was a major source of Dublin's wealth, as fortunes were made from those captured inland being shipped out to the scattered settlements of the Viking diaspora stretching from Scandinavia to Iceland. By the tenth century the town had developed into a thriving commercial centre, much as York was to do under Scandinavian rule in the same period. Occupying a site between the River Liffey and the much smaller River Poddle, the original Viking fort lay in the eastern corner of the expanding settlement. To the north-west, the quays fronted the River Liffey.

The kingdom of Dublin variously fought or sought allies among the nearby Irish kingdoms as it became part of the political complexity of the island. This lasted until about 873 when the death of Olaf's successor, Ivar, saw Dublin once again vulnerable to Irish attacks due to political instability among the Vikings. Once again a significant number of Scandinavians left. As before, some went to Francia and England, while others sought out a new home in recently colonized Iceland. As we have seen, modern genetic studies there have revealed that a large component of the female genetic inheritance of Iceland came from Ireland. Whether this was in the form of female slaves or wives gained by negotiation is now difficult to say; probably a mixture of the two.

For forty years, Ireland experienced a respite from Viking incursions. It became known, as we have seen, as the "Forty Years

Rest". During this time the Irish resurgence was so strong that it even saw the Vikings expelled from Dublin in 902.

THE VIKINGS RETURN

After 914, and facing increased resistance from the English and the Franks, the Vikings returned in force to Ireland. Within just a few years they were re-established at coastal bases from which they could once again raid the interior. The most significant of these were Dublin, Limerick, Wexford and Waterford, from where their areas of settlement spread inland, creating small Norse enclaves.

From 917 the Norwegian Vikings were back in Dublin. An attempt to expel them failed to repeat the Irish success of 902. Instead, the Irish high king of Tara was killed in battle, as were twelve of his sub-kings. Victory went to a Viking warrior named Sihtric *Cáech*. His given name was an Irish form of the Norse name Sigtryggr. He was a member of a powerful Norse dynasty – the *Uí Ímair* – who were to dominate the Irish Sea region and northern England for decades. He not only seized control of Dublin, he also took the other Scandinavian settlements at Limerick, Waterford and Wexford. He went on to rule in York; other Viking rulers of Dublin would also intervene (with differing levels of success) in politics there. Ireland also suffered far-flung raiding from Vikings based in the Hebrides and on Orkney, and the Irish king of the Northern Uí Néill attacked the Hebrides in 941, in an attempt to punish Scandinavians settled there for attacks on Ulster.

The strength of Irish resistance to the Vikings in the tenth century meant that the Scandinavians were never able to establish a strong presence to mirror their earlier settlements in eastern and northern England. Indeed, the temptation to fish in the troubled waters of northern English politics meant that the Viking rulers of Dublin were frequently occupied with expeditions designed to extend their rule to the kingdom of York. This diluted their impact on Ireland and this was exacerbated by rivalry between the Scandinavian coastal towns, so they could not present a united front in the face of Irish resistance. An example of this occurred in 924 when the Dublin Vikings failed in their attempt to capture the Viking settlement at Limerick. They were more successful in 937, when Olaf Guthfrithson defeated the fleet of the Limerick Vikings.

Had Ireland had a more united political system, the Viking settlement in the tenth century would have been eclipsed. As it was, the Scandinavians managed to maintain their position even if, by the late tenth century, they were overshadowed by the Irish kings of Munster in the south and those of Meath in the centre. In 968 the Scandinavians were even expelled for a year from their base at Limerick, by Mathghamain, the king of Dal Cais. The continued independence of the Viking coastal towns was only possible because they accepted their subservient positions and paid tribute to the Irish kings. It was a far cry from the devastation they had inflicted on the Irish in the previous century.

In 1014 this was amply demonstrated at the battle of Clontarf, on Good Friday, when an alliance of the Vikings of Dublin and Leinster was decisively crushed by Brian Boru, the king of Munster. Although Brian was killed in the battle, the Irish were victorious. Later Icelandic legend, recorded in the thirteenth-century *Njáls saga*, claimed that Brian would not fight on a Christian fast day (i.e. on Good Friday) and so was protected by a shield wall of his bodyguard. But a Viking warrior, named Brodir, broke through the wall and killed him. The saga recounts how Brodir was swiftly captured, had his stomach cut open and his entrails tied to a tree. He was then led round the tree until all his entrails were wound out of his body and he died.

THE CHRISTIANIZING OF THE VIKINGS IN IRELAND

By the time of the battle of Clontarf, the Vikings of Ireland had become immersed in indigenous Irish culture. Many converted to Christianity, they adopted the Gaelic language and they intermarried with local Irish families, which further accelerated assimilation. They became known among the Irish as *Ostmen* (east-men) to differentiate them from both the Irish and from unassimilated Scandinavians. The mixed nature of this Norse community is apparent in the account in *Njáls saga* of supposed supernatural events which occurred in Viking communities elsewhere as a result of the battle of Clontarf. On Caithness, Scotland, and in the Faroes, mysterious women (valkyries?) were supposedly seen weaving with men's entrails. On Iceland, it was alleged that blood appeared on a priest's stole as he celebrated Mass and the garment had to be removed. Again on Iceland, a priest saying Mass was shocked to see a vision of the sea and a battle appear beside the altar.

These were clearly later legendary traditions of a kind often claimed to have marked events of great historical importance and, in this case, of great violence. But, as well as revealing something of the mixed Christian and pagan traditions of thirteenth-century Iceland, they also reveal something of the religious complexity of the event in 1014. It would have been both Christians and pagans who died in the defeated armies of Dublin and Leinster and this (according to the legends) was reflected in strange events discernible to both Christians and pagans. But this reality was obscured in later traditions, such as those recorded in the twelfth-century Irish work *Cogad Gáedel re Gallaib (The War of the Irish with the Foreigners)*, which portrayed Brian Boru as the heroic Irish Christian king who had finally vanquished the pagan barbarians. The reality at Clontarf was, as the hints in *Njáls saga* remind us, more complex and untidy, with Christians fighting on both sides in the battle.

This was the culmination of a century and a half of mixing the two cultures and should be set alongside the evidence for pagan Viking destruction of Irish communities. As early as the second half of the ninth century Olaf the White, the first king of Dublin, married the Christian daughter of an Irish high king. Such a marriage could only have been accompanied by some kind of concession to Christianity, since evidence from similar events elsewhere indicates that giving a daughter in marriage usually involved conversion of the husband or toleration of Christian activities. By 873 the death of Ivar, king of Dublin, was marked by an Irish chronicler with the words he "rested with Christ".[14] This is clearly significant and it is difficult to imagine why the Irish writer would have included this unless Ivar had made a clear step towards Christian faith.

This might not have meant full conversion. In a number of areas where Vikings settled, they adopted a curious practice, termed *prima signatio* (first signing) by early medieval Christians. This involved a

Christian priest making the sign of the cross on the forehead of the person in question. It was a preliminary step towards baptism and full membership of the Christian church. However, for many this became the final destination. Having been first signed, they were then eligible to trade with Christians, who would not now be condemned for collaborating with pagans. So many who underwent *prima signatio* never progressed beyond it, and it became a simple strategy to allow access to economic activity with Christians. The compromise suited both sides since it promised economic benefits to both. There is plenty of evidence for this across the Viking world, once the initial phase of raiding developed into trading and settlement. It could even occur during the first phase, since Vikings were highly opportunistic. Trading and raiding, as we have seen, could occur on the same expedition, depending on the strength of the opposition and where the advantage lay. Set against this apparently cynical spiritual compromise, for many communities it was the first step towards eventual conversion, even if this occurred in a later generation.

As the Vikings became enmeshed in Irish politics and society in the tenth century, the adoption of Christianity accelerated. Olaf Sihtricson – the grandson of Sihtric *Cáech* of the Norse dynasty of the *Uí Ímair* – was formally baptized as a Christian in 943 and died in 980 as a monk on the island of Iona. This king, who was known in Ireland as Amlaíb Cuarán, had made a career out of looting churches in enemy kingdoms and yet, according to the twelfth-century *Chronicon Scotorum* (*Chronicle of the Scots*), he ended his life after "communion and repentance". The irony of this Christian death on Iona was profound since it had been earlier Vikings, often operating from bases in Ireland, who had devastated the monastic community on Iona in the ninth century. *The Anglo-Saxon Chronicle* explains that Olaf's baptism occurred at the instigation of Edmund, king of the West Saxons, in England. Edmund would have been keen to bring the king of York[15] into the religious and diplomatic community of Christian rulers. The complex religious beliefs of the man, as of the communities he ruled, were revealed in the silver coins he had minted at York in the early 940s, bearing the *triquetra* (a trefoil knot, symbol of the Trinity) on the obverse and a banner, probably the raven banner of Odin, on the reverse.

His son, Sihtric II Olafson, also known as Silkenbeard, consolidated Christian rule in Dublin. During his time as king of Dublin he proclaimed his Christian faith through the short-cross coins that he minted. He probably became king of Dublin in the year 989 and, though there were several interruptions in his reign, he ruled on and off until he abdicated in 1036. Sihtric II was forced to submit to the Irish high king, Brian Boru, in the year 1000. He later joined the revolt against Brian and, according to *Cogad Gáedel re Gallaib* (*The War of the Irish with the Foreigners*) and also *Njáls saga*, he was the main Norse leader at the battle of Clontarf in 1014. However, he survived the defeat and kept his throne. He is credited with travelling on pilgrimage to Rome in 1028 and he may have done so more than once.

Tradition names him as the founder of Dublin's first cathedral, Christ Church, shortly after 1028. The cathedral was sited on high ground overlooking the Viking settlement at Wood Quay on the River Liffey. It came under the authority of the Anglo-Saxon archbishop of Canterbury, a relationship which lasted until 1152.[16] This was a cunning move because, by placing the cathedral outside the control of the native Irish church and looking towards Anglo-Scandinavian England, the Christian Vikings of Dublin preserved an idea of their separate identity.[17] The new church was not the first within the city, since an earlier Irish church, of St Martin, had been included within the town's defences. By the 1120s there were at least ten significant churches there. These owed payments to Armagh, the Mother Church of Ireland, as a poem of the 1120s explains:

> *Every tenth of these loads* [materials traded in Dublin] *that reaches the Vikings is known to be owed to Patrick* [Armagh].[18]

One of the churches with a later dedication – to St Audoen/Ouen – had earlier been dedicated to St Columba, underscoring the close connection between the Dublin area and the Hebrides in the tenth and eleventh centuries, which built on the connections between Ireland and the Western Isles that pre-dated the Vikings. The later church was built in the 1190s, replacing an earlier building.

The Irish annals record that Sihtric II died in 1042, aged seventy-two. By this time many of the Vikings of Ireland had been Christian for a century. This is reflected in the way that Irish sources steadily dropped the term *genti* (heathens) to describe them after the 940s. After this point, if used, it was more to denigrate Norse communities than a strict indication of religious beliefs. Curiously enough, it was from the later twelfth and thirteenth centuries that Irish literature referred to "heathen Vikings" as a common literary expression to convey a sense of alien and threatening other.[19] In the same way, Icelandic literature of the same period became increasingly preoccupied with representing the violent Viking past, albeit giving it a more positive spin than the one found in contemporary Irish literature.

It was in this same period, in Ireland, that the Scandinavians who had fought at the earlier battle of Clontarf (1014) were retrospectively described (indeed misrepresented), in *Cogad Gáedel re Gallaib*, as a "wrathful, foreign, purely pagan people". This tells us more about twelfth-century Christendom than it does about the Scandinavians fighting Brian Boru at Clontarf. At a time when the concept of the "just war" was being defined and popularized, war against pagans was presented as a "just" form of war (as opposed to wars between Christian states). In such a context the retrospective reinvention of the Scandinavians of Dublin and Leinster as pagan opponents served to justify the representation of Brian Boru as an example of a ruler conducting a "just war". But it tells us little about the real Christianized inhabitants of these Viking towns. As the Irish historian Dáibhí Ó Cróinín has memorably put it, *The War of the Irish with the Foreigners* is "about as good a source of information on the Vikings as *Star Trek* is for the American space programme".[20]

What the rulers of Dublin were resisting at Clontarf was the loss of their autonomy as an international trading city at the hands of Brian Boru, who was attempting to absorb them into his kingdom.[21] This was not a revolt of Viking pagans but of new Christianized entrepreneurs of Scandinavian extraction, keen to protect their political and economic independence. That does not make for such a catchy headline but is clearly what was at stake.

The battle was not over religion, because the cross of Christ had already triumphed over the hammer of Thor in Dublin and the other Viking towns of Ireland. In fact it was the power of Viking longships, from Dublin, Limerick and Waterford, that had allowed Brian Boru to assert himself as high king of all Ireland and sail his host around the northern coast of Ireland to make the point.[22] The Norse traditions of seamanship were now in the service of the Christian Irish high king.

The Christian conversion of the Viking settlement at Dublin was assisted by the influence of Irish monasteries that survived in its hinterland, including those at Dunleer, Dromiskin, Clondalkin, Swords, and Tallaght. Their survival reminds us that the early period of raiding and looting had damaged but by no means destroyed the Irish church. Rather, the institution that had once seemed to be the chief victim of the Vikings in Ireland had survived, prospered and eventually absorbed the newcomers. By the twelfth century the churches in the Viking towns of Ireland were at the forefront of reforms in the Western church that saw the reduction of the power and influence of monasteries in favour of bishops and their episcopal territories based on cathedrals in major towns. In 1052, Diarmait, the Irish king of Leinster, seized Dublin and inherited the overlordship of its influence, which stretched as far as Wales. But now this city, with its web of trade and political power, was under the control of an Irish king. When the Irish ruler, Muirchertach, became king of Munster and overlord of Ireland in 1086 he kept Dublin as his capital. His power extended across the Irish Sea to Man and the Western Isles. When the last great Viking fleet – that of Magnus Barelegs, king of Norway – sailed down through the Irish Sea in 1098, Muirchertach defused the threat by marrying his daughter to Magnus's son. It was an alliance of two Christian kings, for Norway was now a well-established Christian kingdom.

In 1171 Dublin fell to the Anglo-Normans and a new chapter in Irish history began. The age of the Irish Vikings was long past by then.

CHAPTER 6

The Duchy of the Northmen

For many people, the Normans only really cross their minds when considering the events of the eleventh century that led to the Battle of Hastings in 1066. But by that time, they were second or third generation immigrants to northern France. They had originally come from Scandinavia and their origins lay in the same waves of Viking raiders and settlers that had impacted on Britain and Ireland and led to widespread seizure of territory there in the late ninth and early tenth centuries.

The origins of these Norman settlers lie in their larger than life but clearly historical ancestors who had seized land on the coast of the Frankish Empire. The foundation myth of Normandy named a Viking named Rollo (or Rolf), who turned raiding into settlement, in about 911. Rollo's name is a Latinized form of either the Old Norse personal name *Hrólfr* or *Hrollaugr*, probably the former. But he is now generally remembered as Rollo. To confuse things, he took on the baptismal name of Robert, and is also known as Robert I. To confuse things even more, he is sometimes just referred to as Robert, with the number (i.e. Robert I) being reserved for Robert the Magnificent, the ruler of Normandy between 1027 and 1035. It is easier just to call him Rollo.

Describing Rollo as larger than life is more than just a figure of speech: he is generally considered to be the same Viking leader described in later Icelandic sources as *Göngu-Hrólfr*, with an Old

Danish form of *Ganger-Hrolf* also being known (meaning: walker Hrólfr or Rolf the Walker). The implication is that he was so large that no horse could carry him. Stories of Rolf the Walker are found in the thirteenth-century Icelandic works *Heimskringla* (*Circle of the World*) and *Orkneyinga saga* (*Saga of the Orcadians*). The identification is not certain, though, since the written sources in Normandy and France never actually refer to the founder of Normandy as *Ganger-Hrolf* and the Icelandic works date from 300 years after the activities of the founder of Normandy. But it is likely that they were one and the same person.

Be that as it may, Rollo's ethnic origins are also a little confused. Later medieval sources do not agree, but he was probably a Norwegian Viking who led a force of mostly Danish adventurers.[1] Like those who eventually settled in England, Ireland and elsewhere, he had been campaigning in the region for some time, and had taken part in the siege of Paris in 886, where he was defeated. This was followed (as with Guthrum and King Alfred) by a strategy designed to neutralize him, by bringing him into the political game as a subservient player. So, in the year 911, Rollo was granted land to act as a frontier lord on behalf of the Frankish king. Thus, from the start, this Viking statelet on the coast would be heavily influenced by Frankish practices and culture. The name used to describe these newcomers was *Normands* in French and *Nortmanni* in Latin. The land they were granted became known as *Normannia* (the land of the Northmen), reflecting their Viking ancestry.

The extent of the territory that was granted to these Northmen was established by the formal treaty of Saint-Clair-sur-Epte, between King Charles III (Charles the Simple) of West Francia and the Viking Rollo. The agreement was described as a *foedus* – a formal treaty – in later sources. The land in question, between the River Epte and the Atlantic coast, lay within the former Frankish sub-kingdom known as Neustria. Once again the policy of "set a thief to catch a thief" was in operation, so they would provide protection against further Viking raids along that section of coast. Today we would describe the area as Upper Normandy as far as the River Seine, and the area under Viking rule was soon extended west of the Seine. Under Rollo's son, William Longsword (ruled

927–942), the rule of the Northmen expanded to the Cotentin peninsula, the Channel Isles and the area around Avranches (the Avranchin). Like Rollo, William was an astute politician and offered his services to first one player and then another in the interminable civil wars that beset Francia in the mid-tenth century. This, alongside advantageous treaties made with neighbouring rulers, saw Normandy expand to its largest extent and set the stage for future influence in France and further afield. In 987, the ruler of Normandy, Richard I, the Fearless (ruled 942–996), was able to establish virtual independence from his nominal overlord, Hugh Capet (the new king of France).

Unlike the Viking rulers of Dublin, York, and East Anglia, the rulers of Normandy were not titled as "king" (nor as "Grand Prince", as they were in Kiev: see Chapter 10). Instead, they were originally described in Latin records as *comes* (count). Consequently, Rollo was known as the "count of Rouen". However, his descendants had their eyes on a more prestigious title. Rollo's great-grandson, Richard II, the Good (ruled 996–1026), adopted the title "duke", derived from the Latin *dux*. From his reign onwards, we can talk of the dukes of Normandy, the most famous of whom was Richard II's grandson, renowned in history as Duke William of Normandy (duke 1035–1087) and King William I, the Conqueror, of England (king 1066–1087).

THE CHRISTIAN VIKINGS OF NORMANDY

The Vikings who at first raided and then settled in Francia were pagans, but these Viking Norse-speaking overlords soon adopted Christianity as part of the political package that saw them gaining control of the coastal lands. As we have seen, Rollo took on the new name of Robert when he was baptized as a Christian.

Again, what is striking is how fast the transition from paganism to Christianity occurred. In just over a century, as we shall shortly see, the recently pagan Normans became such enthusiastic supporters of church trends and reforms emanating from the pope in Rome that Duke William of Normandy could even merit a papal banner from Pope Alexander II (pope 1061–1073) in 1066, alongside a commission to reform key areas of the Anglo-Saxon church. We rarely think of the Norman Conquest as a church-sanctioned reforming crusade but, as we have seen, that was how Duke William presented it. It is a striking sign of how the Christianization of the Vikings of Normandy had transformed them, their culture and connections in just over a century.

This accompanied fairly rapid assimilation to local French culture. Despite their Viking past the Old Norse language was rapidly replaced by what is known today as *Nourmaund* (Norman), a regional form of French. The earlier form of this language, used in Normandy by the eleventh century, is now usually described as Norman French. But it is a language that rapidly lost the vast majority of its Scandinavian history. At most, its vocabulary today shows *some* influence of Old Norse roots and this may have affected *some* aspects of pronunciation. In short, the descendants of the victorious Rollo were soon speaking a language which was French with some Scandinavian influences. This was a Romance language (the family of languages, including ones such as Italian, French, Spanish, derived from Latin) and not a North Germanic one (such as Danish, Icelandic, Norwegian or Swedish). Looking critically at the combined evidence of place names, personal names, and language indicates that only small numbers of elite Scandinavian settlers took part in Rollo's apparent takeover and rapidly intermarried with the local Frankish families. Thus, by as early as the mid-tenth century, there were very few speakers of Old Norse in Rouen,[2] with the northern language surviving in Bayeux for only a generation beyond that.[3] Not a single object carrying runes has been identified in Normandy: it is clear that Viking culture there rapidly assimilated to local Frankish customs and language.[4]

In short, the Viking settlers rapidly became Frenchified, in religion, culture and language. Counts William Longsword and Richard I, the Fearless, both married French princesses. Although the king of France interfered in the troubled years of the early 1040s in Normandy (during the minority of William the Conqueror), he eventually knighted the fifteen-year-old William, in about 1043, and went on to assist him in his victory over his

Norman rivals at the Battle of Val-ès-Dunes, near Caen, in 1047, which secured the duchy for the nineteen-year-old duke. Soon the duke of Normandy would become more powerful than his overlord, the king of France.

It is intriguing that by 1066 – although the Normans considered themselves distinct from the French, who had their own kingdom and king – the Bayeux Tapestry occasionally describes the Normans as *Franci*.[5] This, though, may be more how the conquered English regarded them, since the tapestry was almost certainly the work of English seamstresses. But, in the aftermath of the Norman Conquest, the legal distinction made between the conquerors and the conquered was expressed in the contrasting terms *Franci et Angli* (French and English).[6] So, not only was the Norman Conquest of 1066, apparently, a Christian crusade, it was also a French conquest of England.

HOLDING ON TO POWER

The newly baptized Rollo was lucky his gaining of the area of Normandy coincided with a time of weaker kingship in the Western Frankish kingdom. The Franks gave him little trouble as he established his powerbase. Nevertheless, Normandy was not an easy place to rule. The complex interaction between the counts (and later dukes) of Normandy and their most powerful followers had a big impact on how it developed. The sometimes anarchic nature of early Normandy caused the local landowners to build defended residences, early castles. These became a regular feature of Norman society and were scattered across the landscape. When the Normans eventually invaded England, in 1066, they brought the technology of castle defence with them. It was a legacy of the way in which the Viking Rollo and his descendants had been forced to share power with an influential group of (originally) Viking followers who expected to be rewarded with land.

Today we often describe these very early Norman castles – both in the duchy of Normandy and eventually in the conquered kingdom of England – as motte and bailey castles. These consisted of a wooden stockade put up around an area which contained the living quarters and also stabling for horses, the bailey. Within it, or built to one side of it, was a defended tower which was constructed on top of a high mound of earth, the motte. Defenders could escape into the tower on top of the motte if an enemy succeeded in breaking into the bailey. Around the defended stockade a ditch was dug which we know as the moat (not to be confused with the motte). This might be a dry ditch or filled with water if there was a convenient local source. In reality, very few early castles in Normandy and England were actually built in this way, despite what is shown in many school history textbooks. Most were just constructed as simple defended ring-works and would have looked like a Wild West fort from the nineteenth-century USA. The famous motte and bailey form seems to have been a slightly later development, which became popular prior to the construction of more elaborate stone defences.

With castles came knights. Between them, these two features of Norman military technology would become synonymous with the Normans and reveal how rapidly they morphed away from the traditional image of Viking foot-soldiers in the context of the challenges of their new home. Knights were a mounted military elite whose life was concentrated on preparing for and carrying out warfare. They were also very expensive, since their horses and equipment cost a great deal of money and grants of land were required to provide them with the necessary resources to fund their military expenditure and lifestyle.

This shift to knightly warfare moulded much of the development of society in the century after Rollo was granted his regional powerbase and converted to Christianity. It eventually grew into a complex system usually referred to as feudalism. This was not unique to Normandy but the Norman version of it was striking and had a huge influence on the way that power and land was organized. It was a hierarchical society made up of a series of rights and responsibilities. At the top of this pyramid stood the duke and the great landowners (barons), each with their own groups of dependent knights. These knights owed their lords loyalty and military service, in return for grants of land. When needed, the duke would call up his own household knights and summon his barons to call up theirs, together creating his mounted army. The barons held their estates directly from the duke (and later from the king after 1066). These developments put the Normans, with their mounted knights, at the cutting edge of military practice in the eleventh century.

Today we have a very elevated image of knighthood, largely the product of the later development of the myths of chivalry that knights encouraged as a way of setting themselves apart from the rest of society (particularly from the lower orders). In reality, most Norman knights by the early eleventh century were relatively poor and there was not enough land with which to reward them. This led to ambitious Normans selling their swords and lances to the highest bidders across a huge swathe of territory. It spread Norman culture and influence over a wide area. It was a strange combination of their Viking military heritage of widespread opportunistic raiding and military adventures, with the new way of fighting that had developed in Normandy. From the early eleventh century this development accelerated.

Normandy faced problems in its lack of centralization and it took a strong grip to hold the place together and overawe ambitious vassals with threats of retaliatory violence if they opposed the ruler's will. An example of this lack of sophistication in centralized government reveals itself in the matter of Norman coinage. While Norman dukes *did* control the coinage in Normandy, its production was spasmodic and lacked consistency. When William (later the Conqueror) became duke in 1035, no new coins had been minted in Normandy since the time of his grandfather, Duke Richard II, the Good. It was against this background of limited power that Duke William launched a campaign of tightening up government control over the local elites and he was successful in bringing them more fully under his control, by punishing those who resisted him. In the same way, the dukes of Normandy lacked what the Anglo-Saxon rulers on the other side of the English Channel enjoyed: the centralized royal record keeping office (the *chancery*), the method of sending out and enforcing their will on the regions (via documents known as *writs*) and the centralized tax raising machinery (via the taxes known as *gafol* or *geld*). This added to the attraction of England as a prize worth fighting for, as it had done for generations of earlier Vikings.

However, we should not overdo this catalogue of weaknesses, for Normandy was still much more orderly and controlled than many neighbouring French regions. The imposition of Viking rule on Normandy after 911 had meant that structures of government that had collapsed elsewhere in France were either preserved or revived there. This was an important achievement. This had created a hierarchy of power in which aristocrats, termed *counts*, held power below the duke; while others, termed *viscounts*, ran the royal estates. These positions were dependent on the will of the duke, which increased his power. Although there were times of civil war and violence (as during the childhood of Duke William) it was generally true that warfare was directed outside of the duchy. And most castles were built by those whose loyalty had been secured by the duke. This contrasted with the building of castles by out of control local elites, and the associated endemic warfare, that were features of life in other parts of France.[7] The descendants of the Viking warlord Rollo might have spoken a form of French and been described, at times, as *Franci* but they had carved out a very distinctive style of rule and military society in Normandy. Their Viking ancestors would, no doubt, have approved.

Nor did the Normans forget their northern roots. They remained "participants in the maritime culture of the world of the northern seas",[8] and most of the Old Norse words borrowed by the French language refer to ships and shipping. Their Viking character had not quite vanished. Other Scandinavians continued to be aware of this, just as other Viking adventurers still recognized kindred connections with the rulers of Kiev Rus at the other end of Europe. So when Viking fleets troubled England in the year 1000, they afterwards sailed to Normandy seeking shelter. Viking connections were not forgotten. When later Robert I, the Magnificent, and William the Conqueror first considered invading England, and then succeeded (in the case of William) in invading England, they were acting consistently with their Viking history. Duke Robert I was apparently reminded of this heritage, by allies, when considering an invasion of England. William's huge array of ships was practical proof of his Viking maritime heritage.

PATRONS OF THE CUTTING EDGE IN CHURCH REFORMS

For the generation after Rollo's baptism in 911 the Christian nature of Normandy was shaky. Clergy who had fled from the Vikings returned and a monastic community was once more established at the monastery of St Ouen in Rouen, but the extent of the new elite's commitment to their new faith gave cause for concern. In the 1020s, the archbishop of Reims wrote to the pope asking what he should do with Viking settlers who, despite repeated baptisms, still killed priests and offered sacrifices to idols. A later tradition held that, when Rollo died, he hedged his bets by both bequeathing gifts to the church in Normandy and also ordering the sacrificing of Christian slaves to the Norse gods Odin and Thor.[9] It may be a legend but it clearly was rooted in concerns about early Norman Christianity.

Things improved after this alarming start. The abbey at Jumièges revived and went on to become a famous centre of learning, patronized by the Norman rulers. Rollo's son, William Longsword, was responsible for the reinstitution of the monastery here, in the mid-tenth century, and it went from strength to strength. In 1040 work began on a huge new suite of abbey buildings. In a way consistent with the Norman dukes' enthusiasm for supporting the latest trends in the church (and gaining reciprocal support from the papacy as a result) these buildings are often described as the first major Romanesque construction in northern France. This was a new architectural style, rapidly patronized by the dukes of Normandy. The building project was overseen by the churchman Robert of Jumièges, who later became first the bishop of London and then, for a short time, the archbishop of Canterbury under King Edward the Confessor.

To return to the later tenth century: under Richard II, the Good (ruled 996–1026), the church expansion accelerated. He invited reforming monks from Cluny to improve the discipline and practices at the monastery of Fécamp, which saw an expansion of the influence of Benedictine monks. New monasteries were set up at Bernay, Bec-Hellouin, Cerisy-la-Forêt, and at Rouen (Holy Trinity). Many of these new or reformed monasteries became centres of learning, powerhouses of Christian intellectual development. One of the Norman scholars, Lanfranc (lived 1005–1089), was one of the most prominent intellectuals in Western Europe and his influence had a huge impact on Normandy and, later, on England where he became archbishop of Canterbury in 1070. All of this also enhanced the influence of the dukes of Normandy, who held the power to appoint bishops. It also pulled Normandy together and gave it a united character; and it drew the dukes close to the papacy.

However, this close relationship fractured at times. When Richard II, the Good, died, there was a disputed succession between his sons, eventually won by Robert the Magnificent (ruled 1027–1035), the father of the later William the Conqueror. Duke Robert clashed with the bishop of Bayeux and the archbishop of Rouen (both relatives of his and serious political players) and the latter was sent into exile by Duke Robert. Duke Robert seized monastic estates and used them to reward his knights. As a result, the archbishop of Rouen placed Normandy under an interdict, which denied church rites to its rulers and their supporters. The duke was soon reconciled to the church, gave back the land, recalled the exiled archbishop and made him a trusted adviser. In 1035, Duke Robert even embarked on pilgrimage to the Holy Land. He died on the journey, leaving seven-year-old William as his heir. The alliance between duke and church had been restored.

This continued in the later reign of Duke William who, as we have seen, was energetic in supporting the church and in gaining the support of the pope for his ambitions in England. This was rooted in his childhood which, although violent and turbulent, was still lived in close relationship with the church. Archbishop Robert of Rouen was a close companion (until his death in 1037), as was the monk Ralph Moine, who acted as his principal tutor. William's devotion to the church, though, was balanced by his own driving desires. He married his cousin, Matilda of Flanders, in 1050, despite a papal prohibition. But he was too important a son of the church to be left under a papal interdict and, in 1059, the pope lifted it on condition that both William and Matilda founded abbeys in the town of Caen.

When William fought at Hastings in October 1066, in the company of a papal banner, it was a vivid demonstration of how far the Viking duchy of Normandy had come in a century and a half.[10] William was certain that God was on his side. And when William eventually won, he would, in return, send the pope "more gold and silver coins than could be credibly told, as well as ornaments that even Byzantium would have considered precious". These gifts included the personal banner of the defeated Harold Godwinson himself. It seemed a fitting act of gratitude for the provision of the pope's banner.[11]

KEY PLAYERS IN THE COMPLEX POLITICS OF THE ELEVENTH-CENTURY CHANNEL COAST

The Viking origins of Normandy continued to influence its foreign policy in the eleventh century. It was not unusual for Viking fleets attacking England to shelter in Norman ports. In 1002, in an attempt to stop this through a diplomatic alliance, Æthelred II of England married Emma of Normandy, the sister of Duke Richard II, the Good. The intention of the marriage/alliance was to "draw the duke away from his Scandinavian allies".[12] The strategy was only partly successful. On the negative side, the English found that, from time to time, Viking fleets still found shelter in Norman ports.[13] On the other hand, it prevented the Normans from cooperating too actively with their Viking allies. If not a firm friend, then Normandy was, at least, not an active opponent.

Its longer lasting legacy was that when Edward the Confessor finally became king of England in 1042 (he would reign until his death in January 1066), he regarded Normans as his natural friends and this paved the way to him making Duke William his heir; an act that led to the Norman Conquest. The offer to William was probably intended, as in the past, to close Norman ports to Viking fleets, since rulers in Norway and Denmark still harboured ambitions regarding the English crown.[14] The pious Edward had spent his formative years in Christian Normandy and he looked to it for candidates for church leadership within the Anglo-Saxon church (e.g. Robert of Jumièges) as well as a potential heir to the throne of England. In this way the Christian descendant of Vikings (William) was made heir, in about 1051, by a childless king (Edward the Confessor) who had been forced into exile, in 1016, by a recently converted Christian king of Viking Denmark (Cnut), and the success of William in the autumn of 1066 was unintentionally assisted by the intervention of the Christian Viking king of Norway (Harald Hardrada). All in all, the Vikings – post-conversion – had a huge impact on the British Isles and Western Europe generally, this remarkable strand of cause and effect being one example.

CHAPTER 7

The Christian Vikings of Denmark

When Harald Bluetooth converted to Christianity in the 960s he set about the conversion of Denmark and its northern territories. It was the first of the Viking Scandinavian homelands to convert to the new faith, and occurred while Denmark was undergoing far-reaching political changes. During the mid-tenth century a more unified Danish state was emerging under King Gorm (c. 936–958). His queen was Thyra, whom he described in a runic inscription on her burial mound as *tanmarkar but* ("Denmark's ornament"). We do not know exactly when she died but this inscription is the first recorded use of the name for the country as a whole, and was surely significant: a united Danish kingdom was being built. Soon it would be a Christian Viking kingdom.

THE CURIOUS LEGACY OF HARALD BLUETOOTH

In the 960s this trend towards unification increased at the same time that Gorm's son, Harald Bluetooth (ruled Denmark c.958–c.986), extended Danish rule into Norway. It is almost certainly at this time of increased centralization of power that the military barracks complex at Trelleborg, on Zealand, was constructed.

These buildings were built in a geometrical pattern within a circular fortress in about 980. The complex, impressive though it is, is not unique, since four such complexes were constructed. The reason for their construction has been debated by archaeologists and historians, but the most convincing explanation is that they were built as military camps to defend royal power against both internal and external threats. They are a testament to the increasing organizational power of the Danish monarchy. The fact that concerted Danish Viking attacks on Anglo-Saxon England resumed at about this time is surely no coincidence. The powerful new Viking state was able to flex its military muscle abroad as well as at home.

Harald Bluetooth converted to Christianity in about 963 and later claimed to have been the ruler responsible for enforcing the Christian conversion of the Danes. His reputation as a strong unifying king has left a curious legacy which is still remembered in the twenty-first century in Bluetooth technology. As an open wireless technology that connects several electronic devices, the Swedish data communication systems company Ericsson took as its logo the combined runic alphabet initials of Harald Bluetooth: H or ᚼ and B or ᛒ. Such a combined set of runes is known as a bind-rune. The form of the runic alphabet from which this bind-rune was chosen in 1997 is that of the so-called "Younger Futhark".

Despite all the uncertainty which surrounds Harald Bluetooth's reign, he is the first Danish king who is more than just a name. From the time when he ruled, the written sources become much richer and we do not need to rely as heavily on the German chronicler Adam of Bremen (who died in the 1080s), our sole source for many other Scandinavian rulers and events of the earlier Viking Age. This means we begin to get a more rounded picture of the Viking rulers from this time onwards. A number of these insights come from semi-literate Scandinavia itself. Runic inscriptions become much more common and the stone which Harald ordered put up at Jelling is of particular importance (see below). Important information can also be gained using dendrochronology (dating a structure from its tree rings) on a number of major building works dating from Harald's reign. There is also evidence from coinage, as

Harald Bluetooth appears to have been the king responsible for the first national Danish coinage. In 2013, a hoard of over 162 half-bracteates (low silver content coins) was discovered at Strandby Skatten in northern Denmark. The motifs on the reverse of the coins testify to the king's Christianity: either one cross created out of four crosses or, in some cases, three crosses placed on top of a triangle (known as a *Golgatha*). Harald was clearly promoting his new Christian faith.[1]

Similarly, Harald asserted on a famous runestone at Jelling that he had ordered it to be erected in memory of his father and mother (Gorm and Thyra) and explicitly stated he was "that Harald who won for himself all of Denmark and Norway and made the Danes Christian".[2] His memorial stone at Jelling is famous for the image of the crucifixion which shows Christ bound by vines and, indeed, technically there is no actual cross portrayed. This is a feature of a number of Viking depictions of Christ's death. Perhaps surprisingly, the third face of the huge stone is occupied by a great beast, in the Mammen Style, with a foliate crest and tail, engaged in a struggle with a snake which is intertwined with its body.[3] Together these striking images show the simultaneous use of Scandinavian animal art with Christian themes and remind us of the high degree of continuity in terms of artistic style which accompanied the conversion. Clearly, even when themes and motifs were partly borrowed from Christian Europe, they were executed in a traditionally Scandinavian manner. This was a very Viking conversion.

THE CLAIMS OF HARALD BLUETOOTH

To return to the momentous claims made on the Jelling runestone… Harald claimed to have been the unifier of Denmark; to have extended Danish rule to Norway; and – most significant for this book – overseen the conversion of the Danes to Christianity. These are three big assertions.

Regarding the first one, there is evidence to support the idea that, by the reign of Harald's son Svein (known as Svein Forkbeard), at the very least the major component parts of medieval Denmark must have already been fully integrated. This is demonstrated by the marriages of both Harald and Svein Forkbeard, both of whom married women from outside of Denmark. Svein Forkbeard married a Polish princess and Harald had earlier married the daughter of a prince of the Slavonian Abodrites. This is in contrast to Harald's father, Gorm, who married a princess from within Denmark. This suggests that, while Gorm married to consolidate his power among the Danish nobles, his son and grandson no longer needed to do so and married to build alliances with other international players. It is clearly significant that both Harald and Svein Forkbeard's wives came from royal houses which were opposed to the Germans, the traditional southern rivals of the Danes.

Fighting within Scandinavia had reached a national scale – as the Viking states began to emerge there – and without a united Denmark, it would have been impossible for Svein Forkbeard to have maintained control on both sides of the North Sea, as he was eventually to do (he briefly conquered England in late 1013). If Harald's claim was also referring to the reconquest of parts of southern Jutland from the Germans, then the marriages just mentioned would have been of particular importance. The Germans were threatening both their eastern and northern neighbours and these marriage alliances reveal Harald allying himself with the kingdoms to the east against the Germans.[4] By the end of the tenth century, the centre of power of the Jelling dynasty (as Harald's family is known) had moved to Roskilde, west of modern-day Copenhagen, suggesting the achievement Harald boasted about was indeed the unification of Jutland with the north islands and parts of the Scandinavian mainland in what is now southern Sweden.[5]

All this seems to confirm that not only can Harald's claim be corroborated, but also that the interpretation of the relocation of the Jelling kings from west to east seems to be consistent with the evidence for his increased power. Perhaps the most important indication of this is expressed by his building projects. The most impressive and unusual are the geometrical fortresses that we referred to earlier. There are four confirmed geometrical fortresses in Denmark: Trelleborg on the island of Sjælland,

Nonnebakken on the island of Fyn, Fyrkat in north-east Jutland, and Assersborg in north Jutland. These were major projections of royal power.

The second claim on Harald's runestone at Jelling is that he won Norway as well as Denmark. His power in Norway, however, is unlikely to have been on the same scale as the control he exercised over Denmark and is more likely to have taken the form of overlordship. If this is correct, then it is given substantial weight by the fact that the *jarl* (earl) of Lade fought alongside Harald against the Germans. The jarls of Lade were powerful local lords in the regions of Trøndelag and Hålogaland in Norway, from the ninth until the eleventh century. (The role of jarls, especially those of Lade, is explored more fully in Chapter 8.) Although Danish power in Norway waned for a time towards the end of the tenth century, it did not disappear completely. The Norwegian king, Harald Finehair, was married to a Danish princess, and his son Erik Bloodaxe (sometime king in York) was married to one of Harald Bluetooth's sisters.[6] Later Danish kings, such as Cnut the Great, would build on this foundation as they also sought to extend Danish rule to include Norway.

The last of Harald's claims was that he "made the Danes Christian". He may have been the first king to make Christianity the official religion of Denmark, but Christianity was by no means a new concept to the Danes. The first attempt to convert Denmark was at the beginning of the eighth century when the Northumbrian missionary saint Willibrord (died 739) extended his mission into Denmark from Frisia. It was unsuccessful and does not seem to have had any royal backing.[7] There were some further attempts under the Frankish emperor Charlemagne, but it was not until the reign of the Frankish emperor Louis the Pious (ruled 813–840) that any serious action was undertaken. One of the outcomes of this was the conversion of the Danish king Harald Klak, who was baptized in Mainz (Germany) in 826. When he returned to Denmark, two missionaries accompanied him on the journey.[8] However, despite this imperial support (and possibly because of this and because he was the first Christian king of Denmark) he was driven out by the still-pagan Danes in 827 and died in exile around 852. Nevertheless, he was the only ruler in Scandinavia who is known to have converted to Christianity in the ninth century.

His successors, Horik I and II, were not baptized, although they were on good terms with Anskar (archbishop of Hamburg-Bremen and a Christian missionary) and allowed two churches to be built in Denmark. Adam of Bremen even claimed that Horik II "accepted the Christian faith and by edict ordered all his people to become Christian" but this was an exaggeration. It is obvious, however, that by the middle of the ninth century, at least some of the most powerful men in Denmark were prepared to tolerate Christianity and respect the Christian God.[9] It does seem likely, as well, that many ordinary Danes had been converted before Harald Bluetooth's reign, either within Denmark or elsewhere in Christian Europe. Some may have accepted Christianity purely for business reasons, whereas others are likely to have been persuaded by the missionaries or by the power of the Christian God as seen in the outbreak of plague among the Viking marauders who had sacked the abbey of St Germain-des-Pres, on the outskirts of Paris, in 845.[10] However, although there probably were converts and priests in Denmark during the early tenth century, wide scale conversion required the commitment of the Scandinavian rulers, rather than just their tolerance.[11] So when Harald Bluetooth came to the throne, Christianity may not have been an alien concept but, since it was not yet officially endorsed by those in the upper echelons of society, it had not become widely accepted.

Harald's claim to the Christianization of the Danes, therefore, had more to do with the implementation of church organization than the introduction of Christianity itself. But this was important, as royal support was crucial to the expansion of Christian influence and the building of churches in the early medieval period. Harald Bluetooth's reign, just over a century after the lifetime of Harald Klak, was therefore the next one of religious significance for Denmark. There is, in fact, strong evidence for the conversion of Harald Bluetooth himself since excavations at Jelling have revealed a contrast between the paganism of Gorm that was practised there and the Christianity of Harald. The role of the priest Poppo in Harald's conversion around 965 suggests that, despite the fact that Gorm died a pagan, priests were still allowed in Denmark at that time.[12] The account of Harald's conversion, as recorded in the writings of the German chronicler Widukind of Corvey (died c. 973), tells the dramatic story of how Poppo demonstrated the power of Christ by carrying a large iron weight, heated in a fire, without suffering burns.

The account of the conversion found in Widukind emphasizes the point that before the conversion of Harald Bluetooth, the Danes had accepted Christ as a god but that it was only after Harald's conversion that other gods were rejected and Christianity accepted as the official religion.[13] Harald was aware of the importance of the decision. He built a large church at Jelling and proclaimed he had made all the Danes Christian. The movement of the body of his father to the new church there can be seen as "dramatically symbolizing the transition to the new faith".[14]

It was also Harald who produced the first explicitly Christian coinage. His conversion would have resulted in at least the abandonment of the pagan rituals in which the king was involved. However, some people still persisted in pagan activities and the acceptance of Christianity was accompanied by compromises, as occurred in Iceland, as we shall see.[15] The archaeological evidence suggests a peaceful conversion, though, with people gradually invoking God and St Michael on runestones rather than Thor. The use of Thor's hammer dramatically reduced in the second half of the tenth century, as did burial with grave goods; but there were still some people being buried with artefacts until around 980 and, even within Harald's fortress of Fyrkat, there are several examples of female pagan wagon-graves, although there are no male horseman-burials, and there are clear Christian features in the burials overall.[16]

Other old habits also took some time to disappear and some Danes continued to worship and sacrifice to the old gods well after Harald's conversion. For example, eating horse flesh (a custom often associated with paganism at this time) and some pagan burial practices were not abandoned until the end of the tenth century.[17] The Strandby Skatten coin hoard (probably buried in the 990s and famous for its use of Christian crosses on coins) still also contained a miniature silver Thor's hammer, representing *Miollnir*. A smith's mould, found at Trend in Jutland, had spaces for two crosses and one hammer; clearly the smith was open for work from both Christians and pagans. But perhaps the pace of conversion is revealed in the fact that he expected twice as much Christian custom. Adam of Bremen claims that the Danish church experienced a setback following the revolt of Harald's son, Svein Forkbeard, against his father, and Svein may have been temporarily harnessing a pagan reaction to further his own political ambitions. Clearly, it took time for the new faith to be accepted across Denmark. But the cultural tide was flowing in Christianity's favour.

Although Svein's revolt will have caused disruption and some bishops may have fled, there is no hint of a widespread revival of pagan burial practices. Svein Forkbeard is, in fact, remembered as a supporter of Christianity who built a church in Lund and in Roskilde, as well as a royal mausoleum. He dedicated both to the Holy Trinity, which may have been due to the influence of Anglo-Saxon Christianity, since this was the dedication of the royal church at Winchester, in England. It contrasted with dedications to the Virgin Mary that were something of a hallmark of churches influenced by Hamburg-Bremen. It seems that it was Svein's lack of support for the German archbishop of Hamburg-Bremen, rather than his lack of Christian faith, which caused Adam of Bremen to condemn him.[18] Adam similarly states that Harald's conversion was enforced by the German emperor Otto I (ruled 962–973), but this also stemmed from a desire, on Adam's part, to see Denmark under the authority of Hamburg-Bremen. This claim does not appear in Widukind's earlier history of Otto, or his account of the conversion of Harald, suggesting that Widukind's version is more persuasive, and it is far more consistent with other evidence. Although Harald's claim on the Jelling runestone may be slightly exaggerated, it is correct to a significant extent. Some Danes *were* already Christian when he came to the throne, while others were still pagan when he erected his great runestone. However, although he was not the first Danish king to convert, he was the first effective and successful king to do so, able to actively support the church and create a situation whereby Denmark would become a Christian nation, even if the conversion of the nation was slower than Harald's runestone would have us believe. And even if the start of this process predated Harald's reign.

A later tradition, recorded by the twelfth-century Danish chronicler Sven Aggesen, that Harald renounced Christianity on his death-bed, is not supported by earlier accounts. Adam of Bremen insisted that Harald died a Christian. While he never was canonized, which may reflect some reservations about him as a model Christian king, there is no reason to accept the assertion made by Sven Aggesen.

In conclusion, Harald's claims stand up to scrutiny. It appears he did bring all of Jutland into Denmark. The spread of a new system of land administration, the distribution of coin hoards and, most importantly, the geometrical fortresses seem to substantiate his claims. The fortresses are of particular importance as they demonstrate not only the area over which Harald wielded power, but also the level of power and the large scale of the resources he had at his disposal. His interference in Norwegian politics and his close relationship with the jarls of Lade make it likely that he did act as an overlord over Norway, although his control there was never on the same scale as in Denmark. Lastly, although he did not introduce Christianity or make all the Danes Christian, he did transform Denmark into an officially Christian nation with the trappings of ecclesiastical organization; even if it was almost a century before the first recorded bishoprics appeared in Denmark (e.g. at Lund in the 1050s). So while the claims that Harald made may be slightly exaggerated, in essence the assertions on the Jelling runestone can generally be substantiated. This Christian Viking king of Denmark had a significant impact on his kingdom.

DENMARK AFTER HARALD BLUETOOTH

This raises the question of what role his son, Svein Forkbeard, played in taking this Christian conversion forward after Harald's death, around 986. Without a shadow of doubt, he has received a mixed press. Adam of Bremen described him as an apostate who repeatedly suffered the wrath of God. The German chronicler Thietmar of Merseburg (died 1018) described him as "not a ruler... but a destroyer... an enemy to his own people".[19] On the other hand, the *Anglo-Saxon Chronicle* treated him as a remarkable military leader. Perhaps more importantly, in the mid-eleventh-century *Encomium Emmae Reginae* (*In Praise of Queen Emma*), Svein Forkbeard is described as a fortunate king who was loved by his people, which caused his father to be envious of him. It then goes on to state that he ruled wisely and actively, and that the loyalty of his men meant that he was able to leave for England knowing that his trusted agents would keep control of Denmark.[20] This is supported by the abandonment of the geometrical fortresses built by his father, suggesting Svein Forkbeard no longer needed them to control the Danes.

The portrayal of Svein Forkbeard as a weak ruler who suffered from revolts and incursions and defeats from abroad seems to have more to do with the biases of Adam of Bremen (reflected in some later histories) rather than being a reflection of political reality. Svein Forkbeard seems to have abandoned the archbishopric of Hamburg-Bremen in favour of English bishops and it is this, rather than an actual lack of control or rejection of Christianity, which led to this negative portrayal. If this is taken into consideration, then it appears that Svein Forkbeard maintained control of a possibly volatile, newly united and Christianizing kingdom, despite spending much of his reign campaigning in England. This implies a strong leader, with loyal retainers.

Yet according to Adam, Svein Forkbeard was subordinate to his neighbours, especially his Swedish neighbours. Adam reports that Svein Forkbeard suffered defeat in numerous naval battles against King Erik of Sweden, who conquered Denmark and drove him into exile.[21] This "exile" may plausibly be explained as a (fictional) elaboration of Svein Forkbeard's repeated absences in England and it is possible that the king of Sweden may have tried to take advantage of this absence; although a conquest of Denmark seems unlikely. According to Adam of Bremen, Svein Forkbeard only regained his kingdom on the death of Erik. He then married Erik's widow but was quickly exiled again by Erik's son, Olof *Skötkonung*, and was only allowed to return because he had married Olof's mother. However, the marriage of Svein Forkbeard to Erik's widow would normally be seen as a sign of male superiority, rather than subordination. In addition, Olof is referred to as *skötkonung* (taxes-king, meaning he paid tribute) in later sources, which implies he was a tributary king of a more powerful ruler. Lastly, the fact that Olof supported Svein Forkbeard in the battle which established Svein Forkbeard's overlordship of Norway would imply that Svein was also Olof's overlord.[22] Olof waited until the death of Svein Forkbeard before asserting his independence. Then, when Svein's successor, Cnut, sent young Anglo-Saxon princes to Sweden to be killed, Olof refused. Instead, he sent them on to Hungary, out of reach of Cnut. Then he married off his daughter to Cnut's enemy, Olaf Haraldson of Norway. Finally, by requesting a bishop who was consecrated at Hamburg-Bremen, Olof *Skötkonung* freed himself from the influence of the English church.[23]

Svein Forkbeard seems to have had an even greater direct control over Norway. Danish interest in Norway can be traced back to the early ninth century and this was a tradition continued by Svein, who seems to have inherited Norwegian overlordship from his father, Harald Bluetooth. However, in 995 the Viking adventurer Olaf Tryggvason, funded by the English crown, returned from raiding England to Norway and was accepted as the king of Norway. Olaf was not to reign for long and in 1000, he was killed by Svein Forkbeard, with the support of the Swedish king, in the naval battle of the Svold. Svein then restored the jarls of Lade to their position as sub-rulers of the country. They acted effectively as the agents of the Danish king and, as such, Svein Forkbeard was able to exercise more direct authority over Norway than he had achieved with regard to Sweden. However, his role in Norway was more of an overlord than a king, even if he did have a large amount of control over the kingdom (and even if the power of this particular overlordship exceeded that of his influence in Sweden). This intervention in Norway continued under his son and successor, Cnut the Great. Svein Forkbeard died in February 1014, and was initially succeeded in Denmark by his son, Harald II, who was reluctant to share the Danish throne with Cnut.

DENMARK UNDER CNUT THE GREAT

So Cnut turned his attentions to England, and in 1016, succeeded in conquering it and becoming king. He gained control of Denmark in 1018, after his brother Harald II died. Cnut was a third-generation Christian and his Christian credentials were enhanced by his conquest of the well-established Christian kingdom of England. Adam of Bremen records that when Cnut returned to Denmark from England, he brought numerous bishops with him. We are used to hearing about Viking invasions of Christian England, so it comes as something of a surprise to hear of this Christian "invasion" of Viking Denmark. From this group, one bishop, named Bernhard, was given responsibility for Scania, Gerbrand for Zealand and Reginbert for Fünen. Their names were not Old English so they were probably continentals who were active in the English church. These appointments were deeply resented by the archbishops of Hamburg-Bremen and, in 1025, Gerbrand was forced to swear allegiance to the German church while travelling through Bremen. It is likely that the earlier appointments were deliberate attempts by Cnut to stop Germans influencing politics in Denmark through the back door.

As well as wishing to stamp his authority on the Danish church, Cnut was also determined to extend his rule into Norway and Sweden, and to resist aggressions from the German Empire and the Slav peoples east of the River Elbe. However, the defeat of the jarl of Lade (an ally of the Danes) by Olaf Haraldson at the Battle of Nesjar, in 1015, meant that Cnut lost control over Norway.[24] Cnut then faced another serious setback in Scandinavia with the death of the Swedish king Olof *Skötkonung* in 1022. Olof was an ally, and Adam of Bremen even tells us that Cnut had intended to conquer Norway (to add to the crown of England) with his support. However, this plan was thwarted by Olof's death.[25]

The next challenge to Cnut's ambition occurred at the Battle of Holy River, in 1026. He was facing the joint forces of the king of Norway and the new king of Sweden.[26] The *Anglo-Saxon Chronicle* reports that Cnut's enemies won; however, contemporary Scandinavian skaldic poetry suggests that Cnut was victorious. It is certain that Cnut's brother-in-law, Ulf, was killed. He had been Cnut's regent in Denmark, until he rebelled and allied himself with the Norwegians and the Swedes. The late twelfth to early thirteenth-century Danish historian Saxo Grammaticus believed that Ulf was assassinated on Cnut's orders in the church at Roskilde.[27] Following the battle, Cnut's opponents negotiated a peace treaty, suggesting they were not dominated by Cnut. On the other hand, Cnut was able to travel immediately to Rome so must have felt fairly strong in Scandinavia.[28] It is likely that the battle was something of a stalemate in which neither side could land the killer blow. Despite this, Cnut, in a letter to his English subjects, claimed he was now king of England, Denmark, Norway and some of the Swedes.[29] He was probably claiming too much, since in 1027 he was buying the support of Norwegian nobles against Olaf Haraldson, who was still on the throne.

He was also not king of Sweden, despite his claims. In fact, the Swedes he claimed to rule may just have been those in his army.[30] And the coins struck in Sigtuna (Sweden) carrying the words *CNVT REX SW* (*Cnut rex Swevorum*) were probably an adaptation of a coin of Cnut and didn't prove that he actually ruled Sweden.[31] He may have enjoyed a loose (and contested) overlordship of both Norway and Sweden but both at this point retained their independent dynasties. There were limits to the greatness of Cnut the Great.

However, in 1028, Cnut struck at Norway. King Olaf Haraldson of Norway's rule had already been weakened by pagan reactions to his determined Christianity. Cnut – though also a Christian – undermined this further by bribing key Norwegians and promising them greater freedom. *Realpolitik* had trumped faith. This led to Olaf Haraldson's death, in 1030, at the Battle of Stiklestad, at the hands of Norwegians allied to Cnut. Olaf's sanctity was emphasized by a later Icelandic tradition, recorded by Snorri Sturluson, that his men charged, shouting: "*Fram kristmenn, krossmenn, kongsmenn alle!*"[32] ("Forward, Christ's men, cross men, king's men all!") The battle-cry was derived from Christian hymn, the Sanctus.

Cnut's ambitions had borne fruit and he appointed Jarl Hakon of Lade as his governor, but when Hakon died, in 1030, Cnut named his own son, another Svein, as king of Norway with the support of Svein's mother, Ælfgifu, one of Cnut's two wives.[33] However, the Norwegians soon grew restless under the taxation and harsh rule of this particular foreign king. This was combined with the growing cult of the dead king (now St) Olaf Haraldson, despite the fact he had died at the hands of dissatisfied Norwegians. The decision to move the body of St Olaf Haraldson to Nidaros (Trondheim) Cathedral, in 1031, could not have occurred without young King Svein's active participation, so it looks as if he was trying to harness (or defuse) the power of this saint's cult. He failed. The Danish position in Norway could not be held and, in 1034, both young Svein and Ælfgifu were forced out.[34] Norway had asserted its independence from Denmark in decisive fashion. Cnut the Great had been out-manoeuvred.

THE IMPACT OF THE CHRISTIAN CONVERSION OF DENMARK ON VIKING ART

As Christianity was introduced to Denmark, the complex intertwined animal art so beloved of Viking craftspeople became increasingly used in conjunction with Christian symbols. One of the most famous examples of this is on the Jelling stone (referred to earlier) which simultaneously used both Nordic animal art and an image of the crucified Christ.[35] Similarly, the decoration on Jelling-style horse collars depicts the Norse myth of Odin being swallowed by the wolf Fenrir next to the biblical story of Jonah and the whale. This shows the complex mixture of influences during this period of conversion. We see a society partly embracing the artwork of their new faith but also unable to completely sever all ties with the old one. In a time of upheaval and change this apparent ambiguity and mix of cultural styles and influences suggests that the process of conversion was initially eased by allying Christian artwork with the familiar and traditional styles.

The influence of Christian iconography can be clearly seen in the depiction of the crucifixion. The earliest complete surviving representation of the crucified Christ to be found in Viking Age Denmark – the Aunslev Cross – dates from the first half of the tenth century (900–950).[36] It was discovered near Aunslev, Eastern Funen, in 2016, and has a figure of Christ made from fine gold threads and small filigree pellets.[37] A comparable figure, dating from the same time (but made from gilded silver), was unearthed in 1879, at Birka, in the Swedish province of Uppland. Earlier fragments from similar crosses (made from silver) had previously been discovered in Denmark in a silver hoard from the island of Omø and in a burial within a wagon at Ketting, on the island of Als.[38] These all stand out as portraying Christ bound to the cross, not nailed. While the image of binding to the cross may not be common with regard to portraying Christ's death, it is a common iconographical image with regard to other biblical figures such as St Andrew and the thieves at Golgotha. This may have led Scandinavian artists to use this image when portraying Christ on the cross.[39] It may also have been derived from eighth-century English poems, which may have been interpreted as referring to binding.

What is particularly noteworthy is that every cross pendant appears to have been buried with women, when a gender could be assigned to the burial. This may be simply because more women than men in these particular communities wore pendants. But this is unlikely. It may be more indicative of a particular attraction of Christianity to women. Perhaps this was because the new faith promised gender equality before God, and heaven for both genders (instead of just Valhalla for men), and banned infanticide. The association of crosses with women may also have been connected with a female responsibility for aspects of pagan cult practice which caused them to be significant players in the actual process of conversion.

The binding of Christ with vines also shows a more definite link to Christian iconography, based on the scriptural reference to Christ in the words "I am the vine". Vines came to be regarded as a symbol of Christ and of members of the church.[40] In Eastern Orthodox art, empty crosses surrounded by vines are recorded from the sixth century. In England, free-standing crosses with carved vine scrolls appear on an important group of eighth- and ninth-century monuments.[41] Surviving examples suggest that this became a normal element in Carolingian art in the Frankish

Empire. The vine and acanthus plant seem to have become interchangeable as scrollwork decoration on scenes connected with the crucifixion.[42] As a result, the Jelling stone and the bound-cross pendants must be seen against this European background, for Christian Viking art had a rich back story in European styles, as well as in the traditions drawn from Scandinavia. So, far from being a barbaric misconception or just a product of the Viking love of complex visual styles, these items belong to a theologically important group in early medieval European Christian art. And to this, the newly converted Scandinavians added their own particular contribution.

CHAPTER 8

The Christian Vikings of Norway

The Christian conversion of Norway appears to have been different from that of Denmark and Sweden as, while the role of the kings and the aristocracy was vital in all of these kingdoms, the Norwegian conversion seems to have been influenced far more by the English church than that of Hamburg-Bremen. Indeed, despite the fact that Anskar of Hamburg-Bremen (died 865) is often referred to as the Apostle of Scandinavia, he never actually made it to Norway and there is very little in Adam of Bremen's account which suggests that any significant missionary activity occurred from Hamburg-Bremen to Norway. Instead, the written sources, and the kings' sagas in particular, give the impression of a conversion which was organized solely through the work of missionary kings; especially Olaf Tryggvason and Olaf Haraldson. However, this is an over-simplification and foreign missionaries must have, in reality, played a larger role in the conversion of Norway. It is unrealistic to assume it could have occurred simply as a result of the efforts of a small number of hyper-active kings.

THE CREATION OF NORWAY: KING, JARLS,
AND EARLY RELIGIOUS CHOICES

According to the later saga evidence (often from thirteenth-century Iceland), King Harald Finehair united the separate mini-kingdoms of Norway into a single country after the Battle of Hafrsfjord in 872. He died in about 930,[1] and was succeeded by his son, Erik Bloodaxe, who had already been ruling before his father's death. However, Erik was killed in England in 954 and he was quickly replaced by his half-brother Hakon *Athalstein's fóstri* (named from being fostered at the court of King Athelstan of England). He was later to be known as Hakon the Good. However, although these were the first kings of a united Norway, they did not have complete control over all areas of the country; many powerful nobles still had significant influence over their various regions.

The most important of these magnates were the jarls – or earls – of Lade whose power was based in the north of Norway. Later, these jarls of Lade were to become rulers of the whole of Norway as agents of Denmark but, during the reigns of Harald and Hakon, they seem to have been content to accept the Norwegian kings as their overlords. However, it is important not to underestimate the importance of the jarls of Lade or the role they played in maintaining these kings in their positions of power. Given the major role they played in the creation and development of the kingdom of Norway, it is necessary to examine the dealings of kings with them in order to fully understand the complex nature of the relationship and the nature of early Norwegian kingship.

It is probable that the office of jarl dates back to an ancient institution of high prestige, in which magical and religious elements were involved as well as political. In contrast, the role of king seems to have been a Viking Age innovation based on the Danish model.[2] This means that the power of the jarls of Lade was based on an older tradition than that of the king and so, within their own areas of influence, their power had become entrenched over generations. This ensured that while both Harald and Hakon were able to ally themselves with these powerful jarls, neither was ever able to ultimately control them. Instead, the jarls of Lade permitted the kings of Norway to be their overlords. This affected later aspects of the Christian conversion, as we shall see.

Hakon the Good tried to convert Norway in the tenth century but gave up in the face of pagan resistance. Missionaries from England and Germany then had some limited success and the coastal distribution of large stone crosses indicates the start of Christian communities there. This was assisted by the reign of Olaf Tryggvason (995–1000). However, it was under King Olaf II Haraldson (St Olaf) that the conversion took off in the 1020s, assisted by missionaries from Normandy, whose Norse roots assisted them in making an impact on other Norse people. The conversion, as we shall see, also included a lot of violence.

The reforming nature of Hakon the Good's reign seems to have been heavily influenced by his earlier fostering by Athelstan, king of England. All of the major texts dealing with Hakon's reign – the late-twelfth-century *Agrip af Nóregskonungasögum* (*Abridgement of Norwegian kings*); the twelfth-century *Historia de Antiquitate Regum Norwagiensium* (*History of the Ancient Kings of Norway*); the early-thirteenth-century *Historia Norwegiae* (*History of Norway*); the thirteenth-century *Heimskringla* (*Circle of the World*); and the thirteenth-century *Fagrskinna* (*Fair parchment*) – all agree that Hakon was fostered in England during the lifetime of his father, Harald Finehair. As a result, Hakon was brought up as a Christian in a Christian country (i.e. England) at a time when Norway was still basically a pagan nation and this meant that, although his actions may have been influenced by his faith, he had to bear in mind the religion of the general populace when introducing his reforms.

There does seem to have been a link between Hakon's later law making, alongside the ideal of Christian kingship he promoted, and Anglo-Saxon influence. By introducing codified laws Hakon was acting in an established Christian pattern of the king as the final judge, under God. While this can be traced back to a model of kingship found in the Old Testament, this tradition was followed consciously in Anglo-Saxon England.[3] However, although this influence was very significant, it was also important that Hakon did not alienate his pagan people. As a result, the influence of the still pagan jarl of Lade was also important, as it counterbalanced these innovative and non-indigenous Christian ideas and methods. Hakon knew this and, as he introduced his new law code, he was politically astute enough to include among his closest advisors a man who was staunchly pagan. But this pragmatism also revealed weaknesses in his power as king. For, while Hakon himself was Christian and persuaded a number of his friends to convert, the people of Trøndelag refused to be converted and forced him to make pagan sacrifices, since this was expected of him as their king.[4]

The accounts in the kings' sagas do not describe this as a wholly spontaneous uprising. Rather, they describe a group of pagan chieftains banding together against a perceived threat to their authority.[5] Hakon's authority in northern Norway relied on the jarl of Lade and although the jarl usually supported him, in this instance he seems to have also had an eye to his own political position, since he urged first compromise with and then submission to the demands of the northern chieftains.[6] The jarl was also strongly pagan and, as such, clearly harboured doubts about this attempt to convert the kingdom and, in particular, his own region to the new Christian faith. Hakon had to tread carefully.

The archaeological evidence from grave goods also seems to support the idea of a particularly strong pagan presence in the north. The petering out of the use of grave goods in Vestlandet, Hakon's main area of control, suggests that Christianity was influential there earlier than in Trøndelag, ruled by the pagan jarl Sigurd Hakonson of Lade.[7] This may be why King Hakon the Good did not persevere in trying to impose Christianity on his people, and why the tenth-century poem *Hákonarmál* (*Hakon's poem*) implies that he died as a reluctant follower of the traditional pagan religion. The poem appears to suggest that, on his death at the Battle of Fitjar, the king was received into Valhalla. One doubts whether Hakon would have been pleased to be so described.

This shows how strong an influence the jarls of Lade had over Hakon and the course of Christian conversion. Their ability to influence him over this issue of great significance to him shows just how much power they wielded, as does their control over the local chieftains. This sudden flexing of political muscle was probably due to the jarls' strong feelings about the introduction of Christianity, and the way Hakon was developing kingship in a more proactive manner than in the past, in which both the jarl and the king were more dependent on each other to get things done. This dependence could, as in this instance, stand in the way of the Christian state-building Hakon appears to have been attempting. Christianity finally came to be accepted as the dominant religion of the Norwegians under later kings.

CHRISTIAN KINGS OF A MORE ASSERTIVE NORWAY

As we have seen, it was after the decisive naval battle of Hafrsfjord, in 872, that Harald Finehair came to dominate a more united Norwegian kingdom, even if the northern regions remained frustratingly beyond his control. After Harald's death, the unity of the new Norway disintegrated. Sometimes the direct descendants of Harald ruled and at other times power was held by jarls who accepted a foreign Danish overlordship. This continued until the late tenth century, when Olaf Tryggvason briefly held the Norwegian throne independent of Denmark. He was a descendant of Harald Finehair (father of Hakon the Good and Erik Bloodaxe) and ruled Norway from 995 to c. 1000. Like other members of the Norwegian royal family before him, raiding England had given him a detailed knowledge of the country.

Given the way that Olaf Tryggvason played an active role in promoting the Christian conversion of Norway, it is frustrating that the historical information about his life and activities is very limited. There are some brief mentions in the *Anglo-Saxon Chronicle*, but the only other near-contemporary account is found in Adam of Bremen's *Gesta Hammaburgensis ecclesiae pontificum* (*Deeds of Bishops of the Hamburg Church*), written in about 1070. Then, in the late twelfth century, Olaf featured in two Icelandic sagas.[8] The most famous of these is called *Ólafs saga Tryggvasonar* (*Saga of Olaf Tryggvason*) and was compiled in the monastery of Thingeyrar on Iceland. However, the most detailed description of his activities was written (again in Iceland) by Snorri Sturluson, in a work later entitled *Heimskringla* (*Circle of the World*), which aimed to tell the history of Norway from prehistoric times to 1177. Written around

1230, it was one of many insights into early Norwegian history compiled in Iceland. This was because there was an historic connection between Norway and the Viking settlers in Iceland. So when there was a revival of interest in the Viking past on Iceland in the thirteenth century (resulting in the compilation of many sagas, "histories" and collections of myths) this tended to reveal as much about Norway's past as Iceland's.

In these later sagas, we learn that Olaf Tryggvason gained his first military experience in the Baltic, where he raided the Slavs and the Balts on the southern and south-eastern shores of the sea. Far more historically trustworthy are the near-contemporary Anglo-Saxon sources which record that he raided Folkestone (Kent), in 991, with a fleet of ninety-three ships, only to be bought off with 10,000 pounds of silver. Then, in 994, he seems to have converted to Christianity and was confirmed at Andover (Hampshire), with Æthelred II acting as his sponsor. He then returned to Norway to take the throne and there he promoted Christianity. He did the same regarding the conversion of Orkney, on his way home to Norway in 995, indicating his conversion was more sincere than simply an attempt to gain English support in his assertion of independence *vis-à-vis* his one-time Danish allies in the raids on England.

Olaf Tryggvason died in the year 1000, when he was ambushed off the island of Svolder (in the western Baltic) by a combined fleet of Swedes, Danes and Wends (a tribe from Pomerania). These allies against the assertive new king of Norway were accompanied by the ships of the sons of the still-pagan jarl of Lade. Their father, Hakon Sigurdarson, had been killed in 995 just as the newly Christian Olaf Tryggvason was seizing control of Norway. Hakon Sigurdarson had not been killed by Olaf Tryggvason, who opposed the power of such pagan nobles, but, following an internal dispute with the people of Trøndelag, had been forced to flee and was memorably killed by his own slave and friend while hiding in a pig sty. His sons came to oppose both Olaf Tryggvason's political dominance and his religious beliefs. Once more the pagan north of Norway was opposing the religious conversion espoused by Christian kings. At the sea battle of Svolder, Olaf Tryggvason fought courageously from his longship named *Ormrinn Langi* (long serpent) until, facing overwhelming odds, he leapt overboard and vanished.

After this, the Danes dominated Norway, along with their allies the Norwegian jarls of Lade, until another independent Norwegian king, the Christian Olaf II Haraldson, emerged in 1015. Following the death of Olaf Haraldson (later known as St Olaf) in 1030 at the Battle of Stiklestad, the Danish king Cnut the Great reasserted Danish control over Norway. Olaf Haraldson had died as the result of Norwegian nobles once again allying themselves with a Danish king because they resented Olaf's dominance. However, as we have seen, only a year after his death he was canonized and became a symbol of Norwegian national independence in the face of an increasingly resented Danish overlordship. Today King (St) Olaf is the patron saint of Norway, remembered as a key figure in the Christian conversion of Norway; a legend that almost certainly overemphasizes his influence. He died while trying to become independent of the Danes (who were also Christians).

Following Cnut the Great's death, in 1035, Olaf Haraldson's son, known as Magnus the Good, took the throne of Norway. He was succeeded by Harald Hardrada, who died at the Battle of Stamford Bridge in England, in 1066.

THE ROLE OF MISSIONARY KINGS

The written sources for Norway tend to describe passionate, missionary kings who were baptized abroad and came home to convert the people with missionaries in tow.[9] So, unlike in Denmark and Sweden, there is little evidence for individual missionaries to Norway and no written accounts of the lives of individual missionary saints active in the Norwegian conversion. These sources therefore give us the traditional picture in which Norway was converted in roughly thirty-five years by Olaf Tryggvason and Olaf Haraldson (St Olaf). It is only fair to say that these two kings and the English priests they brought with them were very important in this process. However, it would have been impossible to Christianize the kingdom in such a short space of time and the conversion process must have begun much earlier than 995.[10] We have already seen how Hakon the Good tried (with limited success) to spread Christianity among the Norwegians. So it appears, despite the emphasis put upon the role of Olaf Tryggvason in the written records, his missionary activity consolidated a process which had begun decades earlier. His main contribution was his conquest of the area called Trøndelag which until that point had been resolutely pagan.[11] But even this did not fully neutralize it.

The conversion of Norway should be seen as the result of two factors. On the one hand, there was an expansive Western European church working on the conversion of the Norse in general, which had a forceful, developed missionary strategy, devoted and well-educated missionaries and a close relationship with worldly power. Both the church in England and its competitor in Hamburg-Bremen featured in this. On the other hand there was a strong movement on behalf of the Norwegian kings and aristocracy towards closer integration with European culture. The king and prominent magnates offered the men of the church shelter, protection and the opportunity to work in the country. This practice of installing priests on the estates of kings and magnates, in institutions which resemble English minster churches, appears to date back to the days of Hakon the Good.[12] In order to unearth the important work of the missionaries it is necessary to strip away the role of the kings to view the people whose work lay behind the throne, and to reveal the ordinary Norwegians whose lives changed as a result.

One of the most commonly used tools to measure Christian conversion and early missionary activity is through burial. This technique is not without its difficulties and it is hard to define a grave as categorically Christian. Just because it has few or no grave goods (or contains Christian objects), is east-west orientated and is an inhumation, it does not mean that it is unequivocally Christian. A lack of burial goods may well be an indication of lack of disposable wealth, and many Christian objects had been plundered from foreign monasteries.[13] However, when more than one of these characteristics appears to occur in a group of people buried at the same time, it is generally fair to assume that this indicates a change in belief. This is particularly true given the conservative nature of burial customs, which makes it more likely that real religious change was occurring.

The earliest Christian graveyard, identified by the above criteria, is on the island of Veøy in Møre og Romsdal county, in western Norway. Here the proximity of this graveyard to pagan burials suggests that Christian and non-Christian groups co-existed in the Romsdal area.[14] This would fit both chronologically and geographically with the Christianizing actions of King Hakon the Good. The burial evidence also seems to show that Norway was the subject of regional variations. There seems to be no Christian influence before the eleventh century in the interior of eastern and northern Norway or in Vestfold. In contrast, Østfold, Rogaland and some parts of Møre appear to have been significantly influenced by Christianity earlier, soon after 950.[15] This would suggest successful missionary activity in Norway from the mid-tenth century and so the conversion effort must have been well underway by the start of Olaf Tryggvason's reign in 995.

One of the most interesting categories of evidence of this is crosses on runestones and free-standing crosses, which not only show that the conversion occurred earlier than the reign of Olaf Tryggvason but also reveal an English influence. Unlike the rest of Scandinavia, western Norway has roughly sixty free-standing stone crosses and it seems there was a link between heathen grave-markers (*bauta*) developing into runic inscribed monuments, which themselves developed into inscribed crosses, and then finally into free-standing crosses. There appear to have been two schools of influence on these crosses, producing what we might call Norwegian-Anglian crosses (English influence) and Norwegian-Celtic crosses (Irish/Scottish influence).

The Kuli-Stone from Møre (in the northernmost part of western Norway) is of particular importance. It tells us that "Thore and Hallard raised this stone after Ulfljot. Twelve winters had Christianity been in Norway." The Old Norse word for twelve (*tualf*) is a very early form and, consequently, the stone is unlikely to have been erected later than the tenth century. The word for Christianity (*kristintumr*) is a loan word from Old English and surely indicates where this new religion originated, in this case at least.

119

This stone is too early to refer to either of the Olafs (Tryggvason and Haraldson) and may instead be a reference to the missions of Hakon the Good.[16]

The geographical location of these stone crosses – mostly along the western coast between Rogaland and Sogn og Fjordane – shows they were also placed within the sphere of influence of Hakon.[17] This "invasion of cross-worked runestones and free-standing crosses" throughout the tenth and eleventh centuries in western Norway shows conspicuous signs of English and, potentially, Scottish missionary activity.[18] So, even after the end of Hakon's reign, the English missionaries he probably brought across the North Sea with him continued their work to convert the Norwegian people, as evidenced in the archaeological record.

MORE ON THE ENGLISH CONNECTION

The argument for an "English connection" is based on more than the suggestive evidence of the crosses. Norwegian Christianity, in other respects, has a definite English character, seen in Christian laws and aspects of church language. One important piece of evidence is the earliest liturgical fragment discovered so far in Norway, which appears to be part of an English missal from roughly 1000 and strongly resembles works produced at Winchester. The organization of the Norwegian church also appears to echo the English minster church system, suggesting strong connections between the two churches.[19] There also seems to be shared venerations of saints' cults. St Botulph in particular stands out, featuring in the liturgy and dedications of a number of churches in Norway (and in Denmark and Sweden). In Norway there were two churches in Slagen and Ignarbakke (both in south-eastern Norway) dedicated to him, and the unusual personal name Botulf is also attested in thirteenth-century Norway. This implies church books (missals and breviaries) – and possibly clerics – were brought from eastern England, and East Anglia in particular, and spread to all areas of Scandinavia, including Norway. This is perhaps one of the most enduring signs of the Anglo-Saxon role in the Christian conversion in Viking Scandinavia.[20]

Despite this, very few specific English churchmen can be connected to this conversion effort, but one Englishman can be discerned from the written records. A list found in William of Malmesbury's twelfth-century *Antiquitate Glastoniensis Ecclesiae* (*History of the Church of Glastonbury*), commemorating monks of Glastonbury who were bishops, contains a reference to a *Sigefrifus norwegensis episcopus* ("Sigfridus Norwegian bishop"), probably a missionary in Norway.[21] Careful analysis of this work suggests that the list originally dated to the beginning of the 1030s, so Bishop Sigfridus/Sigfrid must be earlier than Olaf Haraldson, and probably a separate person to Bishop Sigfrid of Sweden, who converted King Olof *Skötkonung* of Sweden.[22]

There is also a passage from the late-twelfth-century *Chronicon Abbatiae Rameseiensis* (*Ramsey Abbey Chronicle*) which contains a reference to a Bishop Siward who seems to have been involved in Olaf Tryggvason's conversion attempts in Norway. Traditionally it has been assumed that Olaf Tryggvason recruited missionaries in England in roughly 995, led by Siward (or Sigfrid). However, there are no contemporary sources to bear this out and the earliest evidence is from Adam of Bremen, who refers to Olaf's bishop in the words: "The first bishop, a certain John, came from England to Norway, and he converted and baptized the king with his people."[23]

The next reference to Olaf Tryggvason's bishop comes from the thirteenth-century Icelander Snorri Sturluson, who refers to a Bishop Sigurth (or Sigurd) but does not mention a nationality. It is not until c. 1300, when *Óláfs saga Tryggvasonar en mesta* (*Great Saga of Olaf Tryggvason*) is thought to have been compiled, that the record becomes explicit, with a claim that a man named Sigurd was the king's bishop, and was also known as Sigurd the Great. The writer stated that the king brought Sigurd with him from England. It seems reasonable to equate the "Sigurd" of the sagas and "Sigfrid" of William of Malmesbury with Adam of Bremen's "John"; and it may have been that John was his baptismal name or perhaps that John was his real name and he acquired the name Sigurd/Sigfrid in Scandinavia.[24] Whatever the detail of this, it shows clear evidence of an English missionary working alongside Olaf Tryggvason to convert the Norwegian people.

The main reason for this English influence appears to have been Norway's historic links with England and, in particular, those of its missionary kings. The settlement of many western Norwegians in the British Isles must have had some impact upon the more rapid conversion of that area of Norway, compared with other regions, as they could have transmitted their new faith back to their home area.[25] Given the direct sea routes and trading connections between Norway and England across the North Sea, this would have provided a perfect vehicle to spread English Christian influence.

However, perhaps the most important link to England was through a succession of Norwegian kings baptized in the British Isles. The first of these, as we have seen, was Hakon the Good who, according to the sagas, was brought up in the court of Athelstan of England and who took missionaries with him when he went back to Norway. The two main missionary kings, Olaf Tryggvason and Olaf Haraldson (St Olaf), were both converted abroad. Olaf Tryggvason was baptized in England in connection with a peace agreement and Olaf Haraldson was baptized in Normandy, possibly in connection with the exiled English king Æthelred II (the Unready). Adam of Bremen gives two different accounts of the baptism of Olaf Tryggvason and has him baptized in both England and by Danish missionaries, probably in Norway. The Norwegian-Icelandic sources all agree that he was baptized in England but give different accounts of the circumstances. Olaf Tryggvason's baptism in England is confirmed by the *Anglo-Saxon Chronicle*. The Norman historian William of Jumièges tells us that Olaf Haraldson was baptized in Rouen in 1013 or 1014, and this is likely to be correct. This is also referred to by the twelfth-century Norwegian monk-chronicler Theodoricus Monachus, who also refers to an alternative Norwegian-Icelandic tradition whereby Olaf Haraldson was baptized as a child by Olaf Tryggvason. This, though, is almost certainly fictitious.[26] The preponderance of sagas and histories focused on the deeds of Norwegian kings inevitably places these missionary kings at centre-stage. This makes it difficult to discern the missionaries who were working for them, although their English nationality does not seem to be in doubt.

OTHER MISSIONARY INFLUENCES

Despite the apparent English dominance over the mission to Norway, the English were not the only missionaries. In the early-twelfth-century Icelandic *Íslendingabók* (*Book of Icelanders*) the writer, Ari Thorgilson, refers to three Armenian bishops: Petrus, Abraham and Stephanus. These three apparently came to Scandinavia with Harald Hardrada in about 1045, as a result of his Russian or Byzantine connections. If true, this suggests an eastern influx and influence on Norway during the reign of Harald.[27] This may have extended to missionary activity in Iceland too.

More in line with the rest of Scandinavia, there does also seem to have been some activity from Hamburg-Bremen and Denmark. When Olaf Haraldson became king he brought with him many priests and bishops from England but, according to Adam of Bremen, also established contact with Hamburg-Bremen and asked for missionaries to be sent from there. Adam tells us that these missionaries were named Grimkjell, Siegfried, Rudolf and Bernhard, and these names suggest a German origin.[28] The Norwegian region of Østfold may well have been subject to influences from Sweden and Christian Danes. This latter contact may have brought some German involvement via Harald Bluetooth and strengthened Danish influence in Norway. Sixty-two Christian graves have been found in St Clement's Church in Oslo and, according to the sagas, King Harald Bluetooth sent two jarls to this area to convert the people living there.

This may also be the mission referred to by Adam of Bremen, who writes that many were converted when German missionaries came to Norway in the time of Archbishop Adaldag (died c. 988). There is, though, nothing to suggest that political pressure from their German neighbours played any role in the Christianization of Norway.[29] However, despite these snippets of evidence and the important work that these missionaries no doubt undertook, Hamburg-Bremen was not to dominate this conversion, as it did in Sweden and Denmark. The Norwegian connections to the British Isles and the flow of missionaries from England that resulted meant Hamburg-Bremen was left out of the picture.

As with much of the history of Scandinavia, the actual details of the conversion, particularly the missionaries involved, are difficult to discern. However, the majority of the missionary work appears to have been carried out by the English, starting in the mid-tenth century, before the reign of Olaf Tryggvason. The English bishop Sigfrid or Sigurd is the only confirmed missionary, and even he is fairly elusive in the records compared to the king he followed to Norway. The nature of the evidence, therefore, makes it difficult to know whether missionaries did cross the sea independently of the Norwegian kings. However, we know they did cross the sea, even if we don't know why, and they, with their English-baptized kings, must have been responsible for the English flavour of Norwegian Christianity.

THE BENEFITS OF CHRISTIANITY TO THE RULERS OF NORWAY

Christianity eventually spread throughout Norway because of the benefit it brought to the kings of Norway. After the breaking of the major European powers by the Viking raids and the disintegration of the Frankish Empire, conversion was no longer seen as subordination to the West but, rather, a better way of integrating and strengthening the power of kings over their people. The connection between Christianization and royal power is clear in the Scandinavian traditions. They are explicitly connected on the Jelling stone (Denmark) and both the Olafs in Norway linked their attempts to gain kingship with the introduction of missionary bishops. This was reinforced by the literacy of the Christians, meaning that Christianity contributed to the development of a literary national consciousness and royal administration.

Missionary activity was initially directed towards the leaders of society and carried out by preaching and royal sanctions against those who opposed it. Given the way in which some pagan elites had contrived to thwart and then kill some early Christian kings in Norway, the latter method was predictable. There was, therefore, a close connection between conversion and the expansion of royal power, due to the legitimacy conferred by Christian kingship, and

Christianity was preached as a religion of success and power. For Norwegian kings, Christianity offered an effective ideological alternative to paganism. Hierarchical church organization also defined social hierarchy and introduced divine legitimacy for kings and elites. The Old Testament tradition of sacred kingship, in particular, established a sacred immunity of authority for Scandinavian kings, and provided the ideological platform for the shift from family-centred societies to a state society.

Harald Finehair sent his son Hakon to be fostered in England because he realized that Christian ideology would provide support for his new kingship. The conversion of both Olaf Tryggvason and Olaf Haraldson at the hands of the English king Æthelred II (the Unready), and his funding of their campaigns for kingship, shows being allied to a Christian ruler was very beneficial for Norwegian claimants to the throne back home. In Norway, Olaf Tryggvason then converted the kingdom with the sword and used Christianity to control the kingdom. Olaf Haraldson carried out his campaign of conversion through evangelization, force and legislation. Although Christianity must have spread due to the initiative of many men and women – and not just due to the conversion of kings – Norwegian kings had much to gain from the conversion and played a significant role in pushing it forward.

High status women benefited too. In Norway, many more women became nuns than in the other Scandinavian kingdoms. This can be seen as an empowerment of these Norwegian women as although the step from pagan shield maidens to holy virgins may seem a leap, both groups were able to abandon their traditional roles and assert their independence, using chastity as their weapon. Clearly, it was not just claimants to the Norwegian throne who found their role enhanced by the new faith.

CHAPTER 9

The Christian Vikings
of Sweden

Scandinavia finally moved from a period of pre-history to history during the Scandinavian conversion. The Christian church brought literacy and record-keeping to areas that were either pre-literate or only employed writing to a very limited degree. So for Sweden, the last kingdom to be converted, history arrives very late indeed. All that we know about Sweden before it became Christian is limited, very sketchy and incomplete.

THE PEOPLES OF SWEDEN

In the twenty-first century we are so familiar with the idea of nation-states and their borders that it is easy to forget how recent a historical phenomenon nation-states are for many Europeans. It is particularly easy to forget this in England, where a unified English state has existed since the late tenth century. In Scandinavia, nation-state formation came later than in England, but earlier than in some other parts of Europe, where nation-states did not develop until after the Middle Ages. While Denmark led the way in this development among the Scandinavians, for Norway and Sweden the situation remained fluid longer. And the situation in Sweden was particularly complex, since Denmark ruled much of the south of what we now call Sweden (as part of Greater Denmark) and the rest of the country lacked political unity. Even Norwegian kings (who were themselves used to Danish interference) intervened at times in Sweden. Here, from the ninth century, we read of petty kings who are mentioned in the written sources, although all of these sources were compiled outside of Sweden. From the fairly fragmentary evidence it appears that there were two main political units in what we would now call Sweden until as late as 1172.

Those known as the *Svear* had a royal and religious centre at Uppsala. They are first mentioned in the first century AD by the Roman writer Tacitus, who knew them as the *Suiones*. It is from *Svear* that the national name Sweden is derived. Today the early centre at Uppsala is known as Gamla (old) Uppsala in order to differentiate it from the modern-day town of Uppsala. The former site was a hugely important political, religious and trading centre. Here the kings of Svealand – the legendary Yngling dynasty – held power. The earliest surviving Scandinavian written sources[1] refer to the kings of Sweden as "kings at Uppsala". The "*Thing* (assembly) of all Swedes" was held there into the medieval period, along with a huge fair and religious sacrifices. It became the seat of the archbishop of Sweden in 1164. By this point the pagan religious sacrifices had ceased and the market had been moved from late winter to the Christian feast day of Candlemas (2 February). The three large "Royal mounds" are still a distinctive feature, and Viking mythology claimed that the Norse gods Thor, Odin and Freyr were buried there. In reality, they are probably the burial mounds of earlier rulers from the Yngling dynasty.

The other main political focus was that of the *Götar*. Their settlements were centred on the plains of Östergötland and Västergötland, near Lake Vättern.[2] They dominated a large area of what is now southern Sweden and are referred to by the Roman geographer Ptolemy in the second century AD. The rulers of the *Götar* were independent of the Swedes or *Svear*. While the matter is obscure and complex, it is possible the later Goths who troubled the Roman Empire may have roots that (in part at least) extended back to this area of what is now Sweden. But that is another story.

The *Svear* and the *Götar* were closely related and there is some evidence that some kings of the *Svear* were from the royal family of the *Götar*. Certainly the first king who ruled both peoples was Olof *Skötkonung* (c. 995–1022). However, it was not until the twelfth century that a single Swedish kingdom emerged.[3] Nor did increasing Swedish unity prevent kings of Denmark from overshadowing the emerging kingdom. Cnut the Great (ruled Denmark 1018–1035) succeeded in being recognized as overlord of the Swedes.

He was also nominally king of Norway from 1028 to 1035 but faced a lot of resistance from that quarter. At the Battle of Holy River, in 1026, Cnut attempted to subdue the kings of Norway and Sweden who were attempting to challenge his authority. In a letter written by Cnut to his English subjects after the battle, he claimed victory and asserted that he was king of all England, Denmark, and of the Norwegians and some of the Swedes too. In reality, the king of Norway hung on to power until 1028 and Cnut never imposed himself on the Swedes as king. Even in Norway, Cnut's control was overthrown by 1034. From this time onwards three distinct Scandinavian kingdoms were emerging. There was even a brief time (which ended in 1046) when the ruler of Norway ruled in Denmark. This certainly indicates how rapidly Cnut's empire fell apart following his death in 1035. Sweden then became independent of Danish control. A fully united kingdom took time to emerge and the *Svear* and the *Götar* were not permanently united until the reign of Knut Erikson (in 1172), when a united Sweden emerged, over 200 years after the forging of a united English kingdom.

THE ARRIVAL OF CHRISTIANITY IN SWEDEN

The first recorded Christian missionary activity in Sweden occurred in about 829 when a German monk, Anskar, preached and converted a number of Swedes in Birka, on Lake Mälaren. In the face of political unrest he returned to northern Germany and became the first archbishop of Hamburg (Hamburg-Bremen from

864). Pagan resistance resulted in the bishop assigned to Sweden (Gautbert) being expelled in 845. Anskar returned to Sweden in 853–854, where he enjoyed royal support. Today the church in Sweden remembers him as its apostle. However, his impact was limited and Christianity did not flourish.

During the tenth century, missionaries from Hamburg-Bremen unsuccessfully tried once more to evangelize in Sweden, and Anglo-Saxon missionaries were active in Västergötland. By the year 1000, the new faith was established in a number of communities and, over the next century, an increasing number of influential landholders converted. This was encouraged by the official conversion of King Olof *Skötkonung*, who was issuing coins carrying Christian motifs by 995. These were produced by Anglo-Saxon moneyers and the thirteenth-century *Life of St Sigfrid* claims that Olof was baptized by an Anglo-Saxon missionary bishop. Adam of Bremen recorded a tradition that Olof's father had been baptized in Denmark but reverted to paganism when he returned to Uppsala. Adam goes on to say that Olof wished to tear down the pagan temple at Uppsala but faced too much opposition. Nevertheless, by about 1050, a bishop had been established at Skara and by 1100 there were probably two other bishops, based at Linköping and Sigtuna. The Christian influences leading to this were mixed. We have seen the possible English connection and there may even have been some Eastern Orthodox input via returning Viking mercenaries. German missionaries from Hamburg-Bremen were also very influential, although occasionally they faced resistance from Swedish rulers suspicious of German influence.

Sweden was less politically united than Denmark and Norway, so it took some time for Christianity to dominate. There are later traditions of Swedish Christian kings facing opposition for refusing to carry out pagan sacrifices and, as late as 1110, it seems that both the old pagan centre at Uppsala and the new royal Christian centre at Sigtuna were in contemporary operation, despite being only eighteen miles apart[4] and despite the fact the official cults at Uppsala ceased in about 1080.[5] But the days of Uppsala as a pagan centre were numbered. An increasingly confident Swedish royal authority had thrown its weight behind Christianity. Nevertheless, paganism lingered for longer in Sweden than in other areas of the Viking diaspora. As late as 1130, the monk Ailnoth complained: "The Svear and Götar, however, seem to honour the Christian faith only when things go according to their wishes and luck is on their side."[6] He noted that any bad weather, droughts and floods, or threat of enemy attacks, caused them to abandon the new faith. Other evidence corroborates this slow progress of Christianity. On the island of Öland the inhabitants cremated some of their dead into the second half of the twelfth century, despite having had a stone church for a generation. In northern Sweden, paganism was practised until the early thirteenth century. Further north still, most of the Swedish Sami remained pagan, despite attempts to evangelize them from the fourteenth to the seventeenth century[7]

The paths of Swedish unity and Christianization were closely related. Olof *Skötkonung* – like Harald Bluetooth in Denmark and Olaf Tryggvason in Norway – was remembered as a supporter of Christianity as well as a political unifier. This was no coincidence because, as we have seen, Christianity brought a lot of advantages to a ruler intent on unifying his kingdom. First, the new faith had a high regard for divinely sanctioned kingship, and enhanced the position of the ruler as the "Lord's anointed". Kings had been seen as holding sacred authority under the pagan belief system at Uppsala for centuries (associated with religious activities there) but the new approach underlined this holiness and made it even more explicit. This was true for the Swedish rulers as for kings in other contexts.

Secondly, the church brought literacy, which assisted in nation building, taxation and law making and also the creation of "history" (which cannot exist without written records) by which existing rulers could enhance their legitimacy and origins. Churchmen made effective administrators who assisted in the development of royal government, which is why the first bishopric in Sweden was founded at Uppsala. Ecclesiastical power and royal power were closely related, to mutual advantage, seen in the fact that the new archbishop united the bishoprics of Svealand and Götarland and Åbo in Finland. These church arrangements would lead, eventually, to these representing the territorial extent of the kingdom of Sweden.

Thirdly, through conversion a ruler joined the ranks of the Christian monarchs of Christendom, so local power and authority became part of a Europe-wide enterprise uniting communities from the North Atlantic to the Mediterranean. This made relationships with other states easier, and created a sense of common identity and purpose to some extent. Sweden thus became a recognized Christian state, and soon Swedish Christian warriors (with those of Denmark) would be involved in crusades designed to conquer and convert some of the last European pagans. It was not until Finland was finally incorporated into the Swedish kingdom that its Christianization was secure. Later traditions claimed this dated from a mid-twelfth-century crusade under King (St) Erik of Sweden; what is clear is that by 1300, both the authority of the church and the Swedish crown were well established in Finland. This followed two Swedish crusades there during the thirteenth century (the final one being in 1293).[8]

Fourthly, the increased stability (allied with more effective administration and tax-raising capabilities) detached rulers from the destabilizing wealth-creating strategies of raiding and plundering. It would be naïve to assume that this stopped all such destructive warfare but it certainly reduced it and it is no surprise that the end of Viking raiding followed on from conversion to Christianity. In the case of Sweden, a better tax base made Swedish kingship viable, without the need for raiding. This was fortuitous, as the flow of silver from Kiev Rus had gone, as we shall see, and England was no longer a good substitute source of income, following first Cnut's invasion and then that of the Normans.

THE CHRISTIAN CONVERSION AS REVEALED
IN RUNESTONES

Our best source of evidence for the conversion of Sweden – as with much of northern Scandinavia – comes not from written documentary sources but from the inscriptions which can be found on runestones. This will come as a surprise to many, who probably associate runes with paganism, since many modern pagans use them. This form of writing – employing letters formed from straight lines that were particularly well suited to carving or inscribing on stone, bone or metal – was almost certainly a Scandinavian response to the Latin letter forms used further south in Europe but adapted to Scandinavian use. The Scandinavian version of these runes is today often known as the *futhark* or *fuþark* (a name derived from the first six letters of the runic alphabet: F, U, Þ, A, R, K). The Anglo-Saxon variant of the runic alphabet is described as the *futhorc* or *fuþorc* because the letter sounds were a little different in Old English compared with Old Norse. As such, their roots can be traced back into the pre-Christian past of Scandinavia. But then, of course, the same can be said of the Latin alphabet which eventually became widely used across Christian Europe, from the late Roman Empire onwards. It too was originally used in pagan inscriptions before it was adopted in Western Europe by the (originally Greek-speaking) Christian church. Consequently, there was nothing intrinsically pagan about either letter-system; it was the use to which it was put that might make it so.

This is not to deny that ideas developed in pagan Scandinavia about rune-magic, religious characteristics of particular runes and the association of certain runes with particular gods and goddesses. Norse mythology recounted how the god Rig (later assumed to be an alias for the god Heimdall) taught the use of runes to mythical people named "Lord" and "King", the ancestors of later Scandinavian royalty. This tradition is found in an Icelandic compilation known as the *Poetic Edda*, in a poem called *The List of Rig*, which gave a supernatural explanation for the origins of the human social order. Another tradition (known as *The Sayings of the High One*) explained that Odin had hung on a tree for nine nights – sacrificed to himself – before he gained mastery of the magic-making runes. So runes were associated with pagan mythology but they were also letters used for things as mundane as recording who made a comb or owned a brooch. As Christianity replaced paganism, they continued to be used as a way of communicating the new faith.

Runestones appear in Viking Age Scandinavia before the period of conversion but it seems to be the eleventh-century conversion to Christianity which facilitated the massive increase in the number of runestones found there. The runestone became a particularly Viking way of displaying Christian faith and, even though this borrowed ideas from Western Christian artwork traditions, it was done in a particularly Scandinavian way. This suggests that in the areas of Scandinavia where runestones were particularly prominent, the local people did not feel themselves to be subordinate in relation to more established Christian European culture. It is possible that the increased production of runestones, with their increasingly Christian ornamentation, was used actively by Swedish Christians to mark both their distinct Christian identity and their independence from the German church in particular.

Runestone ornamentation seems to have become more Scandinavian over time as the new Viking Christians focused less on displaying their Christian identity (now established) and more on distinguishing themselves culturally from the rest of Europe. The voluntary nature of the Scandinavian conversion – in Denmark and Sweden at least – seems to have led to communities feeling that they did not need to significantly alter their artistic communication or abandon their traditional culture in order to be good Christians.[9]

At the beginning of the Viking period the carving of stone monuments was mainly confined to the island of Gotland, rarely practised in Sweden and unknown in Denmark and Norway. Examples include the picture-stones found on Gotland such as the Stora Hammars picture-stones (from Lärbro parish, Gotland) and the Alskog or Tjängvide picture-stone (Ljugarn, Gotland). Indeed, over 400 such picture-stones have been discovered to date. The earliest were erected during the fifth century and the latest during the twelfth century.

The spread of Christianity, however, changed this limited distribution and, by the eleventh century, stone monuments were common throughout Scandinavia. In many ways, though, the images which were used on these new and more numerous Christian runestones were not all that different from their pagan counterparts. For example, the carved rock at Ramsund (Norway) tells the story of the mythical hero Sigurd, while stating that a person named Sigrid had the bridge built at this spot for the salvation of her father-in-law Holmger's soul. The scroll bearing the inscription also doubles as the ribbon-like body of the mythical dragon Fafnir, who was slain by Sigurd. This applied Mediterranean ideas regarding commemoration to the telling of a northern pagan story, illustrating how pagan and Christian cultures interacted during the conversion.[10] Similar things occurred further east in Sweden, where carving runestones after the conversion became common.

Yet while there is a degree of continuity from pagan to Christian runestones, these old images were used by Christian Vikings, in Sweden in particular, to express very different beliefs. The cross, not surprisingly, played an important role in the conversion and replaced the hammer of Thor on such carvings. This new symbol could be made into intricate and beautiful patterns, but was still associated with the dragons and animals of pagan times, as evidenced by the Hogrän churchyard stone (on the Swedish island of Gotland) and the columns in Uppsala Cathedral. However, these interlaced dragons acquired a new meaning and, so adapted, stubbornly held their own for several centuries.[11] This use of dragon and serpent images was particularly adaptable due to the common portrayal of the devil in these forms. This can be seen in many images of St Michael which portray him as defeating the devil in the form of a snake. So snake-like animal ornamentation and the pagan mythology of Sigurd killing the serpent/dragon Fafnir lent themselves to adaptation for Christian purposes.

This adaption of pre-existing art forms occurred over a number of years, since the conversion of Sweden was a protracted process lasting well over a couple of centuries, as we saw earlier. (The same can be said of Norway and Denmark.) This process had three distinct phases. The first was one of infiltration from further south in Europe which lasted for hundreds of years; the second one of mission activity; the third one of ecclesiastical organization, as churches were built and bishops established. It seems likely that the erection of runestones in Sweden occurred during the second (mission) phase, since the building of churches seems to have mainly occurred after this. So although runestones cannot be seen as objectively Christian, they were generally connected with the spread of Christianity in Sweden. However, what they reveal about the conversion of Sweden and the mind-set of people during this period of religious upheaval is debatable. The runestones can be interpreted as burial markers in consecrated ground. The inscriptions on the Christian runestones directly correspond to the Latin formula *Hic iacet* (here is buried) found on medieval tombstones across Europe. That these occur in consecrated burial grounds suggests they preceded the (later) church building on the site,[12] so were official markers of a place chosen for the burial of the Christian dead, before a church was built. Other experts have suggested these monuments meant that the newly converted could bury their dead in churchyards, while also honouring them in traditional places, such as roadsides or assembly places,[13] explaining why many are found in the countryside and away from churches.

Whatever the motivation – whether to connect to the new religious practice or to reach back to the familiarity of the past – the erection of runestones appears to have answered the religious and social needs of a society during a period of transition. The rituals associated with burial were not only for the commemoration of the dead: they were also a way of demonstrating the status of the living.[14] Since missionaries objected to pagan burial with grave goods, the alternative public erection of runestones, with their Christian inscriptions, was a way of displaying status without attracting criticism for continuing pagan practices.[15] The original tradition may have started as one where both the living and the dead benefited equally[16] but, over time, more emphasis was placed on the role of the relatives responsible for erecting the runestones: "the dead do not need the runestones but the relatives need them to show they have done their duty, not least in the eyes of God".[17]

This action may have served a number of purposes in the newly Christianized areas of Sweden. The change of faith and burial custom cannot alone explain the origin, distribution and uniformity of the fashion.[18] The distribution also suggests that runestones served other functions and were memorials not only to the dead but also to those who raised them. Often the sponsor's name appears first on a runestone, not that of the person it is commemorating.[19]

The Viking Age runestones also seem to have been erected mainly for men, with only about seven per cent honouring women, suggesting only certain individuals (mainly men) were suitable for this honour. This probably signals a newly Christian (male) elite.[20] All of this suggests that the process of erecting runestones was governed by well-understood rules determining who should be so commemorated. It also suggests that the purpose of erecting runestones, while strongly linked to the arrival of a new faith in Scandinavia, had as much to do with perpetuating existing status. These runestones were not simply showing the Christianity of the individual being buried, but also the wealth and power of those who erected the stones; not only indicators of faith but also status symbols, saying as much about secular society as religious belief. They are as revealing of an increasingly hierarchical society as they are of a society undergoing Christian conversion. So we can reasonably assume that there were more Christian converts than the number of runestones implies.[21] The presence of runestones indicates the presence of individuals who were able to express their faith in a monumental way during the conversion but the absence of runestones does not necessarily imply that there was an absence of people who considered themselves Christian.[22]

The relatively few Danish runestones that survive were erected around the year 1000 and, since there are roughly equal numbers of pagan and Christian ones, this suggests a short period of transition[23] and cultural conflict as new converts and recusants alike both used the same medium to express ideological differences. By way of contrast, in the Uppland area on the eastern coast of Sweden, the large number of Christian runestones in a distinct geographical area suggests that the conversion to Christianity was the decision of the local communities, since we know of no central power behind the process.[24] So, in Uppland, people were more likely to display their new faith as a personal choice rather than the official religion. The variation in the numbers of runestones around Scandinavia may, therefore, give us an insight into the different processes of conversion which occurred in the different regions.

Wherever they occur, they show a distinctly Scandinavian form of Christianity. For while the erection of runestones can be seen as a Christian phenomenon in a Scandinavian context, the erection of this sort of monument was very different to practices further south in the Frankish Empire, where religious attention was focused more on the church building itself and the attendant graveyard, rather than on monuments scattered across the landscape.[25] So, while a number of Swedish runestones may reveal the location of new Christian cemeteries, many are (as we saw earlier) scattered across the countryside.

It is also interesting that the style of the runestones (where they are decorated with crosses) and the carvings on them generally do not fit within the Frankish-Christian branch of the Christian church. Instead, the runestones appear to show a British influence, in both the shapes of runestone crosses and the linguistic evidence for the inscriptions. This suggests that there was considerable Anglo-Saxon influence in Svealand (south-central Sweden) during the conversion, in the form of missionaries from England, and that these missionaries influenced the style of the runestones there.[26] The teachings of the missionaries also affected the way God was presented on the Swedish runestones. None contain any references to the Trinity, perhaps emphasizing the unity of God in contrast to pagan polytheism.[27] In order to avoid the misunderstanding that the Christians had three gods, the missionaries may have simplified their teaching by identifying God totally with Christ.[28] Initially at least, this involved less emphasis on the belief in the Trinity, once again demonstrating the specifically Viking style of Christianity reflected on these stones. This was a conversion where some of the old elements of paganism were adapted to fit a Christian context while, at the same time, the Christian message was carefully delivered in a tailored way, designed to avoid confusion with the pagan past. This was a people whose practice of paganism was deeply imbedded in their culture and, consequently, all aspects of it could not simply be swiftly cast aside.

These links with the pagan past can also be seen in the references to the Virgin Mary on a number of the runestones. Among the 1,597 runic texts that survive, there are 248 with a prayer inscribed on them, and 213 of these contain the prayer "May God help his/her soul", while Mary is invoked in thirty-four of these prayers as

God's mother and in combination with God.[29] Almost half of these Mary inscriptions contain a woman's name, either as the subject or involved in the erection of the stone.[30] This female veneration of Mary may have replaced previous emphasis on pre-Christian goddesses, such as Freya, abandoned during Christianization, and Mary's importance can be seen as early as the eleventh century. Women were clearly actively involved in this process, especially in Sweden.[31] The fact that Mary was always invoked as a mother, not a virgin, supports the idea that Mary may have taken over from the abandoned fertility goddesses.[32] It may also have been thought that a female spiritual helper was particularly empathetic to women and their concerns.[33]

While it can be argued that women played a less prominent role within Christianity than they had within the old pagan religion, the strong emphasis on the importance of the individual within Christianity allowed women the opportunity to be seen in their own right rather than simply as part of the wider unit of the kin,[34] suggesting the importance of females as goddesses in the pagan polytheistic faith continued into Christianity through the devotion to Mary, and Christianity gave women the opportunity to be important in their own right as individuals. So, although some aspects of the pagan past found their way into the new faith, these aspects were not carried across without serious adaption, to fit within the new framework of belief. Instead, they were sanitized.

Although the Christian runestones are important to understanding the conversion to Christianity, the story they tell is not simple. The surviving pagan runestones from the same period also give a fascinating insight into the complexities of the situation. These suggest that it was not simply a straightforward transition, and the finding of magic spells and curses on runestones must be seen as explicitly pagan survivals which lasted some time.[35] So while large numbers of the population had embraced Christianity in Sweden by the late eleventh century, others clung on to the old practices and gods. However, some historians argue that the invocations to Thor on runestones do not express pagan beliefs but are an adaptation of the Christian custom of a blessing. It has been suggested that Thor, a sky god who fought against giants and monsters (regarded as the forces of chaos), was more acceptable to Christians than other pagan deities and, as such, his presence on runestones was not an explicitly pagan act.[36] It has also been suggested that the motif of Thor's hammer can be interpreted as a Christian cross but represented via a familiar shape. If so, then the question is whether this ambiguity was intentional and expressed syncretism, or whether it was thought of as a symbol prefiguring the Christian cross.[37]

In conclusion, runestones are important for our understanding of the conversion of Sweden (as elsewhere in Scandinavia). They give us an insight into the reasons for their erection, the process of conversion, the influence of paganism on the newly emerging religion and the peculiarly Viking nature of the conversion. However, while runestones are found across large areas of Scandinavia, the vast majority are located in the south-east of Sweden. This concentration suggests the process of conversion in south-eastern Sweden differed from the other areas of Scandinavia. While in other areas Christianity was imposed from the top down by elites, in south-eastern Sweden Christianization was probably a more gradual process, due to the conversion of individuals and families.

The runestones also show us that some aspects of the pagan past, such as the worship of goddesses, probably found their way into the new religion, albeit in a sanitized form. The very presence of these runestones in south-eastern Sweden suggests that the form of Christianity found there was very different from that of the Frankish missionaries who sought to influence the conversion. These runestones give us an insight into the mind-set of a people who otherwise would not have a voice. But it is an insight that cannot be used to speak for the whole conversion process across the whole of Sweden and, at times, the "voice" is rather more complex, compromised and discordant than it might at first appear.

CHAPTER 10

Vikings in the East

CHRISTIAN VIKINGS IN RUSSIA AND THE BYZANTINE EMPIRE

Beside the driveway of Gripsholm Castle, in Sweden, stands an eleventh-century runestone. Discovered in the early 1820s, built into the floor of a cellar and covered in tar, it had clearly once been used as part of the fabric in an earlier building, before being re-used to make a threshold in that cellar. But its fame lies not in its chequered history but in the inscription discovered on it, when it was finally removed from the cellar and cleaned about a century after it was first discovered. It bears witness to an adventure that went terribly wrong, far from home. Contained within the body of a snake that follows the edge of the stone and then curls into the centre is a runic inscription, which reads: "Tóla had this stone raised in memory of her son Haraldr, Ingvarr's brother. They travelled valiantly far for gold, and in the east gave (food) to the eagle. (They) died in the south in Serkland."[1]

Known today as *Sö 179*, the stone is one of about twenty-six Ingvar runestones, mostly found in the Lake Mälaren region of southern Sweden. They can specifically be located in the provinces of Södermanland, Uppland and Östergötland. They are named from Ingvar the Far-Travelled, who led an expedition to the

Caspian Sea. This single event is mentioned on runestones more than any other in Swedish Viking history. Other evidence suggests that he and most of his companions died in 1041, some in a fierce battle fought at Sasireti in Georgia – to the west of the Caspian Sea – that involved Byzantines, Georgians and also Scandinavian mercenaries. It was a battle fought in a Georgian civil war. Those that did not die in the battle succumbed to disease far from home, including Ingvar himself. The Georgian chronicler who compiled an account of the expedition, in a fourteenth-century addition to the chronicle known as the *Kartlis Tskhovreba* (*Life of Kartli* – a core area of Georgia), added that Ingvar and his men were given slave-women in Georgia: and a twelfth-century Icelandic saga called *Yngvars saga víðförla* (*Saga of Ingvar the Far-Travelled*) claims they died from disease contracted through sex with these slaves.

It was a disaster for most of those who embarked on this expedition to the distant east. According to that later Icelandic saga (which claimed to tell the story of the expedition in detail), some survivors made it back to Russia. Others travelled on to *Miklagarðr* (or *Miklagard*), the Scandinavian name for Constantinople. This was the capital of the Eastern Roman – or Byzantine – Empire. Of the survivors, some it seems eventually got back to Sweden and, as news spread of what had occurred, the runestones were carved by remaining family members to commemorate the dead.

The Serkland referred to on this and four other runestones was the name used by Scandinavians for the Islamic Abbasid Caliphate and other Muslim areas of the east. It was either derived from the word *Saracen* (so Saracen-land) or from *serkr* (gown), referring to the distinctive robes worn by the Muslims living in the east. Either way, it was a long way from home.

The expedition led by Ingvar the Far-Travelled was as much about trade and diplomacy as it was about courage and battle. Regarding one of those who died in far-off Serkland, and commemorated back in Sweden on a runestone, his sons wrote of him: *knari stur* ("He could steer a cargo-ship well").[2] The reference is to a *knarr*, a spacious sea-going cargo ship, not the dragon-prowed longships of Hollywood films, TV series and popular expectations. And the blessing on the dead found on this runestone – "May God help their spirits"[3] – is a formula associated with Christians. Indeed, another of the Ingvar Runestones (*U1143*, from Tierp, in Uppsala County) specifically prays that *Guð drottinn hialpi and [ald]ra kristinna* ("May Lord God help the spirits of all Christians").[4]

The Icelandic saga version of the Ingvar expedition talks of the Viking fleet being attacked by enemy ships armed with flamethrowers. These were probably Muslim vessels equipped with a version of the flammable "Greek-Fire" (a form of flame-thrower) employed by the navy of the Byzantine Empire and clearly now copied by its enemies.[5]

We associate Vikings with the stormy seas of the northern world, Scandinavian fjords, the cold of Iceland, and attacks on the monasteries of north-western Europe. It is less in the popular image to include the rivers of Russia and Ukraine, the Eurasian steppe, the shores of the Caspian Sea, slave markets and Arab traders, flame-throwing ships, the ritual and drama of the Eastern Orthodox Church, and the walls and towers of Constantinople. Yet many Swedish Viking raiders, traders and settlers were beckoned by the road to the east.

GO EAST, YOUNG MAN

Swedish Viking raiders and explorers have hardly featured so far in our exploration of the impact of the Vikings, because we have focused on north-western Europe. Vikings from Sweden played no significant part there, until some sailed with Cnut to England in the early eleventh century. But long before that occurred, adventurers from Sweden had sailed to the east. These eastern Vikings are variously described in ancient sources as *Rus* and *Varangians*. We have come across *Rus* in Chapter 1 as a physical description of the men who travelled among the Slavic communities of the east. The name may, alternatively, have been derived from the Finnish word *Ruotsi*, used to describe Swedes, which itself may have been from an Old Norse term meaning a "crew of oarsmen". The other name was derived from the Old Norse word *várar*, meaning "men who have pledged allegiance".[6] This name first appears in the mid-tenth century. *Rus* was only ever used of Scandinavians living in what we now call Russia, from which the national name derives. The word "Varangian", on the other hand, was generally used to describe Scandinavian mercenaries who travelled as far as Constantinople to be employed as soldiers (the Varangian Guard) of the Byzantine emperor, or who arrived there as traders. Either way, these newcomers got there via communities in Russia which were increasingly assimilating to Slavic culture.

The movement of Swedish Vikings to the east had begun about a century before the first Viking raiding started in north-western Europe, as early as 650. Archaeology reveals the graves of Scandinavians (almost certainly merchants) in eastern Baltic settlements of the Slavs and Balts, such as that at Elbing (now Elbląg in northern Poland). By 750, other Scandinavians were settled in the Finnish trading settlement of Staraja Ladoga (on the River Volkhov, near Lake Ladoga, near the modern-day town of Volkhov in the Leningrad region of modern-day Russia).[7] This was a centre of the fur trade and the Swedes living there would have been involved in the purchasing and westward transportation of this luxury commodity. Some of this was done, no doubt, by peaceful trade; some may have involved tribute-taking (payments demanded from subjugated communities) from groups who had been brought under a loose Viking overlordship. It is now difficult to differentiate between the two, as we cannot always disentangle the power relationships at work. However, we may assume that a fair bit was mutually advantageous trade, with the application of Viking muscle when the occasion demanded it (to ensure a good deal from a Swedish perspective).

This situation developed as a result of Arab trading movements from the south-east. By the 790s, merchants from the Islamic Abbasid Caliphate (centred on Baghdad in modern-day Iraq) were expanding their trading journeys up the River Volga and bringing with them good quality silver with which to purchase the furs, amber and slaves of the northern world. The Abbasids had replaced the previous ruling dynasty in the Muslim empire, the Umayyads, in 750. Initially this political change disrupted the northward flow of silver and would do so again in the next century. However, the period 775–861 brought more relative stability under the new caliphs (though not one of unbroken success for them), sufficient to act as a platform for expanding trading ventures.

These events in the Middle East were to impact on the Swedish Vikings of the south-eastern Baltic. The reappearance of this coveted silver encouraged Swedish adventurers to expand their areas of operation in order to exploit this source of wealth and dominate the trade at its northern end. In this they were assisted by the network of rivers which gave access to the hinterland of Staraja Ladoga and beyond that into the heart of what is now Russia. Their clear aim was to establish direct contact with the silver-rich world to the south and to eliminate trading middle-men so that the Swedish Vikings benefited from direct access to the Muslim traders. As early as 830 (just as the western raids of Danish Vikings were ramping up in Western Europe) the Viking explorers from Sweden established direct contact with Arab traders on the Volga and with the Byzantine Empire at Constantinople.

Writing probably in the late 840s, the Director of Posts and Intelligence in the Baghdad Caliphate, Ibn Khurdadhbih, stated that traders he called *ar-Rus*, who brought merchandise to Baghdad on camels, claimed to be Christians. However, this may have been because this reduced their tax burden rather than evidence for genuine early conversion, as he linked the lower taxes they paid to their apparent conversion. What is equally striking is that they had reached as far as Baghdad. They were Vikings with camels.

This remarkable achievement was assisted by the riverine geography of Russia. Just south of Novgorod (soon to loom large in this story) are the headwaters of rivers which, between them, flow to the Gulf of Finland, the Gulf of Riga (both giving access to the Baltic), the Black Sea and the Caspian. With their strong construction and shallow draughts, Viking vessels were ideally suited to exploit these river routes. Where waterfalls or rapids interrupted travel, these ships could be moved overland ("portaged") to avoid these. In the same way, they could be transported from one river system to another. As a result, the Swedes were soon able to dominate trade from the Baltic to the Caspian and the Black Sea (with the Mediterranean beyond). It was not just peaceful Scandinavian merchants who travelled these rivers, as Viking raiders and conquerors soon followed and attacked settlements on the Caspian Sea and even launched raids against Constantinople itself, although the latter achieved only very limited returns.

THE SWEDISH VIKINGS BECOME THE RUS

In the twelfth century a source of information, the *Pověstĭ Vremęnĭnyhŭ Lětŭ* (now generally known as the *Russian Primary Chronicle*), was compiled at Kiev, in what is now the Ukraine. The original compilation is sometimes referred to as *Nestor's Chronicle*, after the monk (died c. 1114) who, tradition claimed, had begun the work in about 1113. Drawing on lost Slavonic chronicles, legends, Byzantine annals, Slavic oral poetry, and some Norse sources, it purports to tell the story of how Viking adventurers became rulers of the first Russian state. While details may be open to question, the general outline represents the foundation story of the rulers of Kiev and, almost certainly, the gist of what occurred.

According to this account, Viking adventurers (the Varangian Rus) used force to subjugate the Slavic and Finnish tribes living south-east of the Baltic – but were then driven out. However, once free of the Rus, warfare broke out between these tribes and they decided the rule of the Rus was not so bad after all, and invited them back. Three Viking brothers came to rule: Rurik (or Riurik) in Novgorod, Sineus in Beloozero and Truvor in Izborsk. The last two may be Slavic versions of original Old Norse names, Signjotr and Thorvar. All of these settlements were in north-western Russia. A later source, known now as the *Hypatian Codex* (a fifteenth-century compendium of the *Primary Chronicle* and two other chronicles), claims that Rurik originally settled at Ladoga but later relocated to Novgorod. According to the *Russian Primary Chronicle* these brothers were of the Varangian tribe of the Rus. This return as rulers, the chronicle suggests, occurred sometime between 860 and 862. When the latter two brothers died, Rurik amalgamated their lands under his rule and so was formed the nucleus of what would become the kingdom of Rus. The source now called the *Novgorod First Chronicle* (describing events from 1016 to 1471 and drawing, in part, on eleventh-century sources) also records this story of an invitation to foreign rulers to come and bring order and law.

Two other Rus leaders – Askold and Dir – travelled southward down the River Dneiper and captured the settlement of Kiev. This set up two rival Rus states: Novgorod in the north and Kiev in the south. Rurik ruled until around 879. His successor, named Oleg (a Slavic form of the Old Norse personal name Helgi), struck south and seized Kiev in around 882 and relocated his capital there. This was the new kingdom of Kiev Rus, which would last until 1240 when it fell to the Mongols. However, the last *Rurikid* (the dynasty claiming descent from the Viking Rurik) to rule Russia, Tsar Vasily IV, died as late as 1612. It was a remarkable achievement for the family of a ninth-century Swedish adventurer. In time, the Novgorod princes would be appointed by the Grand Prince of Kiev; this Novgorod prince was usually one of the elder sons of the Grand Prince.

In this ancient tradition, we can probably see the general shape of events that led to the foundation of Kiev Rus:

Stage 1: Swedish trading and settlement in north-western Russia.

Stage 2: Trade gave way to political domination and tribute-taking.

Stage 3: The now dominant Scandinavians subjugated the local Slavic and Finnish tribes and set up their Rus mini-states.

Stage 4: The ruler of Novgorod gained pre-eminence among the Rus.

Stage 5: Dissident adventurers broke away and founded a rival centre at Kiev.

Stage 6: The ruler of Novgorod conquered Kiev and made it the capital of an amalgamated state, Kiev Rus.

Corroborative evidence for the early activities of the Rus comes from some surprising sources. In 839, the Byzantine emperor Theophilus sent a diplomatic mission to Louis the Pious, ruler of the Franks in Western Europe. With the embassy from Constantinople travelled some members of a group who called themselves the *Rhos*. They had been sent on a diplomatic mission by their own ruler – Khagan – to Constantinople. Louis was curious and on enquiry discovered that these *Rhos* were Swedes. This intriguing episode is recorded in the *Annales Bertiniani* (*Annals of St Bertin*), a contemporary source documenting events of the period 830–882. This is the very earliest account of the Rus. Incidentally, *khagan* is not a personal name; it is a royal title, used to describe the ruler of the Khazars, living north-east of the Black Sea. It seems the Rus were picking up some of the political vocabulary of their new home.

An Arab writer, Al-Ya' qūbī (died 897), explained that the people he knew as the Rus were of the same race as the pirates who had attacked the Islamic Spanish city of Seville in 843. Al-Ya' qūbī lived variously in Armenia, Khorasan (a region encompassing north-eastern Iran, southern Turkmenistan, and northern Afghanistan), India, North Africa and eventually Egypt. A Shi'ite, he was well informed with regard to peoples from the Caspian Sea to the Mediterranean, so the Rus came into his orbit of interest.

If the story of the rise of the Rurikid dynasty is remarkable, even more astonishing is what came next, for within a century they had morphed into an Orthodox Christian state whose pagan Viking past was rapidly subsumed by a new Christian and Slavic character.

THE RUS AND THE SLAVS

Under the Rus rulers, the mixed Slavic/Norse settlements of northern Russia soon developed into significant urban trading centres. Not for nothing did the Swedes know the region as *Garðaríki* (kingdom of the towns) or just *Garðar* (the towns). When Novgorod (the "new fortress") was founded in the tenth century, it relocated settlement from what had once been a much smaller Slavic trading post on the island of Gorodisce. The fame of the later settlement eclipsed memory of the former site to such an extent that when the *Russian Primary Chronicle* named the seat of Rurik's original power, it named Novgorod, although that settlement had been little more than a staging post on the trade route south, in the 860s. Back in Sweden it was called *Hólmgarðr*. In a similar way, the settlement of Kiev soon became deeply enmeshed in a wide-ranging trading network that linked the Baltic to the Black Sea, the Caspian Sea – and beyond.

However, while the Scandinavians bequeathed a far-flung trading network to the state that was to emerge, we must not credit this entirely to the Swedes, for the Slavic peoples they came to dominate were skilful craft-workers and traders, and their settlements were already on an upward trajectory of development. Furthermore, the Scandinavians rapidly assimilated to their surroundings. Today there are no more than seven loan-words from Old Norse in the Russian language. This amply demonstrates the significance and confidence of the Slavic component in the state of Kiev Rus. It also indicates something of the population imbalance too. As later in Normandy, we should imagine the Rus as an incoming elite minority and not heralding a mass folk movement. There is nothing like the archaeological evidence for an influx of lower class Viking settlers that we see in parts of Lincolnshire, Orkney or Iceland. Even if there had been, such numbers would rapidly have been diluted in the huge areas of the new state which linked the Baltic to the Black Sea. Where there is archaeological evidence for Swedish Viking immigrants (such as Viking-style oval brooches), these were town-based and did not extend to rural settlements, which were undiluted Slavic or Finnish in the north. Even in the developing towns, the Swedes were a warrior and merchant minority. So Slavs were always going to be the majority of the new state, accelerating the transformation of the newcomers, as in England.

The first three rulers of the emerging Rus state carried Norse names and this can be seen through the later lens of Slavonic written accounts. So Rurik was *Rorik* in Old East Norse, Oleg was *Helgi* in Old Norse, and Igor was *Ingvar*. While names do not prove ethnicity, the pattern is surely significant. These men had Norse names that, while adapted by the writers of chronicles who spoke Old East Slavic and drew on traditions written in Old Church Slavonic, are still clearly visible. However, in 945 Igor's son came to power and he was given a Slavic name, Svyatoslav. This reveals both an assimilation of mind-set and a gesture appealing to a subject population, naming a ruler of the state in their language.

In the mid-tenth century there was still a distinction between the language of the ruling dynasty and the rest of the population. The rulers still spoke the eastern form of Old Norse, while the majority spoke Old East Slavic, but the name-giving indicates the way things were developing.

This was not the only Slavic feature in the ruling dynasty of Kiev Rus in the middle of the tenth century. Svyatoslav and his son Vladimir were both worshippers of the Slavic god Perun. Rus Norse paganism had adapted to the local paganism of its subjects. At the same time, Slavic speakers fought alongside the Rus, as soldiers and commanders of armies. But a more dramatic change was soon to occur.

In 989 Vladimir converted to Christianity.

THE CHRISTIAN VIKINGS OF KIEV RUS

The conversion of Vladimir reveals the source of the greatest cultural influence on Kiev Rus in the second half of the tenth century. This was from Constantinople and the Byzantine Empire, not Scandinavia. This shift in the centre of gravity would almost certainly have occurred anyway, given the power and prestige of the Byzantine Empire, but it was accelerated by other factors. While Varangians would continue to travel the well-known paths (or rather rivers) from Scandinavia to Constantinople until the eleventh century, the flow of Scandinavian cultural influence was dwindling and the Viking character of the Rus was not being replenished. From the 960s the silver mines of the Islamic world (situated at Ilak and the Pamir in Central Asia) ceased production. By the first decade of the eleventh century, they were a thing of the past. The "inter-continental monetary-commercial system [based on silver coinage] had during the tenth century disintegrated".[8] There was a silver famine from China to the Atlantic. By the end of the eleventh century, from the Atlantic to the border of Ghaznavid, India, not a single Islamic ruler was minting coins in silver. The impact of this collapse in silver coin production, as we have seen, had been shaking previous trading certainties for over a century before this. Until this occurred, the trade in the Baltic and through the Russian river systems had been dominated by the Swedes, with Sweden accounting for about 800 coin hoards, which in total contain more than 200,000 coins. Of this total, about fifty per cent are Islamic coins, minted before 970. This was already draining silver out of the Islamic lands even before the silver famine.

Not all experts accept the view that the mines ceased production and some argue that the destruction of the Khazar and the Bulghar Empires in western Asia, and the decline of the Samanid Empire (stretching from modern-day Iran to Afghanistan and beyond), caused problems in access rather than supply, which accompanied a growing emphasis on gold (rather than silver) in the Islamic world.[9] Whatever the final verdict (and the evidence for exhaustion of mines seems strong), the supply of silver into Scandinavia collapsed and with it the trade routes to the east. Swedish Vikings turned elsewhere for the rewards of silver and it is from this period that they appear among the armies raiding England.

Clearly not everyone gave up on the hopes of rich rewards to be found in the east, since it was in the late 1030s that Ingvar the Far-Travelled and his companions set out on their eastern exploits. They were clearly hoping that, somehow, the old routes could still be made to turn a profit. They were wrong.

These factors helped reorientate the Rus towards the Christian world of the Byzantine Empire. When this finally occurred, the language of the church of Kiev became Old Church Slavonic, indicating the culture rapidly absorbing the once-Scandinavian Rus. Byzantine stonemasons built the Church of the Tithe in Kiev for the newly converted Vladimir. It was built between 989 and 996 as the premier church for the newly Christian state of Kiev Rus. Its central tower and dome, as well as its general appearance, proclaimed Byzantine influence in Kiev.

The story of how the conversion occurred has the hallmarks of legend. The *Russian Primary Chronicle* recounts how Prince Vladimir of Kiev had decided to abandon the traditional paganism of the Slavs, encouraged by the example of Olga his grandmother, who had already converted to Greek Orthodox Christianity. On top of this, a number of Baltic Slav tribes had converted by 968, and the rulers of both the Danes and the Poles had officially adopted

Christianity in the 960s. Religious change was on a number of contemporary agendas. But which faith should Vladimir adopt? He was undecided. According to one traditional account, he dispatched emissaries to different parts of Europe to explore the religions that they found there. Other versions say he summoned representatives to Kiev. These included representatives of western Roman Catholicism; Jews from among the Khazars who had adopted Judaism in around 865; Muslims from among the Volga Bulghars who had converted to Islam in 922 and finally the Byzantine Orthodox Christians of Constantinople.

One by one, Vladimir rejected the faiths. He turned down Islam principally due to its prohibition of alcohol and pork, despite his initial attraction to the idea of seventy-two virgins awaiting him in paradise; Judaism because the God of the Jews had allowed the chosen people to lose their homeland; and Catholicism because he found its rites dull and disliked its emphasis on fasting.[10] However, when Rus had visited the great cathedral of Hagia Sophia in Constantinople, they were amazed at its beauty and at the grandeur of its formal liturgy. Having weighed it all up, Vladimir decided that the faith of the Byzantines was the best one.

The decision suited the Byzantines too, as it gave them a co-religionist ally north of the Black Sea. This was particularly important as Emperor Basil II was facing the loss of Byzantine Crimea to rebels, and so, in 988, he proposed an alliance with Vladimir and offered him his sister's hand in marriage, on condition that Vladimir accepted baptism. Vladimir went to Constantinople, accepted Christian baptism and also married Princess Anna. She was not happy but accepted her diplomatic and royal conjugal fate.

Once converted, Vladimir was energetic in applying the new faith. The statue of the Slav god Perun was dragged down and beaten, then pulled through the River Dneiper to cleanse it. A mass baptism was arranged in the river and Vladimir let it be known that any who refused baptism would be regarded as his enemy. This had the desired effect. Kiev Rus converted to the Orthodox Christian faith of the Byzantine Empire.[11] The change was profound and, remarkably, it even included the Christianizing of the area around the Sea of Azov, which the later Icelandic historian Snorri

Sturluson considered to be the original home of the Viking gods and goddesses.

The new faith had huge implications for the future development of culture in Kiev Rus. The liturgy of the church would be written in the Cyrillic alphabet, which became the form of writing used in the new state and so in Russia and Ukraine to the present day. This also allowed the use of Greek literature, translated for the Slavic peoples, to be deployed in Kiev Rus. This gave access – via these translations – to Greek science, philosophy and styles of writing history.

After the Great Schism of 1054 between the Roman Catholic and the Eastern Orthodox churches, the church in Kiev kept up communion with both Rome and Constantinople for some time. Eventually, though, it shifted decisively into the Eastern Orthodox camp but, in contrast to other Orthodox churches of the Greek-speaking world, the church in Kiev Rus maintained a generally more positive attitude towards the West.[12]

During the reign of Yaroslav the Wise (1019–1054) this open and integrated outlook was a hallmark of his diplomacy. His granddaughter Eupraxia, the daughter of his son Vsevolod I, was married to the German ruler, the Holy Roman Emperor Henry III. Yaroslav also arranged for his sister and three daughters to marry the rulers of Poland, France, Hungary and Norway (see below regarding this last marriage). He also worked to improve relations with the Byzantine Empire, which had become strained. As a consequence, Kiev Rus stood at the centre of a web of key diplomatic alliances. Yaroslav was also active in furthering Christian government and culture. He issued the *Russkaya Pravda* – the first East Slavic law code. He also had Hagia Sophia Cathedral in Kiev and Hagia Sophia Cathedral in Novgorod built, both named from the great cathedral in Constantinople (*Hagia Sophia* or Holy Wisdom). We know that there was also a Swedish church in Novgorod dedicated to St Olaf of Norway (died 1030). A runestone from Sjusta in Sweden states that the man commemorated met his death *i olafs kriki* (in Olaf's church) in *Hólmgarðr* (Novgorod).[13]

Yaroslav also supported local clergy and the development of monasticism. He even gave up his mistresses. Tradition says that he founded a school system in Kiev which, at the least, showed a commitment to expanding education. It was an approach that outlasted his rule since his sons developed the great monastery of Kiev, Pechersk Lavra, which fulfilled the function of a central educational centre for the church of Kiev.

The newly Christian state of Kiev Rus similarly looked both north and south for its trade, the route to the east being much reduced as we have seen. In the north the continued steady debasement of the Arabic *dirham* coinage (from ninety per cent silver in 1000 to just five per cent silver by 1050) led the merchants of Novgorod to look westward for markets for their furs and amber. This shift of focus was assisted by the fact that they were now Christian, which clearly facilitated increased trade to Christian Anglo-Saxon England and the Christian communities of northern Germany.[14] By a happy coincidence, these latter communities still had abundant silver coinage to exchange for the products of the eastern Baltic, due to the discovery of new sources of silver in the Hartz mountains of Germany in the 960s.

At the same time as these westward trading developments occurred, the eleventh century also saw the Novgorod Rus carve out tributary arrangements with their northern pagan neighbours, the Finns, Ugrians and Sami. In this they strove to fend off competition from other Scandinavians from Norway and Sweden, and from the south-east in the form of the Bulghars, who also traded for furs in the north.[15] According to the later sagas, Yaroslav the Wise's wife (see below), Ingegerd, appointed the Christian jarl Rognvald of Sweden as her governor in the area around Lake Ladoga. The thirteenth-century *Nóregs konunga tal* (*Catalogue of Norwegian Kings*) records how he and his successor, Jarl Eilif, had been employed to "defend the kingdom against pagans". This is not the usual image of Vikings but this was the state of play in Kiev Rus by the eleventh century.[16] Archaeologists have found Christian graves from around this period in the cemetery at Ladoga, of those who were probably members of this group.

HARALD HARDRADA OF NORWAY AND HIS WARS
IN THE EAST

The growing cultural Slavic orientation of the southern Rus was clearly seen by the reign of Yaroslav the Wise, whose court was thoroughly Slavic in character. Under his rule the power and wealth of Kiev grew considerably. It was then that the Golden Gate was built at Kiev with its tiered battlements as a symbol of the grandeur of Kiev Rus. It was his daughter, Elizabeth, who married the Norwegian exile Harald Hardrada, who served in the Varangian Guard of the Byzantine Empire. Her mother, Ingegerd, was a distant relative of Harald and she was also the granddaughter of the Swedish king Olof *Skötkonung*. Harald's brother, Olaf Haraldson, had earlier been in exile in Kiev following the failure of a revolt he had been involved in, in 1028, back in Norway. This reminds us that, though now thoroughly Orthodox Christian and Slavic in culture, there was still a lingering tradition of connection with the distant homeland in Scandinavia. Harald Hardrada was eventually to return home, seize the crown of Norway and then die at the Battle of Stamford Bridge in September 1066.

However, long before he invaded England, he was active in the eastern Mediterranean. These adventures were later recalled in a number of thirteenth-century sagas. One of these was the *Nóregs konunga tal* (*Catalogue of Norwegian Kings*) that we encountered earlier, written possibly in Trondheim, Norway, early in the thirteenth century.[17] While they have some legendary features, these sources clearly recall a general picture of his exploits.[18] After some time in exile in Kiev Rus, he travelled on to Constantinople, to seek employment for himself and his men as mercenaries. The mention of Empress Zoe and Emperor Michael (Michael IV the Paphlagonian) suggests that this occurred sometime between 1034 and 1041. Once in imperial pay, he campaigned in Africa and Sicily, where he indulged in "the harsh sport" (a poetic allusion to warfare). After this he travelled to Jerusalem, where his military prowess resulted in the region coming under his control.

How much reality we can read into this and how much it

represents what a thirteenth-century compiler thought was a suitable achievement for a tough Christian king is now hard to say. Suffice it to say that the later tradition thought that, as a result, it could be expected that "the mighty king's soul [would] live ever with Christ in the Heavens where it is well pleased". While in the Holy Land, Harald bathed in the River Jordan "as was the pilgrim practice", and made gifts to the Church of the Holy Sepulchre, particularly singling out gifts to the shrine of Christ's tomb and the relic of the True Cross. In addition, he imposed order on the road from Jerusalem to the River Jordan and executed robbers who threatened those travelling.

On returning to Constantinople, Harald (according to the *Nóregs konunga tal*) got caught up in a love triangle involving himself, the empress Zoe and a noblewoman named Maria. As a result, he was imprisoned, then eventually rescued by a widow who had been ordered to save him by St Olaf of Norway. On waking his men – who were still in the emperor's service – they seized the emperor and blinded him. Furthermore, they hanged those Varangians who remained loyal to the deposed emperor. The later tradition claims that the emperor so ill-treated was Constantine Monomachos but the tradition has become confused because it was, in fact, Emperor Michael V Kalafates (the predecessor of Constantine IX Monomachos) who was deposed and blinded in 1042. Just what part Harald played in these events of – literally – Byzantine intrigue is hard to say. The later tradition claimed that he was the one who was actually responsible for the deposing and blinding of the emperor. He was certainly involved in the intrigues and politics of the Byzantine court, since another source confirms his high military rank at this time. This late-eleventh-century source, called in Greek *Logos Nouthetetikos* (*Word of Wisdom*), tells how Harald served Emperor Michael IV the Paphlagonian and Emperor Michael V Kalafates and, in this service, fought for the imperial cause in Sicily and Bulgaria. In this time he was granted two Byzantine titles. By this time these were honorific titles within the Byzantine court but, since they had originally been ranks within the emperor's bodyguard, the later tradition may still have reflected a memory of military titles accorded to Harald.

The *Logos Nouthetetikos* makes no mention of an insurrection but does say that when Constantine IX Monomachos came to the throne, Harald asked permission to return to his homeland but was refused. Despite this, Harald "slipped away" and returned to Norway. We are told that Harald "did not complain about the titles" he received in Constantinople, which might suggest that they were later thought unfitting for a man who was eventually a king himself; but this shows the benefit of hindsight. However, we are told that Harald continued to show "good faith and brotherly love towards the Romans [the Byzantines]". There was clearly a bond between Christian rulers who had once fought on the same side in a distant land.

The Mediterranean career of Harald illustrates the opportunities open to Christian Vikings in the pay of the Byzantine emperor. Many of the runestones of Sweden refer to such men who not only travelled to Eastern Europe and Central Asia (to Serkland and to *Garðar*) but went further south still. So, at Skepptuna, we hear of Folkmar who "died among the Greeks"; and at Ed, inscribed on a natural boulder, a man named Ragnvald both commemorated his mother and also proclaimed how he himself "was in Greece as commander of a brigade". The Old Norse is *liðs forungi*, meaning literally "chief of a fighting force". From this we can deduce that he commanded a unit of the Byzantine emperor's Varangian Guard.

Such an adventure could be highly lucrative. A runestone from Ulunda explicitly stated that one man "journeyed boldly, made his money abroad in the land of the Greeks for his heir". Others, such as an unnamed man who was commemorated at Fjuckby, was involved in trade rather than fighting, for he "captained a merchant ship [to] Greek harbours".[19] But the venture, whether military or mercantile, could cost a man his life, as the brothers of a woman (known only as "Gulli's wife") discovered, for both of them "met their deaths on active service in the east".[20] The phrase *i liði* ("in an army") uses the same Viking military term that we came across earlier with regard to the military career of Ragnvald at Ed. Clearly, Harald was not the only Christian from Scandinavia who embarked on the long and perilous journey to the eastern Mediterranean for the military opportunities there – opportunities now more than ever open to Christian Scandinavians in the military service of Greek (Byzantine) co-religionists.

Others who journeyed to the Byzantine Empire and neighbouring states included those specifically travelling due to Christian piety. At Staket, a woman named Ingurin had engraved: "She intends to travel eastwards, as far abroad as Jerusalem." One assumes this was the vow of a pilgrim to the sacred places of the Holy Land. For some, the journey was their last. When Æstrid's husband, Östen, took the same road, "he went out to Jerusalem and died in Greece".[21] This memorial, at Brody, was accompanied by a second commemoration to Östen raised by the man's son, built into a bridge.[22] These glimpses of Scandinavians travelling on pilgrimage to the Christian shrines of Jerusalem are a necessary corrective to the popular image of Vikings on journeys of plunder or even simply selling their swords and axes to foreign rulers. Not all who travelled eastward had violence on their minds, however legitimate it was. Some did so prayerfully and for the good of their souls.

However, the relationship of the more northerly state of Kiev Rus with Scandinavians such as Harald Hardrada was complex and double-edged. On one hand, they were useful swords for hire. It was with bought-in Viking muscle that one Rus leader, Vladimir, had seized the throne of Kiev from his brother when he ruled Novgorod. On the other hand, he did not want these mercenaries hanging around and causing trouble, so he kept a few in his service and sent the rest on to Constantinople. Yaroslav the Wise did the same with Harald Hardrada.

As well as not fully trusting these volatile Varangians, there were now other mercenaries available. With Kiev Rus established as a serious player in southern Russia, its rulers had a number of options open to them when it came to raising armies. Increasingly the advantage lay with recruiting mercenaries from the nomadic steppe peoples who lived further east. These cavalry were more mobile and had the edge over the foot-soldier Varangians, who fought in the traditional Viking way as axe-wielding infantrymen. In 1024 at the Battle of Listven, Yaroslav had seen such infantry defeated by nomadic auxiliaries in the army of his brother, Mstislav. In Russia, the age of Vikings as effective warriors was drawing to a close.

After the death of Yaroslav the Wise, in 1054, the Golden Age of Kiev Rus became overshadowed by growing political instability, in which regional elite families challenged the power of the Grand Princes. A complex succession strategy developed, by which power passed to the eldest member of the ruling dynasty rather than from father to son. This instituted almost constant rivalry within the royal family, with attendant political turbulence. After the death of Yaroslav the Wise, a particularly prolonged and complex period of infighting occurred, at the same time as a reduction in the power of Constantinople and a decline in trade with the Byzantine Empire, which weakened Kiev (the main conduit of the north-south trade route).

During the twelfth century, as Kiev stagnated, the original Rus centre of Novgorod grew more influential and independent. It continued to dominate (and benefit from) trade between the Baltic and the Volga. In 1136 it broke free from the control of Kiev and became an independent city republic known as "Lord Novgorod the Great". But by that time the Viking roots of Kiev Rus were far in the past.

CHAPTER 11

Christian Vikings of
the North Atlantic

One of the most fascinating areas of Viking colonization and then of Christian conversion was in the North Atlantic. The colonists of Iceland, the Faroe Islands and Greenland sought out new homes on the edge of the known world. In such distant places the Christian conversion, when it came, would have distinct characteristics befitting life in these frontier societies.

THE VIKING SETTLEMENT OF ICELAND

The first written reference to Iceland is in the writing of the Irish author Dicuil, who wrote in 825 and believed that Iceland was the island referred to as *Thule* by classical geographers. Dicuil recorded that some Irish monks, seeking distant spiritual solitude, had discovered the island thirty years before but that, after a single expedition, had returned to Ireland in the same year. The later *Íslendingabók* (*Book of Icelanders*), compiled by the Icelandic priest Ari Thorgilson in the early twelfth century, claimed that the Irish seekers after solitude remained in Iceland and only left when the pagan Vikings arrived. Icelandic traditions claimed that the Scandinavians discovered croziers (a bishop's staff, usually with a crook made from metal) and books left behind by the monks. Which of these accounts is correct is now difficult to decide and it was not until the 860s that Iceland caught the attention of Scandinavian adventurers, and not until the 870s that serious migration and settlement occurred. Dateable volcanic ash, sealing the oldest farmstead unearthed in what is now Reykjavik, broadly supports these dates. The settlement of Iceland then progressed very quickly and by the 930s the foundations of Icelandic society had been established.

In common with the colonization of Orkney, Shetland, the Hebrides and the Faroes, medieval traditions referring to the Scandinavian settlement of Iceland attribute the beginnings of the movement to the reign of Harald Finehair. Icelandic sources such as the *Landnámabók (Book of Settlements)*, *Íslendingabók (Book of Icelanders)* and *Vatnsdæla saga (Saga of the people of Vatnsdal)* all suggest that escaping the tyranny of Harald was the main reason for the settlement of Iceland. *Landnámabók* goes as far as referring to Harald by the Old Norse word *ofríki*, a word usually associated with the devil. The increase in the power wielded by Harald is said to have led to chieftains and their families fleeing to Iceland, to preserve their traditional lifestyle. Personal antipathy towards the king's policies became a common motif within the later Icelandic family sagas.

The reality was less simple. As the settlement of Iceland began in about 860, this means that Harald's rule (from the end of the ninth century) may have contributed to increased emigration to Iceland but could not have been the initial stimulus. In the twelfth and thirteenth centuries, when much of this Icelandic literature was first written, Norway was taking an increasingly direct and intrusive interest in the affairs of Iceland. An illustration of this can be found in the fact that the Icelander Snorri Sturluson, who was responsible for the recording of much Viking tradition and mythology, was assassinated at his farm of Reykholt on the orders of King Hakon IV of Norway. Many Icelandic writers of this period wished to distance themselves from Norway and to highlight the tyranny of Norwegian kings, but these may not have been the views of the majority of ninth-century settlers. But the myth of the Norwegian tyranny of Harald Finehair has become deeply embedded in the Icelandic story.

With this in mind, it is necessary to turn to the sources again in search of other possible stimuli for the settlement of Iceland. There is a passage in *Laxdæla saga* (*Saga of the People of Laxárdalr*) which states that the "push of prudence assisted by the pull of opportunity" led to people moving to Iceland.[1] The people "have only two choices: to flee the country or be killed in our tracks" and "good land could be had for free".[2] So the promise of land in Iceland was a major draw for the settlers. Both *Laxdæla saga* and *Vatnsdæla saga* comment on the abundance of natural resources there. *Egils saga Skallagrímssonar* (*Saga of Egil Skallagrímson*) mentions many desirable resources such as whales, walruses and great auk (a large, flightless bird, now extinct). The first settlers found land which was ideal for a traditional Scandinavian lifestyle, overwhelmingly rural and where the focus was mainly pastoral. These new lands offered immense opportunities, easily exploited with minimum effort. There were, in contrast, relatively restricted reserves of new land in western Norway. This was not due to over-population but to the efforts of the king to expand his control of valuable resources. Norwegians had previously been settling in the Faroe Islands but this option was becoming restricted due to the relative scarcity of habitable land there. The advances in ship-building technology, such a feature of the Viking Age, made possible this seaborne expansion.

One version of *Landnámabók* says that the initial discovery of Iceland was made by a Norwegian Viking named Naddoddr, while another says it was a Swede called Gartharr Svavarson, who lost his way in a storm. Another tradition claimed that the first Viking to reach Iceland was Floki Vilgertharson, who used a raven to guide him there. The settlement of Iceland coincided with a reversal of fortunes in mainland Europe. For the first time Viking armies in the west suffered a series of defeats. They were beaten in Brittany and on the Doyle, harassed and pounded in Mercia and Wessex, expelled from Dublin and Anglesey and the Hebrides. In particular, the Irish conquest of Dublin led to considerable movement from there to Iceland.[3] Once started, this emigration to the north-west would eventually encompass Greenland and even North America.[4]

The first group of settlers on Iceland wanted to establish permanent farmsteads and a way of life similar to the one they had enjoyed at home. They sought out places where they could make hay for their domesticated animals, and hunting and fishing could provide food until the domestic animals increased in numbers.[5] Most of the settlers came from Norway but many others came from the Viking encampments and Norse colonies in the Celtic regions. The Norse settlers from Ireland, Scotland and the Hebrides brought with them Gaelic-speaking wives, followers and slaves. Consequently, Celtic names of Icelanders can be found in the sagas, such as Njall, from the Old Irish Niall, and Kormakr, from Cormac.[6]

Once the best coastal sites had been colonized, the settlement of the hinterland began. These areas were covered with woods when the first settlers arrived and were not initially seen as appropriate for settlement.[7] This soon changed and the environmental impact was massive. Today little of Iceland is wooded and that which is, is dominated by dwarf trees and shrubs. Hence the modern Icelandic joke: "If lost in an Icelandic forest, don't panic, just stand up!"

Once the initial settlers had established viable settlements, other settlers came in ever increasing numbers. Easily occupied land became scarce, and competition for land increased.[8] The early immigration established large estates along significant parts of the inhabitable area of coastal Iceland. The later settlement pattern was dominated by medium or small farms in more distant coastal and inland valley sites. This land, of lesser quality, was then divided into smaller sections and sold or rented to the new arrivals to the island.[9] Competition was fierce. The early settlers of Iceland had a distinct "founders' effect" upon the social, political and economic systems which rapidly emerged, and the medieval social order of Iceland reflected the nature of the earlier settlement. In turn, this would affect the nature of the Christian conversion in striking ways.

THE CREATION OF THE VIKING COMMONWEALTH

The society of Iceland was very different from the one they left behind in Norway. Iceland in the "Commonwealth period" was without any direct, executive power. There was no king, no central authority and no one charged with enforcing law and order. Even the eventual *Althing* (national assembly) was a place for discussion and conflict resolution, not a strong governing body.[10] This meant that Iceland lacked an official hierarchy and yet, at the same time, was not an egalitarian society. Much of the political discussion was connected to the legal and political rights of free farmers,[11] since emigration had led to a diminished level of stratification. Until the end of the medieval period, Iceland remained completely rural. There were no towns or even villages and early Iceland was only minimally involved in the trading networks that linked the rest of Scandinavia.

However, although Icelandic society was not as stratified as Norwegian society, it would not be true to say that all men were equal. There were thirty-nine chieftains in Iceland, termed *goðar* (plural). The area over which a *goði* (singular) had leadership was called a *goðorð*. Every household had to choose a *goði* to follow, which did not require any formal responsibility other than following the *goði* to the *Althing* or paying a fixed sum towards the travel expenses of those who did go there. The power of the *goðar* rested upon their following, and unsuccessful *goðar* lost *thingmenn* (assembly men) to more successful ones. This system distinguished Iceland from many other Norse colonies.[12] It was also far from straightforward. Ownership of a *goðorð* was considered necessary for those who wanted to be accepted as leading players. However, it did not, on its own, assure political influence and a weak chieftain would not necessarily become stronger just by inheriting a *goðorð*. Likewise, a chieftain could become quite powerful without having one. In addition, *thingmenn* were not representative of the whole of society under the *goðar* as, in order to be one of the *thingmenn*, a man needed to own a minimum amount of property. This meant that there were many farmers who did not qualify for political participation due to their relative poverty.

As a result, roughly 700 farmers ran the large and small estates and made up the aristocracy of Iceland, living in a loose relationship with the thirty-nine chieftains (the *goðar*). When one considers that there were about 4,000 householders in Iceland, it becomes clear that five-sixths of these householders were both economically and politically dependent on someone else in the Icelandic pecking order. It is the one-sixth, who made up the estate owners, who are represented in the famous Icelandic sagas.[13] Iceland was, for all its political mythology, a very unequal society. A large number of economically dependent and politically powerless people provided the basis for the power of the *goðar* chieftains and their immediate supporters. Among this latter class of powerful landowners – with their shifting support base of allies and dependants – heated debates occurred regarding whether to renounce paganism in favour of Christianity.

THE CHRISTIAN CONVERSION OF ICELAND

The conversion of Iceland was closely related to what happened in Norway, where pagans had feared that Christianity would change the fabric of traditional society by establishing centralized royal authority. Similarly, in Iceland, this desire not to change the established order also seems to have been a major consideration in resistance to conversion. *Íslendingabók* tells us that the decision to convert was made by the law speaker at the *Althing* and that, despite King Olaf Tryggvason sending missionaries, they did not cause the Icelanders to convert. This initial resistance to externally imposed Christianity enabled the Icelanders to later claim they had converted on their own terms even if, in reality, the mounting pressure from Norway was a key reason why they eventually accepted the Christian faith.

Resistance to the conversion seems to have been bound up as much with power politics as with religious sensibilities. This is probably not surprising, given that the pagan Norse belief system was polytheistic, so Icelanders would have had no problem in tolerating other people's belief in a different god. A new deity was not the issue: it was the exclusivity of Christianity that was the challenge. In the long run, it meant that co-existence of the two belief systems was unlikely to be possible. There was also little space for personal religious experience within the Norse belief system and worship was, instead, coloured by utilitarianism. Worship of a particular pagan deity might be abandoned or switched to another if the former object of worship was considered to have failed to support the worshipper. This difference allowed the Viking peoples to more easily make the switch to Christianity for pragmatic reasons.

Belief in the pagan gods was connected to the public sphere in Iceland, and Icelandic chieftains seem to have occupied leading religious and secular roles at the same time. Changing the status quo had far-reaching cultural implications. But the Icelandic laws did not define the status of the pagan gods and there were no common places of worship. In addition, in Old Norse *eddic* poetry, the pagan gods were viewed as being at the mercy of fate and eventually doomed. Christ, for Christians, transcends fate and is, therefore, much more powerful than the pagan gods who even Norse mythology stated would eventually be destroyed on the Day of Ragnarok. So paganism – though well established – was not as secure in the face of potential change as it otherwise might have been. Change was coming.

The major Icelandic sources for the events that led up to the final adoption of Christianity are Ari Thorgilson's *Íslendingabók* and the later family sagas. Although Ari was born sixty-seven years after the conversion, he refers to eyewitness sources and probably gives us a fairly accurate account of these dramatic events. From these sources and church records of early missionary activities, we can piece together what occurred.

After 980 a number of Christian missionaries visited Iceland. The first was a returning Icelander, named Thorvald Konradson, also known as Thorvald the Far-Travelled, who brought with him a German bishop named Fredrik. The mission failed. Meeting mounting conflict with violence, Thorvald was eventually forced to leave Iceland after having killed two of his tormentors.

The accession of Olaf Tryggvason as king of Norway, in 995, was a game-changer. The mid-thirteenth-century *Kristni saga* (*Saga of Christianity*) claims that it was Olaf Tryggvason who had sent Thorvald the Far-Travelled on his mission. Next he dispatched another Icelander, named Stefnir Thorgilson, to convert Iceland. Emboldened by religious zeal and royal authority, Stefnir smashed pagan sanctuaries and idols. The pagan reaction forced him to leave, after members of his own family prosecuted him, under a new law established to punish blasphemy through the intervention of family members. It was clearly framed in order to contrast a traditional family-based pagan society with the institutional whole community adherence to religious teachings, as envisaged by the church.[14]

Next, Olaf Tryggvason sent a priest named Thangbrand, in 997, who had experience preaching in Norway and the Faroes. Several prominent *goðar* became Christians but Thangbrand faced mocking opposition, in the form of abusive poems, leading him to kill two of his mockers in revenge. As a result, he was sentenced to exile. Other violent deaths occurred while Thangbrand was waiting for suitable sailing weather. Returning to Norway in 999, his reports prompted the king to adopt more aggressive measures. Icelandic merchants in Norway were arrested and Norwegian ports closed to Icelandic shipping. Back in Iceland, the supporters of both sides prepared for armed conflict.

In the summer of 1000, the meeting of the *Althing* threatened to descend into civil conflict. Then Iceland's peculiar political institutions came into play. Lacking a strong and decisive executive, it was decided to appoint mediators and submit the matter to binding arbitration. The law speaker of the *Althing*, who was charged with this momentous task, was Thorgeir Thorkelson. He was the *goði* of Ljósavatn, in northern Iceland. He was chosen because, though a pagan, he was accepted by both sides as a thoughtful moderate. Accordingly, for a day and a night Thorgeir Thorkelson lay under a fur blanket reflecting on the future of Iceland.

At dawn the next day he announced his historic decision: Iceland would become Christian. In a further demonstration of the consensual nature of Icelandic politics (based on debate without executive power) it was further decreed that existing laws sanctioning the exposure of infants and the eating of horseflesh would remain. Eating horsemeat was so connected with Germanic pagan rituals that it had been prohibited for Christians since 732. In addition, private pagan worship would be permitted. Each *goði*, each farming household, could make its own decision. This was a very Icelandic conversion. Arbitration had triumphed over civil war. It was in sharp contrast to the violence which accompanied the conversion in Norway.

Thorgeir Thorkelson then made it clear what a momentous decision he had just made. Though he was a pagan priest, he took his pagan idols and threw them into the huge waterfall at Goðafoss (Old Norse: waterfall of the gods), on the river Skjálfandafljót in north-eastern Iceland.

LIVING WITH THE NEW AND OLD FAITHS

There was a great deal of syncretism and compromise in the Icelandic conversion. The decision to adopt Christianity in Iceland provided immunity for people who practised paganism in an unprovocative way, so the old ways often continued in private. This was a huge concession on the part of a religion which was absolutely monotheistic. The conversion in Iceland was, therefore, very much a compromise that occurred in stages and did not result in a sudden break from the old beliefs. This explains why it was so peaceful and lacked a pagan reaction. However, it also meant that the more radical impact of the new faith took longer to take effect (both infanticide and eating horsemeat would eventually be banned). And personal observance could be mixed, to put it mildly. *Landnámabók*, for example, tells of Helge the Lean, who believed in Christ but prayed to Thor when at sea or in a particularly difficult situation.

Norse mythology also provided a major source of poetic content in Iceland (where older material was transmitted and preserved) well into the Christian period. When Snorri Sturluson sought to explain the complex *kennings* (metaphors) found within skaldic poetry, he referred to their roots in Norse mythology. He no longer believed in the old gods, but the complex images, metaphors and similes so common to Scandinavian poetry were rooted in the old myths. The poets continued to regard themselves as the inheritors of a proud Scandinavian tradition, and were regarded as the heirs of the legendary poet Bragi the Old, and ultimately of the giver of the "poetic mead" himself, Odin (even if no longer revered as a god). In time the new Christian hymns and liturgy would come to have a profound effect on the content and structure of skaldic poetry – as well as on whether it was acceptable to preserve older traditions or not – but this took time to develop. An analysis of the occurrence of mythological allusions in the *kennings* found in court poetry shows there was a decrease in mythological allusions, from a high of twenty-five per cent of poems in the late tenth century, to two or three per cent in the late twelfth century. There was then an increase to roughly ten per cent after this point, as it seems that the mythological content had begun to lose its potency and was then considered safe to use once more.[15]

In time, Christian *kennings* emerged which had no relation to old pagan mythology but were written in the same style. The late-eleventh-century Icelandic poet Arnorr *Jarlaskald* (jarl's poet) developed a series of God-*kennings* including *stillir soltjalda* ("ruler of the tents of the sun") and *kongungr dags grundar* ("king of the land of the day"), in a manner that would have been familiar to a Viking poet of an earlier generation.[16] In general, though, these Christian *kennings* are a lot less dense than their pagan counterparts and this reflected Christian teaching, which sought clarity of expression. The writer of the poem *Lilja* (*Lily*) – a skaldic poem dedicated to the Virgin Mary – declared that he wanted to avoid *hulin fornyrðin* ("obscure archaism").[17] This is likely to have been due to the influence of Christian ideology, with its aim of communicating the Christian message clearly and without embellishment. Christianity even had an impact on the metre of poems, and a new metre called *hrynhent* was developed, which seems to have been influenced by Christian hymns and liturgical sequences.

One of the most important contributions of Christianity to the Norse mental world was the emphasis on eternal life as a solution to the problem of mortality, and five of Arnorr *Jarlaskald's* references to God are embedded in prayers for the soul of the hero of the poem. In a similar way, personal confidence in victory over death was linked to the actions of defending angels and we know from runestones that St Michael (who was also connected with the Judgement Day) was widely venerated in Scandinavia and appears in the poetry of Arnorr *Jarlaskald*. However, apart from a new conception of the afterlife, there does not seem to be much evidence for a radical shift in ethical values as a result of Christian influence. Arnorr had no inclination to portray the New Testament values of charity, humility, and peace, and even less to confront the old warrior ideals of dauntless, ruthless courage. And the violent feuding nature of medieval Iceland bears witness to the fact that Christian ethics took a long time to impact on the interpersonal relationships of rival Icelanders. This may have been a direct result of the transitional nature of the Icelandic conversion.

In contrast to kings, it has often been assumed that conversion posed a problem for women because there were no longer any goddesses and the Christian church was headed by men. However, in spite of this, women in the Icelandic context seem to have played an important role in the conversion, such as the wife of Erik the Red who converted before her husband. This may be because the conditions in the Christian afterlife were more desirable to women than the limited experience on offer from Norse paganism. Paradise open to anyone would have been much more preferable to the shadowy Norse "Hel" available for women. Furthermore, the Christian message was not intrinsically violent and the inclusion within Christianity of protection for small children (e.g. the eventual banning of infanticide, which particularly threatened baby girls) may have added to its appeal. Although the church also offered an active role for female religious, the situation in Iceland was complex. In the Icelandic sagas there is mention of only six nuns and, of these, one is Gudrun (who visited Vinland), who had four successive husbands and several children. Only two of the six nuns are said to have been celibate their entire lives. Once again, Icelandic Christianity differed from that found in other areas of the Christian Viking world.

THE CHRISTIAN VIKINGS OF THE FAROE ISLANDS

The Faroe Islands are a group of small islands situated between the Norwegian Sea and the North Atlantic. They lie about halfway between Norway and Iceland, approximately 200 miles (320 kilometres) north-northwest of the mainland of Scotland. Today the islands function as an autonomous country within the overall kingdom of Denmark. Like Greenland, the Viking settlers found that the Faroe Islands were treeless but had abundant grass for pasture, as did Iceland.

Neither archaeological discoveries nor written sources can determine exactly when the Faroes began to be settled by Scandinavians. But it is reasonable to assume that they were occupied before Iceland was.[18] What is certain is that the Vikings were not the first to settle there. The archaeological evidence points towards two earlier waves of settlers before the Scandinavians. The first of these waves occurred between about 300 and 600, while the second wave occurred between 600 and 800. The recent discovery of ancient cereal pollen from domesticated crops supports this view regarding pre-Viking settlers.[19]

The origins of these earlier settlers are obscured by myth and legend. A Latin account of the legendary voyages made by an Irish saint named Brendan the Navigator (traditionally lived c. 484–578) includes a reference to northern *insulae* (islands) which might refer to the Faroes. More reliable is the early-ninth-century account written by the Irish monk Dicuil. In his geographical work *De Mensura Orbis Terrae* (*Concerning the Measurement of the World*) he described Irish monks visiting the Faroes as well as Iceland. Dicuil dates the arrival of the first Scandinavians to around 825 and explained that fear of them drove away the Irish monks who had used the islands as a place of retreat for more than a century.

What is clear is that the Viking settlers of the Faroes were well established by the tenth century and it seems likely that the early settlements were destroyed by rising sea levels, since they would almost certainly have been on the coast.[20] The evidence from the sagas also gives a settlement date in the early ninth century, so it does seem likely that Norse colonization of Iceland was an extension of the pre-existing settlements in the Faroe Islands. Some of the Faroese settlers may have come direct from Norway, and *Færeyinga saga* (*Saga of the Faroes*) maintains the same tradition as found on Iceland: that they fled the tyranny of King Harald Finehair. But many others will have reached there from Norse and Norse-Gael communities around the Irish Sea, the Outer Hebrides, Shetland, and Orkney. It is significant that the name of the first to reach there, according to *Færeyinga saga*, was a man named Grímur Kamban, whose second name was of Irish origin.

Although the Faroes appear, like Orkney, to have been dominated by chieftains and large landowners, it still seems that the ultimate authority there was the *Althing* (the assembly of free men) in Tórshavn.[21] It was to the Faroese *Althing* that Sigmundur Brestison (died 1005), the first Faroese to convert to Christianity, brought a decree from Olaf Tryggvason of Norway in 999, commanding the islands to convert. Sigmundur Brestison was almost killed by the angry pagan response. Rethinking his methods, he then went in the company of armed supporters to the home of the chieftain, Tróndur í Gøtu, forcing entry by night. Tróndur í Gøtu was told to accept Christianity or be beheaded. He converted, but his sincerity is in doubt. The nature of this particular "conversion" is revealed in the fact that Tróndur í Gøtu got his revenge by attacking Sigmundur Brestison (also at night) at his home on the central Faroe island of Skúvoy. Brestison only survived by a long swim to Sandvík, the northernmost village on the island of Suðuroy. Landing exhausted, he was murdered by a local farmer and his sons for the gold arm-ring he was wearing.

Despite this, Norwegian royal support ensured that Christianity was eventually triumphant. Over the next century a bishop was established at Kirkjubøur on the island of Streymoy, under the oversight of the archbishop of Nidaros (later Trondheim). Norwegian royal rule, religious control and taxation were imposed and this rule by Norway (united with Denmark after 1397) continued until 1814, when the union between Denmark and Norway ended following the Treaty of Kiel, and Denmark kept control of the Faroe Islands.

THE CHRISTIAN VIKINGS OF GREENLAND

The famous Viking explorer known as Erik the Red first visited Greenland from Iceland in 983. There had been rumours of the place since its sighting by a storm-driven Viking sea captain in about 930. Erik gave the island its name in order to make it sound more attractive to other settlers. He had many enemies and was looking for a place he could settle after having been exiled from Iceland. The climate was milder in the North Atlantic compared with today and it was even possible to grow some arable crops on Greenland. But, unlike Iceland, it was treeless. At its height the eventual Viking colony on Greenland numbered about 4,000. According to Ari Thorgilson's *Íslendingabók*, the first Icelandic explorers discovered a number of deserted huts, parts of boats, and stone implements which indicated that others had visited the area before and which clearly had been left behind by the indigenous people of what is now called the paleo-Inuit Dorset culture, whom the Vikings contemptuously dismissed as *skrælings* (wretches). Eric named his settlement Brattahlid (meaning "steep slope"), in what became the Eastern Settlement. In time there developed three areas of settlement: the Eastern Settlement, the Western Settlement and the Middle Settlement. All were sited on fjords in south-western Greenland.

Erik's son, Leif the Lucky, visited Norway, where he was converted to Christianity by King Olaf Tryggvason. He was then sent back to Greenland, with some missionaries, to convert the settlers there. This seems to have resulted in a swift (even if nominal) conversion. The details are poorly recorded but what we can glean from later sagas suggests that a range of religious practices were found in the colony in the first couple of generations. In the surviving literature in which Greenlanders feature, we find pagan rituals carried out by the seeress Thorbjorg; Christian belief and practice associated with Erik's wife, Thjodhild; and the remarkable exploits of a woman named Gudrid who, as well as journeying to Vinland, later went on pilgrimage to Rome and died as an anchoress (a form of nun) on Iceland.

All of this rather challenges the impression from the meagre conversion sources that the process was swift and uniform. This is not surprising, given the distance of the colony from areas of royal rule in Norway, and the Greenlanders' experience seems not to have conformed to the official version of "sudden, dramatic, and emphatic change, in favour of a different understanding of religious practice". This Greenland experience "may have had more room for religious diversity than Christian sources would allow".[22] Overall then, this points to a fairly long period of religious diversity in which traditional pagan practices co-existed alongside new Christian behaviour. Only when the Christian church succeeded in establishing formal institutional controls and organization was it possible to insist on Christian norms of behaviour across the whole Greenland community.

Sixteen parishes were eventually founded to serve the scattered communities, and a number of churches built. There were even a few small monasteries established. In time Greenland was formed into the diocese of Garðar, under the archbishopric of Hamburg-Bremen. According to the sagas, it was a wealthy Greenlander named Sokki Thorison – who farmed in the Brattahlid area – who drove this idea forward and gained the approval of the king of Norway for the plan. The first bishop of Garðar, named Arnaldur, was finally ordained by the archbishop of Lund in 1124. Oversight shifted from Hamburg-Bremen to the archbishopric of Lund, in Sweden, from 1126 to 1152. It was then brought under the oversight of the newly appointed archbishop of Nidaros – later called Trondheim – in Norway (along with Iceland, the Isle of Man, the Orkney Islands and the Faroe Islands) in 1152. Perhaps as many as eighteen bishops, of various nationalities, occupied (or were nominated to) the see of Garðar before the Greenland colony finally failed. However, we know little or nothing about most of their activities on Greenland. There is one exception, since a later tradition claims that Bishop Erik Gnupson took part in an expedition, in 1121, aimed at reaching Vinland (North America), which had been discovered around 1000.

The nature of the hunting settlement on Greenland is apparent from the fact that Greenland's contribution to the Church of Rome (known as "Peter's Pence") in the first half of the fourteenth century was paid in walrus ivory.

No bishop visited Greenland after the start of the fifteenth century and by this time the colony was in terminal decline. The last bishop nominally appointed was Vincenz Kampe, in 1537, but by then the Christian community on Greenland was extinct. The fate of the settlers is uncertain, though many may have died as climatic change overwhelmed the colony and glaciers advanced in the Little Ice Age, which started in about 1300 and lasted until about 1850. Desperately trying to maintain their Scandinavian farming economy to the end, they failed to learn from the more successful lifestyle of the people of the proto-Inuit Thule culture, who had replaced those of the Dorset culture. Survivors were probably assimilated by the pagan indigenous peoples, although conflict with them may have physically eliminated the Norse. In 1721, a new Danish colony was established in Greenland with the aim of converting the Inuit inhabitants there to Christianity; but by that time the Viking colony was long gone.

CHAPTER 12

The First
American Christians

Today, if one asked a modern citizen of the USA or Canada to name the first Christian buried in North America, they might come up with the name of one of the sailors who accompanied the voyage of Christopher Columbus in 1492. If they couldn't think of a name, they would probably suggest that such a person must have accompanied that voyage or one soon afterwards. They might think the first Christian born in North America was either a Spanish colonist or a *Mayflower* settler, and the first native American baptized as a Christian would be someone converted during the Spanish settlement in the Caribbean. Or perhaps they might jump forward in time and name Pocahontas, who converted to Christianity in Virginia in the early seventeenth century.

It is highly unlikely that anybody would suggest that the answer to the first question is Thorvald Erikson, brother of Leif the Lucky. Or that the answer to the second question is Snorri Thorfinnson, the child of Thorfinn Karlsefni and Gudrid Thorbjornsdottir, who had sailed to North America from Brattahlid on Greenland. Or that the answer to the third question is two *skraeling* children, captured on *Markland* by the companions of Thorfinn Karlsefni and Gudrid Thorbjornsdottir.

The fact that all these people lived in the early eleventh century and were Vikings would astonish many people. But, if the sagas are to be believed, these names are the answers to those three questions. Evidence discovered in the twentieth century gives us a great deal of confidence in the general witness of the saga accounts. Traditions that were long dismissed as tall Norse tales now appear to be corroborated, in outline at least, by the findings of archaeology. These were, indeed, the first Christians anywhere in the Americas.

THE MYSTERY OF THE LOCATION OF VINLAND

Two thirteenth-century Icelandic sagas tell the remarkable stories of Viking Age voyages to North America. These sagas are *Eiríks saga rauða* (*Erik the Red's Saga*) and *Grœnlendinga saga* (*Saga of the Greenlanders*). Together they tell the story of the discovery of a place called Vinland, located west of Greenland. The accounts differ in a number of ways but often one source adds detail and atmosphere to an event which is only recorded in general outline in the other. However, each also contains information independent of the other, and sometimes they tell decidedly different versions of what was clearly a related tradition.

A straightforward example of the latter concerns the ship used to make an exploratory voyage. *Eiríks saga rauða* states that it was Thorstein Erikson (i.e. Erik the Red's son) who purchased a ship from the father of a woman named Gudrid Thorbjornsdottir, in which to explore to the west. In contrast, *Grœnlendinga saga* says that the ship was bought from a seafarer by the name of Bjarni Herjolfson, by Eric's son Leif. Even supposing it was possible to fully untangle these complex matters and decide between the two traditions where they conflict, this would not be the place in which to attempt this. It would involve overly complex unravelling of sources, motifs and themes, and the compilers of these sources were producing works of Icelandic literature, rather than subjecting their material to the scrutiny of twenty-first-century source criticism. As a consequence, it is not now possible to decide between these traditions where they conflict with each other. The most we can say is that there was a body of Old Norse tradition which gave rise to these works of Icelandic saga-literature which insisted that Viking adventurers, in around the year 1000, sailed far to the west of Greenland and discovered new lands. That there was some reality behind these claims is now certain, and that those named played parts in this adventure we can be fairly sure, even if we cannot nail down every aspect of the journeys and the personages involved in them.

What is indisputable is that Scandinavians sailed the wild seas of the North Atlantic and were the first recorded European discoverers of North America. They did this almost five centuries before the voyage of Christopher Columbus and those that followed him westward to make landfall on the mainland of the North American continent. The first landing in the Americas was a Viking achievement and one accomplished by Scandinavian adventurers who included Christians among their number. These were, indeed, the first American Christians.

The far western lands that were discovered, according to these medieval accounts, were for a long time regarded as legendary and the products of thirteenth-century Icelandic imagination. That has changed over the last century. As a result of more critical study of the medieval texts themselves, comparison of their accounts with the geography of North America, and conclusive archaeological evidence of Norse settlement in Canada, it is clear that Norse voyages this far west did occur.

The archaeological evidence comes from a coastal site known as L'Anse aux Meadows, on the northern tip of Newfoundland, Canada. Discovered in 1960, it is the only indisputable evidence of Viking settlement in North America. Unearthed at a site once known as "the old Indian camp", between 1961 and 1968, the evidence here comes in the form of grass-covered mounds concealing eight complete buildings and the remains of a ninth.[1] Made from earth walls around wooden frames, the buildings were a mixture of dwellings and workshops. From items discovered, it seems clear that these workshops included a smithy (Building J) which contained a forge and iron slag from blacksmithing; a carpentry workshop (Building D); and an area where boats were repaired. This last area was identified from the worn iron rivets discovered there. Artefacts recovered from the excavations included an oil lamp made from stone, a whetstone, a bone knitting needle, a bronze pin, and part of a spindle used in textile production. This latter identification is corroborated by stone loom-weights discovered in Building G and it seems that weaving had occurred in this building.[2] This, along with the characteristic pin, indicates that women as well as men lived at the site. In total the site produced about 800 wooden, bronze, bone and stone artefacts.[3]

Estimates of the possible population at any one time have ranged between 30 and 160.[4] Food remains included butternuts, caribou, fish, seals, walrus and whales, as well as many types of bird. Remains of fox, lynx, marten and wolf may point to animals hunted for their fur. Bears may have been hunted for both food and fur. Harsh winters mean that this coastal site was probably only seasonally occupied and further settlement sites may await discovery further south. The three dwellings, one forge and four workshops are sited on a narrow terrace which overlooks a peat bog and a small brook. These peat-turf buildings and attendant artefacts bear striking similarities to evidence from Viking Age Greenland and Iceland.[5]

Evidence of more turf-walled buildings and the smelting of bog iron (found by archaeological work in 2015) may indicate a further habitation site was located at Point Rosee, in south-western Newfoundland. The matter, though, is open to some debate, although Norse settlers seem the most likely explanation for the site. Another possible site is that of Tanfield Valley (or Nanook) on the southernmost tip of Baffin Island, Nunavut, Canada. This site may contain medieval Scandinavian textiles and metalwork, while wooden items found in excavated sites associated with people of the now-extinct indigenous paleo-Inuit Dorset culture (named from Cape Dorset, at the southern tip of Baffin Island) may suggest trade with the Norse. The people of the Dorset culture were the original inhabitants, rather than the Inuit (who later inhabited these regions). However, the Vikings may have also encountered the Thule people, the ancestors of all modern Inuit, as these migrated into the region. What is certain is that the Vikings disparagingly referred to them as *skraelings* (wretches, shouters, savages).

We cannot be certain but there is a likelihood that the site at L'Anse aux Meadows may correspond to the camp called Straumfjörð in *Eiríks saga rauða* (*Eric the Red's Saga*). There are also debates concerning the other places mentioned in the sagas. The place the sagas know as Helluland takes its name from the Old Norse word for flat stones, and today many experts believe that this was Baffin Island, now in the Canadian territory of Nunavut. The place called Markland in the sagas is derived from the Old Norse word for forest and probably referred to the coast of what is Labrador today.

The key name of Vinland itself has given rise to much more speculation. This is where the furthest settlement took place and so marks the furthest extreme of Viking exploration. At first glance, the place was named from the Norse word for grapes or wine. If so, it probably refers to an area stretching southwards from Newfoundland to the Gulf of Saint Lawrence and it may have encompassed a region as far south as north-eastern New Brunswick, the northernmost growing range for wild grapes (hence *Vinland* or wine land).

However, the matter is more complex. The actual name Vinland was first recorded before the thirteenth-century compilation of the Icelandic sagas and is found in the writings of Adam of Bremen, in Book IV of his history of the Hamburg-Bremen church (written c. 1075). In this book, the place name appears in the German form *Winland*. Adam implied that it referred to wine, which links it to the idea of grapes. It is this name which later appears in the thirteenth-century Icelandic account *Grænlendinga saga* (*Saga of the Greenlanders*). The use of the term there suggests that the reference was to the Old Norse word *vínber* (wineberries). This term was used for a number of plants from which wine could be made: grapes, currants, bilberries. This opens up the geographical range considerably, since these plants have very different growing ranges. The matter has been thrown even further open by the suggestion that the term *vínviður* (grapevines) found in *Grænlendinga saga* should actually have been the word *viður* (wood). If this is correct then *vínber* need not have referred to grapes at all. Instead, it could have been a reference to any berries observed growing on trees.[6]

As a consequence, we cannot be entirely sure whether the thirteenth-century Icelandic accounts refer to wild grapes – a word derived from the wine-making plants mentioned earlier by Adam of Bremen – or some other wild berry capable of being fermented in order to make wine. Nor can we be entirely sure how far down the eastern coast of North America the eleventh-century Vikings reached. What is absolutely clear is that they certainly did not find wild grapes growing at L'Anse aux Meadows, currently the only certain Viking site on the North American continent.[7] So, we can definitely conclude that L'Anse aux Meadows was not Vinland. That must lie further south (whatever berries lie behind the name Vinland).

The dig at L'Anse aux Meadows unearthed clues concerning more southerly journeys by the Viking settlers who built the houses and workshops there. This evidence was in the form of remains of butternuts (or white walnuts), which grow in the eastern United States and south-eastern Canada. Their coastal range stretches from New Brunswick to Connecticut, although they are not present continuously along the coast. A cautious conclusion can therefore be reached that Vinland may have been as far south as the St Lawrence River and parts of New Brunswick. This is because this is the northernmost limit for the growth of butternuts (white walnuts) and wild grapes. Between them, these provide a triangulation which suggests the most likely location of the furthest Viking exploration of the North American seaboard.

Before we leave this matter, it is worth mentioning that there is one other possible reference to Vinland. This occurred on the Hønen Runestone which was noted in 1815, at Norderhov, Norway, but is now lost. This runestone disappeared from the farm at Hønen between 1828 and 1834. However, it had been painted in 1823 and this painting (also since lost) was copied in 1838. The form of the runes has led to an approximate date of 1050 being suggested for the original inscription.

In a runic inscription in Old Norse, these words (translated) can be read as: *Vínlandi á ísa* ("from Vinland over ice"). However, it may be better interpreted as representing *vindkalda á ísa* ("over the wind-cold ice").[8] Whichever is correct, it does not give us a geographical fix on the actual location of Vinland. Consequently, though intriguing, it does not add to the locational information gleaned from the thirteenth-century Icelandic sagas.

This just leaves the Kensington Runestone, from Douglas County, Minnesota, and named from the nearest settlement. This large slab of greywacke stone is covered with runes on its face and side. It was discovered by Olof Ohman, a Swedish immigrant, in 1898. The area in which it was found had been settled by a large number of Scandinavian immigrants.

The inscription on the stone claims to tell the story of a fourteenth-century journey to the area by a joint group of Swedish and Norwegian explorers. It was swiftly declared a forgery after its inscription was studied at the University of Minnesota and by linguists in Scandinavia. As well as there being no persuasive fourteenth-century context which would explain the presence of such a memorial runestone in Minnesota, aspects of its language, grammar, rune-forms and use of a calendar date (1362) all point to it being a nineteenth-century forgery, produced in an area with a strong interest in Scandinavian history, by someone wishing to create a local connection to their original homeland. It is also uncharacteristically detailed in comparison with the evidence from authentic medieval runic inscriptions. However, belief in its authenticity continues in some quarters, despite the strength of the academic evidence against this.[9] Today, the Kensington Runestone is displayed at the Runestone Museum in Alexandria, Minnesota.

This said, it is reasonable to assume that further archaeological investigation will eventually find more evidence for Norse settlement on the eastern coast. When this occurs it will add to the persuasive archaeological evidence from L'Anse aux Meadows.

THE OUTLINE OF EVENTS AS FOUND IN THE SAGAS

As we have seen, the voyages to Vinland are found in two thirteenth-century Icelandic sagas.[10] The account found in *Eiríks saga rauða* (*Erik the Red's Saga*) opens with a party of newcomers arriving in Greenland from Iceland. These include a woman named Gudrid Thorbjornsdottir. Half the immigrants die on the journey but Gudrid ends up living in Erik's residence.

It is about this time that King Olaf Tryggvason of Norway instructs Leif, Erik's son, to convert the Greenlanders to Christianity. Leif is blown off course and chances on a land west of Greenland. Here he discovers self-sown wheat, grapes and maple trees. Sailing back to Greenland he rescues shipwrecked people, and thereafter Leif Erikson is also known as Leif the Lucky.

Following this, Erik's other son, Thorstein, buys a ship from the father of Gudrid and spends a summer sailing the Atlantic, but fails to get to Vinland. On returning to Greenland, Thorstein marries Gudrid. But he soon dies and then rises from the dead to tell her fortune. Gudrid moves to live in the settlement of Brattahlid on Greenland. There she marries Thorfinn Karlsefni, who has recently arrived. Together they set off for Vinland in the company of Erik's daughter, Freydis, and Thorvard her husband, and also Erik's son, Thorvald.

They pass different lands that they name *Bjarneyjar* (bear islands) and much further on *Helluland, Bjarney* (bear island) and *Markland*. At a place they call *Kjalarnes*, they discover the keel of a ship (a hint they are not the first to sail this far west). They pass an area they call *Furðustrandir* (wonderful beaches) and stop at a place called *Straumfjörð* (possibly L'Anse aux Meadows?) where they discover a beached whale. From there one ship sails north around Kjalarnes, while Thorfinn Karlsefni sails south to a place he names *Hop*. Here they settle and trade with natives they call *skraelings*. These are frightened away by a bull brought by the settlers. Eventually a conflict breaks out with the *skraelings* but they are frightened off when Freydis bears her breasts and slaps them with the flat of a sword. Leaving there, Thorfinn Karlsefni kills five *skraelings* he discovers asleep on the shore in skin sleeping-bags.

Sailing around Kjalarnes, Thorvald Erikson is killed by a one-legged creature, with an arrow. There he is buried. Back in Straumfjörð, the settlers quarrel over women and we learn that they have been in Vinland three years, since that is the age of the son of Thorfinn Karlsefni and Gudrid, who was born in this new land. Leaving there, they sail to Markland, where they come upon five *skraelings*. They capture two of them who are children. They lose a ship on the way back to Greenland, but Thorfinn Karlsefni and Gudrid finally go on to Iceland the next summer, where they settle and stay.

In *Grænlendinga saga* (*Saga of the Greenlanders*) a number of these events also feature but there are significant differences too. A Viking explorer, Bjarni Herjolfson, is blown off course and reaches land west of Greenland but does not land there. Leif Erikson buys his ship and sails off to explore the strange land to the west. Erik the Red elects not to accompany him after falling from his horse and injuring himself. Leif discovers Helluland, Markland and Vinland and later rescues shipwrecked people. These include Thorir (the husband of Gudrid), who dies the following winter. This is the same woman that we met in *Eiríks saga rauða*.

It is then that Thorvald Erikson sets out for Vinland. In this account he leads the expedition, rather than simply accompanying it – in the company of Thorfinn Karlsefni and Gudrid – as he does in *Eiríks saga rauða*. His ship is damaged after being driven ashore at *Kjalarnes*. Finding nine *skraelings* sheltering under three boats made from animal hide, they kill eight but one escapes. A large number then attack them and an arrow kills Thorvald Erikson, who is buried at a place they call *Krossanes*.

Back in Greenland, Thorstein Erikson marries Gudrid and they set off for Vinland to retrieve the body of Thorvald Erikson. This is completely different from the account found in *Eiríks saga rauða*, where Thorvald Erikson travels with Gudrid and her husband, and is killed as part of this joint expedition. Anyway, to return to *Grænlendinga saga*, the mission is abandoned and they return to Greenland, where Thorstein Erikson dies, rises from the dead to tell the fortune of Gudrid and is eventually buried at Brattahlid on Greenland.

Thorfinn Karlsefni arrives in Greenland and there he marries the twice-widowed Gudrid. They decide to emigrate to Vinland and take their livestock with them. They reach a place they know as Leif's Camp, where they find a beached whale. There they gather grapes and hunt. They stay there for the winter. In the spring they meet *skraelings* who come to the camp to trade but are frightened of the bull. Gudrid gives birth to Thorfinn Karlsefni's son, Snorri. They are attacked by the *skraelings* but fight them off. The next year Thorfinn Karlsefni and Gudrid sail back to Greenland with timber and skins.

Finally, we come to the voyage of Freydis Eriksdottir and her husband, Thorvard. Consequently, in *Grœnlendinga saga*, she has her own voyage, rather than sailing in the company of Thorfinn Karlsefni and Gudrid, along with her brother Thorvald Erikson, as she does in *Eiríks saga rauða*. Incited by Freydis, this expedition ends in bloodshed at Leif's Camp. In this violence, Freydis slaughters the five women of the men who have already been killed at her bidding after the men in her company are reluctant to do this. After these murders, she and her company take possession of the ship belonging to the slaughtered men and sail back to Greenland, meeting up with Thorfinn Karlsefni, who is preparing to sail on to Norway. Leif Erikson eventually hears of the crimes committed by his sister. He condemns her but takes no action against her.

The saga ends with Thorfinn Karlsefni and Gudrid having a successful trip to Norway and finally settling on Iceland, where they prosper.

THE FIRST CHRISTIAN SETTLERS IN NORTH AMERICA

According to the saga accounts, the voyages to Vinland took place at an important point in the history of Christian conversion in the North Atlantic. It was in the year 1000 that Iceland officially converted to Christianity after a period of tension between Christianity and the pagan beliefs of the Viking inhabitants (see Chapter 11). In addition, a number of those present on the Vinland explorations had strong ties to both Norway (recently converted to Christianity, see Chapter 8) and the Irish Sea region and the Western and Northern Isles, where Norse settlers had been influenced by indigenous Christian beliefs and culture to varying degrees (see Chapters 5 and 14). As a result of this, we should not be surprised to find that Christians sailed alongside pagans in these western adventures. In this way *Grœnlendinga saga* opens by telling us that Herjolf (the father of the discoverer of Vinland,

Bjarni Herjolfson) emigrated to Greenland with Erik the Red in the company of a Hebridean poet who was a Christian. Overall, though, "Heathen were the people of Greenland at that time."[11]

Later we are told that Erik the Red died before Greenland had converted to Christianity but at least one of his sons (Thorvald) is described as being a Christian in the account of his death (see below). In the same way we are told, in a roundabout way, that Thorstein Erikson was also a Christian. This Thorstein Erikson had married Gudrid Thorbjornsdottir (the widow of Thorir the Norwegian) and he and his wife were invited to stay at the farm of a man named Thorstein the Black. When giving the invitation, Thorstein the Black said that he was of a different religion to Thorstein Erikson but that the latter had the better religion. Given that Gudrid is described as a Christian and Thorstein Erikson later rises from the dead to prophesy her future Christian pilgrimage, building of a church on Iceland and taking holy orders, it is clear that we are meant to assume that Thorstein Erikson was a Christian, as was Gudrid. To reinforce this conclusion, the compiler of *Grœnlendinga saga* earlier tells us that Greenland converted to Christianity immediately before his account of the marriage of Thorstein Erikson to Gudrid. *Eiríks saga rauða* explicitly states that both Gudrid and her father Thorbjorn are Christians.

THE FIRST CHRISTIAN BURIED IN NORTH AMERICA

Grœnlendinga saga contains a record of the first Christian buried in North America. Its account of the death of Thorvald Erikson includes the Norse explorers being warned of an impending attack from *skraelings*. They are warned by an unidentified voice, and we are not sure whether the compiler intended this voice to be identified as fate (prevalent in Old Norse pagan beliefs) or the Christian God. What comes next, though, is unambiguous. Thorvald Erikson receives a fatal arrow wound in the armpit. Before he dies he requests that he be buried in the newly explored land, with the significant detail that his companions should "mark my grave with crosses at the head and foot".[12] For this reason the spot was remembered as *Krossanes*, which means Cross Point. With this telling detail we have the first record of any Christian buried in North America. It is not now possible to identify where this took place. The saga account indicates that it occurred in a sheltered cove on a forested cape, within fjords to the east of *Kjalarnes*. The exact location is the subject of much speculation. It may have been somewhere on the coast of Newfoundland or perhaps the coast of Labrador or Cape Breton Island. The matter will probably always remain uncertain.

THE FIRST CHRISTIAN BORN IN NORTH AMERICA AND THE FIRST NATIVE AMERICANS BAPTIZED

Grænlendinga saga also contains a passing reference to the first child born to a Christian family in North America. After Gudrid and her third husband, Thorfinn Karlsefni, sail to the new lands, they eventually establish their settlement at Leif's Camp, in Old Norse *Leifsbúðir*. As with many of the locations in the sagas it is not possible to definitively locate this place but it may have been on the northern tip of Newfoundland. Here they spend a winter and a summer and, after trading milk and milk products (but not weapons) with *skraelings*, they eventually build a defended stockade around their farm. It is here – in autumn and just before the start of their second winter at the site – that Gudrid gives birth to a son. So Snorri Thorfinnson has the historic fame of being the first child born to a Christian family in North America.

It is following this that the *skraelings* attack the camp but are beaten off with many casualties in a battle in which the bull of the settlers is used to lead the defence of the farm, the natives being afraid of the bull. Snorri survives to be taken back to Greenland, as a three-year-old, by his parents (a detail included in the account found in *Eiríks saga rauða*). From there the family eventually move back to Iceland. *Eiríks saga rauða* tells of how, after three years in the new lands, Thorfinn Karlsefni leads his group back home by way of Markland (probably Labrador), where they capture two *skraeling* children, two boys. These they teach Old Norse and baptize them. One hesitates to call these converts, since it is not clear that they had any choice in the matter. However, what one can say is that they were the first recorded Native Americans to be baptized as Christians.

OTHER CHRISTIAN FEATURES OF THE SAGA ACCOUNTS

Eiríks saga rauða opens with an account of the voyage from Caithness to Iceland, via Orkney, of a woman named Aud, the "deep-minded". On settling in Iceland we are told that she prayed on a hill called *Krossholar* (cross hills) where she had crosses erected "for she was baptized and a devout Christian".[13] Later in the saga we are introduced to Gudrid Thorbjornsdottir after she has emigrated to Iceland. The settlers are finding life tough and "a seeress who was called the 'Little Prophetess'"[14] visited the settlement where Gudrid lived and was asked to carry out magic rites in order to foretell the future of the settlement. At first, the saga explains, Gudrid refuses to take part in these because she is a Christian woman. Eventually, though, she is persuaded to assist because she is told it will help the household. This she does and we are told she chants the songs well and is rewarded with a prophecy of the successful future of her family. It is interesting to note that Gudrid's father is not present because he has refused to remain on the farm "while such heathen practices were going on".[15]

As well as revealing that Gudrid comes from a Christian family, this story gives us an interesting insight into the complexity of this period of conversion, when Christian beliefs and pagan practices co-existed. The same saga also recounts how Leif Erikson was commissioned by King Olaf Tryggvason of Norway with the task of converting Greenland to Christianity and how it was on the journey back to Greenland from Norway that he inadvertently ended up in North America as a result of a stormy ocean-crossing. On reaching Greenland he preached the new faith and it was accepted by his father's wife but not by Erik himself. As a result she built a church some way from their farm and refused to sleep with Erik because he was a pagan. Erik was not happy.

The same saga underscores the Christian faith of Gudrid by stating that, before she faced her dead husband Thorstein Erikson (who had briefly risen from the dead), she was advised to "cross herself and ask the Lord for help". In a revealing statement, her recently dead husband announces that he is briefly returning from the dead by "God's will" and that in revealing the future to Gudrid he will, he says of himself, "improve my prospects".[16] The implication is that the Christian God has granted him this prophetic insight and that, in sharing it, he will make more certain his place in heaven. This may also be an oblique reference to easing a passage through purgatory, as understood by medieval Catholic Christians. When he speaks to Gudrid, he asks to be buried at a church and not in unconsecrated ground at the farm, as has been the traditional practice.

The theme of conflict between the new and the old faiths is vividly made clear in Vinland itself during Thorfinn Karlsefni's exploration. Suffering hunger that first winter, the saga-writer explained that they prayed to God. But one of their number, Thorhall the Huntsman, rejected their reliance on Christian faith and claimed that a beached whale they had found was a reward for his composing a poem in honour of the pagan god Thor. "Didn't Old Redbeard prove to be more help than your Christ?"[17] But the whale meat made them sick and so they threw it away, called on the mercy of God and the weather improved so they could go fishing. The saga-writer went on to say that Thorhall the Huntsman (who continued to compose pagan poetry, this time referring to Odin) was eventually driven ashore in Ireland by storms, and was enslaved there.

Grænlendinga saga closes with the story of Gudrid after her adventures in Vinland. She and Thorfinn Karlsefni take trade goods to Norway and then eventually settle in Iceland, at Glaumbær, Skagafjörður, in northern Iceland. After Thorfinn Karlsefni dies and their son Snorri marries, Gudrid makes a pilgrimage to the south. It is likely that Rome is implied here but the saga-writer is not explicit. When she returns to Iceland, she finds that Snorri has built a church at their farm, where she lives out her days as a Christian nun and anchoress (one living a solitary life of prayer). From Snorri were descended three bishops in the later Icelandic church. That the saga ends with these statements reveals the Christian faith of the compiler and the role of Christianity within the lives of this family of Vinland explorers.

CHAPTER 13

A Christian Viking King of England

Between 1016 and 1035 England was ruled by a Viking Christian king, monarch of Denmark and England, and was part of a powerful North Sea Empire. The ruler who presided over this was Cnut the Great. This raises the question of how Christian faith and the church were affected by what was, in effect, a Viking Conquest. How did Vikings act as Christians when they were rulers in England?

THE SHOCKING RETURN OF THE VIKINGS

Most people are aware of the Norman Conquest of 1066 but far fewer have heard of the Viking Conquest of 1016, despite the fact that, more than any other single factor, the unintended consequences of this Viking Conquest led to the Norman Conquest.[1]

The Viking attacks on Anglo-Saxon England fell into two great phases. The first of these phases began in the late eighth century, then escalated during the ninth century. They were frustrated by the resilience of Wessex under Alfred the Great, and rolled back by the campaigns of Alfred's son Edward the Elder and grandson Athelstan. The attacks were finally ended with the death of Erik Bloodaxe (the last Viking king of the kingdom of York) in 954. Under the rule of Edgar (959–975), political stability was established, accompanied by an impressive system of coinage, well-organized taxation, and a national fleet capable of deterring Viking raiders.[2] It looked as if the Viking problems of the past were finally over.

It was not to be. From around 980, the Vikings returned, with devastating effect. The ruler who faced them, Æthelred II (ruled 978–1016), later gained the famously unflattering nickname of *unræd* and so most people now know him as "Æthelred the Unready". In fact, the Old English word *unræd* (meaning "no counsel or wisdom", or perhaps "badly advised") was a biting parody of his actual name, which meant "royal counsel or wisdom".[3] It had, in fact, nothing to do with being unprepared. Æthelred II's death, in 1016, coincided with the culmination of this second phase of Viking Wars and the Viking Conquest of England by Cnut of Denmark.

The return of the Vikings was a shock and prompted a lot of heart-searching by Anglo-Saxon Christians. One of these was Wulfstan (sometimes called Wulfstan II), the archbishop of York until 1023. He is famous for a dramatic sermon that he preached in 1014. It may originally have been written in 1009 and there is evidence that it was reissued and updated several times as disaster unfolded.[4] Its title translates from the Latin original – *Sermo Lupi ad Anglos* – as *The Sermon of the Wolf to the English* and it was a play on his name, which meant "wolf-stone". Wulfstan recorded a great catalogue of sins that stood against the English nation. These were religious, political, social and sexual, and all, in his opinion, stood in the scales against the people of Anglo-Saxon England. His sermon contains one of the relatively rare examples of the term "Viking" being used in Old English literature. It appeared in an example of the inversion of the social order that disturbed Wulfstan. He recounted how a slave might desert his master and "become[s] a Viking". Then, when he killed a socially superior Anglo-Saxon, no compensation (Old English *wergild*) was paid to the victim's family, since Vikings were not about to pay for a dead Anglo-Saxon. But, in contrast, the Viking army would demand compensation for the runaway and newly fledged Viking if he was killed by an Anglo-Saxon. It seemed that, as well as bringing death and destruction, the Vikings were upturning the whole social order.

Wulfstan did not explain exactly why the Vikings had returned at this time, beyond detailing the specific sins of the English that had led, in his opinion, to this punishment. Along with many contemporaries, Wulfstan oscillated between seeing the Vikings as a punishment sent by God as judgment on a sinful nation (which might be averted by repentance), and as an inevitable accompaniment to the end of the world and the Second Coming of Christ. Such apocalyptic interpretations of the troubled years of the late tenth and early eleventh centuries were not restricted to Anglo-Saxon England. On the Continent, others too reached similar conclusions. Just a little earlier, in the 950s, continental writers had viewed the invasions of Magyar raiders as heralding the revealing of the antichrist and the events leading to the end of the world.[5]

Historians have explored the key question of why the Viking attacks resumed and identified a number of causes that we have encountered. First, after about 965, the exhaustion of the silver mines that had previously supplied the Islamic world caused a silver famine.[6] This was a major problem for Scandinavian elites who had previously relied on recycled Islamic silver coins to produce the prestige items used to reward followers.[7] We have seen (Chapter 10) how this silver trade had drawn Swedish Vikings far down the rivers of Russia. At the same time, the stability brought by the creation of the Viking state of Kiev Rus meant that it was more difficult for Vikings to seize the silver that they had once taken via trade. The free for all in Russia was drawing to a close.

This helps explain the presence of Swedish Vikings in the new phase of Viking attacks on England, as their old routes to the east were being closed down. The discovery of new silver sources in the Hartz mountains in the 960s made Western Europe comparatively rich in silver, and it became a tempting target. Growing centralization of power in the Scandinavian kingdoms made them a more formidable force. The new attacks would be led by kings or would-be kings and were soon on a scale that dwarfed previous invasions. Lacking developed home-grown tax systems, raiding Western Europe was a convenient way to finance kingship in Scandinavia. In the case of England this would eventually lead to the conquest of the country by the king of Denmark.

THE CONQUEST OF ENGLAND BY THE VIKINGS

England was targeted for raids by King Svein Forkbeard of Denmark (ruled c. 986–1014), the son of Harald Bluetooth who had earlier unified Denmark (see Chapter 7). Having deposed his father, he teamed up with Olaf Tryggvason of Norway (see Chapter 8) in 994, in a campaign against England. It proved to be very profitable.

The attacks grew in severity. In 991 the invaders achieved a crushing defeat of the Anglo-Saxon army at the Battle of Maldon (Essex). This inspired a fine Anglo-Saxon heroic poem but this was little consolation to the suffering people of England. As the attacks escalated, huge amounts of money were paid by the English in attempts to buy off the attackers. This has traditionally been described as *Danegeld* (Dane tax) but this term did not actually get coined until decades later and, at the time, it would have been simply described using the Old English word *gafol* (tribute). Runestones in Scandinavia offer testimony to the vast amounts of silver extorted from England. One from Uppland, in Sweden, records that "Áli had this stone put up in his own honour. He took Knútr's *danegeld* in England."[8] Another, also from Sweden, records that Ulf "took three payments of *geld* in England. The first was the one that Tosti paid, then Thorkel, then Cnut".[9] About 35,000 of the silver coins paid to such Vikings have been discovered in Scandinavia.[10]

These extortions and acts of violence led to violent retaliations by the beleaguered Anglo-Saxon state. The most famous occurred on 13 November 1002 when, the *Anglo-Saxon Chronicle* records, "the king [Æthelred II, the Unready] ordered to be slain all the Danish men who were in England – this was done on St Brice's day – because the king had been informed that they would treacherously deprive him, and then all his councillors, of life, and possess this kingdom afterwards".[11] This sounds like ethnic cleansing but, in reality, it probably affected only Scandinavian mercenaries, prominent Danish settlers and merchants who had arrived in England during the previous decade or so.

Physical evidence of retaliation against Viking raiders (but difficult to date to a specific decision such as the St Brice's Day Massacre) have been found at two significant archaeological sites. In 2009, archaeologists working on the Olympic 2012 Weymouth Relief Road (Dorset) found fifty-four headless bodies, accompanied by fifty-one skulls, deposited in an abandoned quarry high up on the coastal ridgeway. These skulls all had at least one cervical vertebra attached, evidence of a head severed by a sharp blow. The absence of belt buckles indicates that they had been naked at the time of death. All were male and the killing represents a single event. Most of those who were executed there were aged between eighteen and twenty-five. This is a similar age range to a comparable mass grave excavated in Oxford, where the bodies of thirty-seven males were removed from a similar execution cemetery.

Radiocarbon dating of the Dorset skeletons indicated that they had died around 970–1025. Analysis of the strontium and oxygen isotopes in their teeth and the study of the collagen from their bones indicated that they grew up in various places within Scandinavia. Since a number of the skulls were missing (i.e. more bodies were present than skulls), it is possible that these missing heads had been taken away as trophies.[12] In a number of cases, it was clear from the bones that it had taken several blows to sever the head. Viking Age warfare was a messy business, but then warfare in any period is never as clean and tidy as non-combatants sometimes like to believe. Regarding the Oxford mass grave, study of the bones indicated that they had eaten a great deal of seafood during their lives. Once again it is very likely that these too were Scandinavians, but in this case we might be more confident in identifying them as Viking mercenaries killed in the St Brice's Day massacre in 1002.[13]

Then, in 1011, the Vikings took Canterbury (Kent) and made the archbishop, Ælfheah, a hostage. The next year they murdered the archbishop, pelting him with bones and ox-skulls before finally striking him on the head with the back of an axe.[14] In the words of the *Chronicle* they were "greatly incensed against the bishop because he would not promise them any money, but forbade that anything should be paid for him. They were also very drunk, for wine from the south had been brought there".[15] The combination of hardened warriors, the cleric's reluctance to sanction payment of a ransom and alcohol produced a lethal cocktail, which shocked even some in the Viking army. One leading member, Thorkell the Tall, deserted to the English.

In 1002 Æthelred II married Emma of Normandy in an attempt to close off Norman ports to Viking fleets attacking England (see Chapter 6). But nothing could save his kingdom from conquest because the attacks continued until, in 1013, Svein of Denmark again took command of the Viking forces invading England. Landing in the Humber estuary, he quickly received the submission of the Northumbrians and the Danish settlers in the *Danelaw* region of the eastern Midlands and East Anglia. Following this, he secured the submission of Oxford, Winchester and Bath. Only London held out because Æthelred was sheltering there and this clearly boosted morale. But the onslaught was now unstoppable and at the end of December 1013, the royal family fled to Normandy. To escape Vikings, they had to flee to the descendants of Vikings. Consequently, Svein of Denmark found himself king of England too. His teenage son Cnut was at his side.

Then, on 3 February 1014, he died suddenly, and the English elites switched sides, sending messengers to Æthelred asking him to return. Cnut was forced to depart to Denmark where his brother had succeeded Svein, as King Harald II, as we have seen. However, in 1015, Cnut invaded again. In April 1016, Æthelred II died and his son, Edmund Ironside, succeeded to the kingdom. He then fought a series of battles against Cnut. Following one fought at Ashingdon (Essex), Edmund and Cnut finally met at Alney (Gloucestershire) and agreed to divide England. By this treaty, Edmund took Wessex, and Cnut took Mercia and the Danelaw. But within a matter of months, Edmund Ironside died and Cnut became king of the whole of England. In 1018 he also succeeded to the throne of Denmark following the death of Harald II, his brother.

A RESURGENCE OF PAGANISM IN THE SECOND WAVE OF VIKING ATTACKS?

At first glance it might seem obvious that a second wave of Viking Wars, culminating in a Viking Conquest of England, would lead to the revival of paganism in England. As we have already seen (in Chapters 3 and 4) the first phase of the Viking Wars had led to the conversion of these new Scandinavian settlers to Christianity (at least nominally) during the tenth century. So much so that the last Viking ruler of the kingdom of York (Erik Bloodaxe), who died in 954, was, according to some evidence, a Christian – at least in name. Then the Vikings appeared again and this seemed to threaten to undermine all that Christianity had achieved in eastern and northern England.

However, things were more complex. A number of the new invaders had been converted to Christianity in Scandinavia or rapidly converted once they moved to England. This needs to be remembered, despite the fact that the Anglo-Saxon sources uniformly describe the new set of invaders as enemies of Christianity, even as precursors of antichrist and the imminent end of the world. However, the despoiling of English monasteries in the late tenth and early eleventh centuries is more readily explainable as economic exploitation than an expression of anti-Christian sentiments.

A key example of this complexity comes from the royal family of the Viking conquerors. As we have already seen (in Chapter 7), Cnut's father, Svein Forkbeard, had converted to Christianity during his time in Scandinavia. Despite his earlier pagan background, there is evidence that he then went on to promote Christianity in both Denmark and Norway. It has to be admitted that this followed a youth of paganism. In explaining this shift we need to recall that it was his father – Harald Bluetooth – who had converted to Christianity and promoted this among his Danish contemporaries. Svein was not the first young noble to be hungry for power and to establish an opposition to a reigning father in pursuit of his own ambitions. This probably accompanied the creation of a "pagan party" but it did not last. In addition, this phase of his life got more attention because he and a number of Danish rulers sought to limit the influence of Germans in Scandinavia and fell out with the archbishop of Hamburg-Bremen, from where key histories of Scandinavia in this period would eventually be written. These later writers were not fans of the earlier kings of Denmark and this influenced how they portrayed them.

This political and religious spin affected more than Svein. The Norwegian Viking Olaf Tryggvason, who later became ruler of Norway (995–1000), was a Christian. In 994, he was confirmed at Andover (Hampshire), with Æthelred II acting as his sponsor. He went on to promote Christianity in Norway (see Chapter 8). Despite this, the German chronicler Adam of Bremen, writing around 1080, appears unsure of whether Olaf had died a Christian. But once again we are seeing the influence of the promotion of Hamburg-Bremen, since it seems that Adam wanted to play down English influence in the conversion of Scandinavia. More convincingly, mid-thirteenth-century Icelandic saga writers state that Olaf was an active Christian, who encouraged the conversion of Iceland.[16]

So, by the time Svein and Cnut conquered England, they were officially Christian (Cnut a third-generation one), as were many of those who followed them. The new king of England was at least semi-Christian and his Christian character and credentials became more pronounced after the conquest of 1016.

A CHRISTIAN VIKING KING OF ENGLAND: CNUT THE GREAT

Once in power (he ruled 1016–1035) Cnut actively cooperated with Archbishop Wulfstan of York in the legal reinforcement of Christianity and the active suppression of paganism. Just three years after his victory, in 1019, he wrote from Denmark promising that he would be a good Christian king in England. This would be shown in practical terms through his upholding of the laws of the powerful mid-tenth-century Anglo-Saxon king Edgar. In addition, Cnut called on those who read the letter to confess their sins, keep the Sunday fast, honour the saints, and work towards gaining "the bliss of the heavenly kingdom".[17] Not words we normally associate with a Viking ruler.

In 1020 Cnut founded a church at the site of the Battle of Ashingdon, an earlier event that had played a major part in his conquest.[18] When he visited Denmark in 1023, he returned to England with Bishop Gerbrand of Roskilde for the archbishop of Canterbury to anoint. This was the action of a Christian king who wanted the Christianity of Denmark to be sanctioned by association with a much older and highly respected church (i.e. that of England). That same year, the body of the martyred Ælfheah – the murdered archbishop of Canterbury – was brought with great ceremony from the church of St Paul's in London to Canterbury (Kent). Cnut accompanied the body when it was carried across the Thames to Southwark, and Emma, his queen, accompanied the procession on the final part of its journey to Canterbury. It is difficult to imagine a more striking contrast with the pagan past. It is reminiscent of the way in which earlier Viking converts to Christianity had come to revere the martyred King Edmund of East Anglia in the late ninth century (see Chapter 3). The translation was not popular with the monks of St Paul's or with the Londoners, since they felt they were losing relics of a venerated martyr. In a further gesture towards the church at Canterbury, Cnut gifted it the port and revenues of Sandwich (Kent). Emma continued this promotion of Canterbury when she acquired the arm of St Bartholomew from Benevento, in Italy, and gifted it to Canterbury.

Cnut made himself a loyal son of the church. The Old Norse poem *Knútsdrapa* (*Cnut's poem*) describes him as being "dear to the emperor [the Holy Roman Emperor],[19] close to Peter [the papacy]". In 1027 Cnut went to Rome to witness the crowning of Emperor Conrad II. In a letter to his English subjects, Cnut explained that he had also visited Rome to seek forgiveness of his sins and the security of England. As a patriotic Danish-Englishman, while there he had negotiated a reduction in the amount that English archbishops had to pay when they journeyed to Rome to collect their pallium (symbol of office) and he also gained assurances that English and Danish merchants could travel to Rome toll-free. But his anglophile tendencies only stretched so far in the *Realpolitik* of international relations for, in his need to improve relationships with the German emperor, he thereafter ceased promoting Canterbury (as opposed to Hamburg-Bremen) as the source of missionary activity in Scandinavia.

In a splendidly decorated document, called the *Liber Vitae* (*Book of Life*) of the New Minster at Winchester, Cnut and his queen are depicted presenting a gold cross to the minster. Christ is seated in majesty above the scene, the Virgin Mary and St Peter flank him, an angel places a crown on Cnut's head and points to Christ and a similarly pointing angel holds a veil over Emma's head. Below the king and queen we can see the monks of New Minster. The cross in question was lost in the twelfth century but the picture survives. It shows how Cnut and his queen were understood as standing in a spiritual hierarchy. Above them was Christ (who made the kingship sacred) but they were linked to him by the heavenly host (the angels) who blessed their rule.[20]

Cnut also ordered a valuable gold shrine to be constructed for St Edith at Wilton Abbey (Wiltshire) and he donated the gold-and silver-encased arm of St Cyriacus to Westminster Abbey. In addition, he patronized the cult of St Edmund of East Anglia – not the first Viking to do so. The cult of sacred relics was, therefore, as integral a part of Cnut's kingship and authority as it was of any other early medieval ruler.

Arguably the most enduring image that exists for most modern readers is Cnut failing in his attempt to hold back the tide, and getting his feet wet. This story has even influenced the Latin name of a wading bird, called the knot. In Latin it is *Calidris canuta*, because of its habit of feeding along the shoreline, imitating Cnut whose feet were in the sea. The story first appears in the twelfth century in a chronicle written by Henry of Huntingdon, who recounted a tradition that Cnut had his throne placed by the seashore and there commanded the tide to halt. Despite this royal command the waves:

> *Dashed over his feet and legs without respect to his royal person. Then the king leapt backwards, saying: 'Let all men know how empty and worthless is the power of kings, for there is none worthy of the name, but He whom heaven, earth, and sea obey by eternal laws.'*

He then hung his gold crown on a crucifix, and never wore it again, "to the honour of God the almighty King".[21]

The story may have been an expansion of one told by the late eleventh-century chronicler Goscelin of St-Bertin. He described how Cnut placed his crown on a crucifix at Winchester, but made no mention of the sea "with the explanation that the king of kings was more worthy of it than he".[22] Henry of Huntingdon may have embellished this tradition with an even more graphic image of the impotence of human kingship in the face of the workings of God's creation. Although this is usually presented as an example of the arrogance of Cnut,[23] the story was actually designed to illustrate his humility and his recognition of the power of God.[24] It is noteworthy that the contemporary source known as the *Encomium Emmae* (*In Praise of* [Queen] *Emma*) makes no mention of this tradition, so it probably never happened. This is particularly likely to be the case, since this work depicts Cnut as a pious Christian king and so would have found the story very useful. Although the story is clearly legendary, it shows a fitting association of a Viking king with the sea.

Although keen to present himself as a Christian king, Cnut was also a ruthless ruler. He executed a number of leading Anglo-Saxons who might prove difficult in future. These included Eadric Streona, earl of Mercia, who had betrayed both Æthelred II and Edmund Ironside when Eadric finally backed Cnut, and Uhtred, earl of Northumbria. Edmund Ironside's pregnant wife and little son were sent to Sweden to be killed but were spared by the reluctant king of Sweden. They eventually had to go as far as Kiev Rus and Hungary to escape the long arm of Cnut's vengeance. That Kiev Rus featured in their exile tangles yet more Vikings into the story. Eadwig, the younger brother of Edmund Ironside, was executed.

Cnut promoted other Anglo-Saxons who owed their positions to the new regime. Among these was Godwin of Sussex whose son Harold would eventually become king in January 1066 and then later meet his death at Hastings in the October of that same year. Cnut elevated some of his followers to high rank in England. He placed a leading Norwegian, Erik of Lade, as earl of Northumbria, and Thorkell the Tall (who earlier had gone over to Æthelred II after the murder of the archbishop of Canterbury) became earl of East Anglia. But he was careful to avoid the impression of Danes making a clean sweep, with all the resentment that would prompt. These appointments were those of a shrewd young man, but accompanied by a willingness to use unflinching violence.

He had also married Emma, the widow of Æthelred II, which strengthened his connections with Anglo-Saxon government and Normandy. Since Æthelred II's two sons by Emma were sheltering in exile there, this helped encourage the Normans to go no further in their support for these half-Norman Anglo-Saxon royals. When Cnut married Emma, he was already married to a woman named Ælfgifu of Northampton, but this did not stop him from putting her to one side. However, this did not mean that Ælfgifu of Northampton was treated with disrespect, since she acted as Cnut's regent in Norway between 1030 and 1034 and it was her son (not Emma's by Cnut) who seized the English throne on Cnut's death in 1035.

In Cnut's England, other Scandinavian Christians also had a positive impact on the life of the nation. At Kirkdale (North Yorkshire), the sundial at St Gregory's Minster records:

Orm, son of Gamal, bought St Gregory's church when it was completely ruined and collapsed, and he had it constructed recently from the ground to Christ and St Gregory, in the days of King Edward and in the days of Earl Tosti [Tostig].[25]

While this inscription dates from 1055 to 1065 (Cnut died in 1035), it indicates how Scandinavians had integrated into the culture of Christian England by the middle of the eleventh century.[26] We can rightly imagine many more like Orm who did not leave a written record of their actions.

So, what are we to make of the pagan motifs that influenced art and culture in Cnut's kingdom of England? For these certainly existed. The poem known as *Knútsdráper*, probably written for Cnut's Christian English court, still apparently celebrated the mind-set of the northern pagan world. The poet, named Hallvarthr, referred to Cnut three times with a title based on the name of a pagan god. Twice he referred to *Miðgarðsormr*, the world-serpent who appeared in Norse mythology as a huge monster encircling the world and causing destruction at the end of the world. In addition, he referred to Odin's horse and also to valkyries. Another poem, *Liðsmannaflokkr* (*Poem of the Men of the Fleet*) – preserved in a late-fourteenth-century Icelandic manuscript called *Flateyjarbók* (*Flat-island book*)[27] – similarly used pagan Viking references to gods such as Odin, to goddesses and to a valkyrie. Mythical Norse beasts were engraved on stonework, such as a grave-slab discovered in St Paul's churchyard, London, and also appear on brooches. A slab of stone that once formed part of a decorative frieze on the Old Minster, Winchester (until it was demolished under the Normans in 1093–1094), illustrated a scene from the story of Sigmund and a terrible she-wolf, which occurs in the late-thirteenth-century *Völsunga saga* (*Saga of the Volsungs*).

All of this should not be overstated, though. In the poem written by Hallvarthr, Cnut's power is described as coming from the Christian God, despite the pagan language of some of the poetic expressions.[28] Cnut banned pagan practices in the 1020s, and this can clearly be seen in the law code known as *II Cnut* and also in the document known as the *Law of the Northumbrian Priests*. In *II Cnut* it was spelled out exactly what constituted pagan practices that were now outlawed:

> *...if one worships idols, namely if one worships heathen gods and the sun or the moon, fire or floods, wells or stones or any kind of forest trees, or if one practices witchcraft or encompasses death by any means, either by sacrifice or divination, or takes any part in such delusions.*[29]

Any unintended encouragement of paganism that accompanied a Viking victory was to be strongly resisted. The literary and artistic features just described might seem to indicate non-Christian beliefs, but they were no more than "cultural paganism".[30] They referred to, perhaps even celebrated, Scandinavian roots but they did not promote belief in the old gods. This means that there was, in a memorable phrase, a "light pagan colouring"[31] to late Anglo-Saxon England but, despite this, Cnut's England was firmly Christian. This was the faith that he actively promoted across his North Sea Empire.

Cnut died in Shaftesbury on 12 November 1035. He was the most powerful king that England had ever known. His sons only had short reigns after him. Harald Harefoot (son of Cnut and Ælfgifu of Northampton) ruled 1035–1040; and then Harthacnut, his half-brother (son of Cnut and his Norman wife, Emma), ruled 1040–1042. After that, Edward (called "the Confessor" from his perceived holiness) became king until 1066. He was the only surviving son by Emma and her first husband, Æthelred II. At the accession of Edward the Confessor, the twenty-six years of England being part of a Viking North Sea Empire were at an end.

CHAPTER 14

Christian Jarls of the Northern and Western Isles

This chapter explores the character of Viking rule in the Orkney and Shetland Islands, and the Western Isles. We will see how Vikings acted as Christians when they were rulers there. We will also revisit the *Uí Ímair* dynasty of the Irish Sea region (last mentioned in Chapter 5) to see how they ruled their mixed Norse and Celtic domain.

THE ISLANDS IN QUESTION

An arc of islands lies to the north and west of Scotland and extends down into the Irish Sea to include the Isle of Man. To the north of the Scottish mainland lie the Orkney Islands and beyond them the Shetland Islands to the north-east of the Orkneys. Further to the north-west are the Faroe Islands (explored in Chapter 11). Today Orkney and Shetland are part of the United Kingdom and the Faroes are part of Denmark. All, though, are reached by sailing due west from Norway and this explains the connection with Norway that was so important a feature of these islands and their history in the Viking Age.

West of the Scottish mainland lie the Hebrides. These are differentiated as the Inner Hebrides, comprising from north to south: Skye and its associated islands; south of Skye are Canna, Rùm, Eigg, Muck and other smaller islands; then Coll, Tiree, and Mull and its associated islands, which include Iona; and finally a chain of islands which includes Seil, Luing, Scarba, Colonsay, Oronsay, Jura, Islay and finally Gigha. Beyond the Inner Hebrides lie the chain of islands known as the Outer Hebrides which includes (again from north to south): Lewis and Harris; North and South Uist; Barra and other smaller islands which complete the chain; with St Kilda lying far off to the west, in the Atlantic.

The Northern and Western Isles look out into the great stormy wastes of the Atlantic Ocean. Or at least that is one way of looking at their geographical position. Another way is to describe them as being situated on a huge water highway that links Ireland, Wales and north-western England with western Scotland, and on to Norway to the north-east, and Iceland to the north-west. It is all a matter of perspective and the latter view would certainly have been that of the Viking adventurers who sailed west from Norway and then south towards Ireland. For these great chains of islands, that lie like a scattered necklace to the north and west of the northernmost part of the British mainland, were joined together by their proximity to this great water highway and, consequently, shared much common history in the Viking Age. This was true with regard to both the initial period of raiding and settlement and then after the conversion to Christianity.

The ninth century witnessed a programme of colonization and expansion by the people of Norway. This expansion was particularly concentrated in the North Atlantic and led, as we have seen, to Norwegians creating colonies not only in Orkney but also Shetland, the Faroes, Iceland, Greenland and Vinland. All of these colonies lay some distance away from the kingdom of Norway but all were linked to each other and to Norway by ships and mutual trade, as well as a related culture. Although separate entities, all retained some form of connection with the Norwegian crown as the kingdom of Norway emerged.

THE VIKINGS OF ORKNEY AND SHETLAND

What eventually became the Jarldom of Orkney was noticeably different from the other Norse colonies. For a start, its settlement occurred very early. Some of the early settlers of Iceland, such as Thobjorn Jarlakappi, who are mentioned in the *Landnámabók (Book of Settlements)* are said to have originated from Orkney.[1] This suggests a date in the late eighth and early ninth centuries for the original colonization there, thus making Orkney potentially the oldest of all the Viking colonies outside of Scandinavia. This means that Orkney was settled before the mass movement of Viking settlers and raiders occurred in the later ninth century. If so, then Orkney was settled before the occurrence of conflicts within Scandinavia that led to the settlement of Iceland around 870. While the picture may have been simplified, the impression given by the account in the later *Orkneyinga saga (Saga of the Orcadians)* suggests that a single, great fleet conquered Orkney and Shetland in one expedition, thus opening the way for settlers. The islands offered good agricultural opportunities and occupied a key position on the route to western Britain, Ireland and beyond.

This settlement of Orkney, before the mass exodus to the other North Atlantic colonies, meant that the kings of Norway were able to maintain a large element of control over both the original colonization and the subsequent political developments there. Indeed, by as early as 900, the Norwegian kings of Vestfold had established loose control over the Orkney Islands. This was very different from the situation in Iceland and Greenland, which developed into separate political entities. Although the kings of Norway were able to retain some influence in these latter colonies, their later date of colonization and the relative size of this vast Norse diaspora meant that the Norwegian kings lacked the resources that would have enabled them to dominate Iceland and Greenland in the way they did Orkney. This was enhanced by the relative proximity of Norway and Orkney. When, in 1066, Harald Hardrada of Norway invaded England, he sailed via Orkney and his wife and daughters remained on the island during the campaign.[2] The fact that a later Norwegian king moved to abolish the semi-independent Jarldom of Orkney and captured both the jarls operating from there, in 1098, shows the extent to which he was prepared to meddle in Orkney's affairs. But this brings us back to the question of just what kind of society had developed there prior to this.

In Orkney and Shetland, the Scandinavian settlers appear to have completely overwhelmed the original inhabitants. As in the Western Isles, this seems to have totally obliterated Pictish culture. On Orkney, Shetland and in Caithness almost all surviving place names are derived from Old Norse. The Pictish heritage was subsumed by the newcomers. The Picts were a Celtic people who spoke a language (Pictish) similar to that spoken by the British Celts further south. Pictish became extinct in the early medieval period, at about the time of the Viking raids. Whether the Picts vanished from the Northern Isles due to ethnic cleansing, assimilation to Norse culture or emigration in the face of Viking land seizure is difficult to say, and experts differ in their interpretation. But, suffice it to say, the Picts vanished. An account in the early-thirteenth-century *Historia Norvegiae* (*History of Norway*) describes how the indigenous Picts and Irish monks were destroyed by the Viking arrival. That this same source describes the Picts as pygmies whose strength diminished in the middle of the day, leading them to hide in holes in the ground, does not make one confident about using it as an historical source. On the other hand, this account may chart the pattern of behaviour by which Norse dehumanization of the Picts accompanied (and justified) their elimination.[3] The *papar* (Norse for priest) place names found in the Northern Isles may be an echo of these lost communities, since similar names on Iceland were later recorded as indicating where once Irish monks had lived, before fleeing from the incoming Vikings.[4]

THE RISE OF THE JARLS OF ORKNEY

The chieftains who came to dominate the settlement on the Orkney Islands were the jarls (a Norse title that became "earl" in England). According to the *Orkneyinga saga*, the origin of the jarldom lay in a gift from the Norwegian king, Harald Finehair (ruled 872–c. 930), to Rognvald Eysteinson, jarl of Møre (western Norway), as compensation for the loss of his son Ivar in battle. The saga states that Rognvald was unwilling to remain on the island, so he passed the title of jarl on to his brother. The thirteenth-century Icelandic source *Heimskringla* (*Circle of the World*) says that this brother was, indeed, the first to carry the title. However, information from Irish sources and the early-thirteenth-century *Historia Norvegiae* claims that Orkney was colonized by the jarls of Møre a full generation before Harald Finehair's rule.[5] It has also been suggested that the jarldom was not formally established until much later, by Sigurd Hlodvison, the Stout (died 1014).[6] Be that as it may, chieftains based on Orkney were making their presence felt in the Irish Sea region and northern Scotland long before this later period.

The Jarldom of Orkney had a markedly aristocratic and military character. The jarl was surrounded by a warrior elite who acted as his counsellors, and who also commanded his warships and had legal and administrative responsibilities in the local districts where they owned land.[7] In contrast, in Iceland and Greenland the unifying force was not a jarl or chieftain, but the *Althing* (assembly) and what was known as the Common Law. This gave the Icelanders and Greenlanders a much more republican outlook than was found on Orkney, plus a system of government which had no central state power.

The Jarldom of Orkney was tributary to the king of Norway. This meant that although the jarls were fairly independent, this arrangement brought Orkney into a hierarchical system.[8] Orkney did have a *thing* (assembly) but it was very different from Iceland in that the Orkney *thing* played a much less important role in affairs. There are frequent references in the sagas to disputes being submitted to the arbitration of the jarl rather than the judgment of the *thing*. Unlike in Iceland, the Orkney *things* were far from free assemblies where peasant farmers could speak their minds. At the *thing* under Jarl Einar Sigurdson (also known as Wry-mouth), free speech was a very risky business. One powerful local lord, Thorkel Fosterer, ended up being driven into exile for simply suggesting that the war levies he owed for Irish expeditions should be reduced.[9] In addition, quarrels between competing jarls were often resolved by appeals to the Norwegian king and this royal authority greatly strengthened the king's position with regard to Orkney's affairs. In 1195, Orkney's position as a vassal of the king of Norway was finally formally settled. This was in stark contrast to Iceland and Greenland, which were not dominated by the Norwegian crown until the 1260s.

THE CONVERSION OF ORKNEY TO CHRISTIANITY

The original Viking settlers of the Northern Isles (as in western Scotland) were pagan. About 130 pagan burials have been found on Orkney, Shetland and western Scotland. Adomnán (abbot of Iona 679–704) wrote that monks from Iona had established a hermitage on Orkney and it is reasonable to assume that the Pictish community there was Christian before it was destroyed by the Vikings. Whether this earlier Christian community influenced later developments is difficult to tell and the evidence for any continuity seems tenuous.

However, Norse Orkney not only had links back to Norway but also to Ireland and the Hebrides. This relationship brought the Norse in Orkney into closer contact with the Christian world from an early period which meant that they were responsive to its teaching.[10] The leaders of Orkney were also a highly mobile group and the *Orkneyinga saga* mentions visits to the royal courts of Scotland, Norway, Sweden, England, Russia and the German Empire; and also contacts with Rome, Jerusalem Constantinople and Provence.[11] The complexity of the relationship between Orkney, Norway and the British Isles is apparent in the leadership contest between two warrior chieftains who contested control of the Orkney Islands in the early twelfth century: Magnus and Hakon. Where Hakon was supported by the Norwegians, Magnus relied on Scottish support.[12]

This same saga claims that the conversion of Orkney to Christianity occurred in 995, because of the intervention of the Norwegian Viking warlord Olaf Tryggvason (king of Norway 995–1000). Olaf had been confirmed in 994, in England, and on his way back to Norway he compelled the jarl of Orkney, Sigurd

Hlodvison, the Stout, to convert to Christianity or face death and the destruction of the islands' settlements. The twelfth-century compiler of the *Historia de Antiquitate Regum Norwagiensium* (*Ancient History of the Norwegian Kings*, the earliest surviving kings' saga), the Norwegian monk Theodoricus Monachus, claims that Olaf threatened to kill Sigurd's three-year-old son before his eyes if he did not convert. Sigurd converted, though it is reasonable to assume that such a forced conversion meant little to the jarl, and he was later thought to have fought under a pagan banner at the Battle of Clontarf, where he met his death.

Nevertheless, the power of the Norwegian crown ensured that the conversion was not reneged on and Adam of Bremen recounts how a bishop was established at Birsay, around 1048, by Jarl Thorfinn Sigurdarson, the Mighty (died 1065). *Orkneyinga saga* says that its foundation followed the return to Orkney of Thorfinn after a trip to Rome, during which the pope absolved him of all his sins. The close proximity of the minster of Christchurch at Birsay and the hall of the jarl reveals the close relationship of bishop and jarl, and was part of Thorfinn's attempt to work with the church to unite all the areas under his control (Orkney, Shetland, Caithness, Sutherland and the Western Isles) into one stable political unit. By the early twelfth century this scheme had failed, as the areas fragmented, but it had been an impressive attempt and the Christian church was a key part of Thorfinn's strategy.[13]

Despite these dramatic events, it seems likely that the conversion to Christianity began before the historic date of 995. There are hints, in a source known as the *Life of St Findan*, concerning an Irish-speaking Orcadian bishop around 850, which suggests he had a congregation there. In addition, small churches at Newark Bay and the Brough of Deerness may date from the mid-tenth century, and burial with grave goods seems to have ended at about this time. What happened between then and the intervention of Olaf Tryggvason may have been a situation of either mixed practices (syncretism) or of distinct rival Christian and pagan factions.[14] Whatever the situation, the intervention of Olaf seems to have been decisive.

After the conversion to Christianity, the church on Orkney came under the authority of the archbishops of Hamburg-

Bremen. So they were more connected to the wider European network than settlers on Iceland and, as such, experienced a cultural renaissance where the influences from the Celtic areas and the south – including England and France – blended with their Norse heritage. Consequently, by the second half of the twelfth century, Orkney was no longer a Viking colony but a rich part of mainstream European culture. Eventually the church on Orkney became part of the Norwegian archdiocese of Trondheim.

One of Orkney's most famous Viking Christians was St Magnus Erlendson or Magnus the Martyr. A gentle Orkney jarl who refused to engage in warfare, he was eventually executed on the island of Egilsay, on the command of his cousin and rival for rule of Orkney, Hakon, in 1115. He was buried in Christchurch at Birsay. In 1135 a shrine was built there for his remains but, in 1136, work began on a new cathedral at Kirkwall that would be named after the martyred king. It was the largest building ever constructed on Orkney and masons from Durham worked on its construction. It was a fitting tribute to the way in which the Jarldom of Orkney had embraced Christianity.

THE POLITICAL BALANCING ACT OF THE CHRISTIAN JARLS OF ORKNEY

Although Orkney had links to many European countries, perhaps the most important relationship was with its nearest neighbour, Scotland. This led to a complex relationship. Jarl Sigurd Hlodvison the Stout (died 1014), of Orkney, seized land on the Scottish mainland and married the daughter of the Scottish king Malcolm II. This marriage was a mutually convenient alliance against the common enemy of the earl of Moray. It guaranteed Scottish support for the Orkney jarls, and was an important ingredient in the success of the Orkney jarldom.[15] It also meant that the conquered provinces of Caithness and Sutherland could be ruled by Sigurd's son, Thorfinn, as a fief from his royal grandfather. So began a complex situation in which the jarls held their possessions on the Scottish mainland as vassals of the Scottish king, but were subordinate to the Norwegian crown in the Northern and Western Isles.[16] In the last days of Sigurd the Stout and his son Thorfinn Sigurdarson, the Mighty (1014–1065), the Orkney jarldom dominated the north of Scotland and extended its influence over the Hebrides, the Isle of Man and Ireland.[17] There seems to have been an agreement in 1040 which ceded much of the north of Scotland to Thorfinn's nominal leadership.

This gave the jarls of Orkney an independence not enjoyed by other subjects of the Norwegian crown. Their close geographical position to Scotland meant that contact with the Scottish kings was more logical than a relationship with the kings of Norway. However, this complex balancing act between two different overlords meant that the jarls of Orkney had to be politically astute to avoid the disapproval of both and to use these two relationships to their own advantage. In this way the earlier dependence on Norway, that had distinguished Orkney from the other North Atlantic Norse colonies had by the eleventh century given way to a more complex web of allegiances, but one which still differentiated it from the less complex political positions of the other Norse colonies in the North Atlantic.

However, we cannot assume this meant there was no latent hostility regarding the Scots, since influential Orkney families (all of Viking heritage, as the Picts seem to have vanished by this point) interfered in disputes in Scotland, backing one side against another, if they saw an advantage for themselves. For example, Malcolm Canmore, who deposed the infamous Macbeth in 1057, was married to an Orkney woman.[18] In a similar way, the Scots crown backed Magnus Erlendson in his leadership contest with Hakon in the early twelfth century. Magnus was just one in a long line of claimants to the divided earldom whom the Scots kings manipulated to increase their own influence.[19]

Orkney finally passed from Norwegian control to that of the kingdom of Scots in 1472. It was only then that the administration of the church on Orkney (the diocese of Caithness) was transferred from the archdiocese of Trondheim (Norway) to that of St Andrews, in Scotland. The very long Viking connection with Orkney was finally severed.

THE VIKINGS OF THE WESTERN ISLES

Piecing together the story of Viking settlement in the Western Isles is not easy. From 840 to 880 the Hebrides were under the rule of a Norse aristocrat named Ketil Flatnose[20] but the original colonization had occurred a generation earlier.

Scandinavian settlement affected diverse communities. In the outer islands, as further north on Orkney and Shetland, the Viking newcomers impacted on Pictish communities. Further south, in what is today south-western Scotland and the southern Inner Hebrides, the population of the Scots kingdom of *Dal Riata* (or *Dalriada*) spoke Gaelic, and had strong links to Ireland (from where settlers had originally come in earlier centuries). Further south on the western coast were the Welsh-speaking communities of Strathclyde. But documentary evidence for the experiences of the outer islands is sparse.

The monastery on Iona was an early victim of Viking raids, with the earliest dated to 795, but (as with a number of other religious settlements) these raids did not lead to the abandonment of the community. On the outer islands the impact was more profound, and Norse replaced Gaelic and Pictish as the dominant language. By about 900, Scandinavians – mostly Norwegians – settled from Galloway to the Moray Firth and on the Western Isles.[21] The main problem regarding the Western Isles is that much of the evidence is from a later period, when Gaelic had reasserted itself and replaced Old Norse as the dominant language. This has led to much debate as to the extent of Gaelic survival during the period of Scandinavian settlement.[22]

The place names of the Western Isles (as in the Northern Isles) do not show any evidence of original Gaelic or Pictish names being turned into Norse ones. This suggests a huge ethnic displacement of the pre-Viking population. The once-Pictish Outer Hebrides in particular are one of the most completely "Norsified" areas in the British Isles. If place names are anything to go by, Viking settlement was much less intense on the western coast of the Scottish mainland. This division within western Scotland can be seen in the later Gaelic distinction between the *Innse Gall* (islands of the Scandinavians) and the *Airer Goidel* (coastline of the Gaels). This is also reflected in Old Norse terminology which referred to the mainland as *Skotland* but never used this term for the islands which were, instead, referred to as the *Suðreyjar* (southern isles). This distinction probably dates to the ninth century. Cut off from easy access to Ireland by the Viking settlement on the islands, the Gaelic-speaking peoples of the kingdom of what had once been known as Dal Riata, in Argyll, refocused their settlement along the coast of western Scotland. In some areas this seems to have involved cooperation with the Scandinavian settlers from the mid-ninth century onwards. In this way, while Pictish was obliterated by the Viking arrival, in time Gaelic reasserted itself at the expense of Old Norse across the whole of the Western Isles.

Scandinavian sources corroborate this idea of Norse-Gaelic intermingling, through references to people from the British Isles with a Scandinavian first name and a Gaelic by-name – for example Helgi Bjolan, where "Bjolan" was a Norse version of a Gaelic by-name meaning "little mouth". Such Gaelic by-names could not have existed without some knowledge of Gaelic within the local community, while the Norse element suggests a Norse-speaking population.[23] This mixed Norse-Gael population became known in Ireland as the *Gall-Gaedhil* (foreign Gaels) and gave their name to Galloway in south-western Scotland.

The Scandinavian people of the Western Isles adopted Christianity early, a direct result of their mixing with Gaelic-speaking Christians. This can be seen in the three cross-marked stones and a cross slab with a Norse runic inscription found at Cille Bharra (Isle of Barra). Another important cross slab is from Reilig Òdhrain (Iona) – also known as St Oran's Graveyard – which appears to date from the late tenth or eleventh century and contains a runic commemorative inscription. This stone tells us that two Norse-speaking brothers had the wealth and social standing to acquire a burial place close to the shrine of St Columba and it seems likely that they would have belonged to a leading family in the district.[24] This particular site is claimed as the burial place of at least seven earlier kings of the Scots, including Kenneth MacAlpin (died 858). In later centuries powerful clan chiefs, including those of the MacKinnons, MacLeans and MacLeods, were buried here.

Reilig Òdhrain continues to be used for burials and, in 1994, John Smith, the leader of the Labour Party, was buried there. With no recorded Viking raids on Iona after 825, the same kind of assimilation to Christian culture found across other areas of Viking settlement was clearly also occurring here. Cille Bharra and Reilig Òdhrain were in continuous use as places of Christian worship and burial right through the Viking period, despite the earlier upheavals.

Under Thorfinn Sigurdarson, the Mighty (died 1065), jarl of Orkney, the Western Isles became part of his united church structure, with a bishop based at Birsay on Orkney. While Thorfinn's unified realm and church structure did not last, the faith did. From 1000 to 1300, despite being geographically on the very edge of Western Europe, the Western Isles shared in the major cultural and social trends affecting the rest of Europe. This can be seen in how the Kings of the Isles adopted feudalism and the idea of knighthood and the building of castles; as well as becoming lavish patrons of the church.

THE VIKINGS OF THE ISLE OF MAN

During the ninth century the sheer number of Norse inscriptions (there are more pre-1100 Norse inscriptions here than in any other area of Britain or Ireland) suggests that Norse may well have been the dominant language on Man and definitely the language of the elite.[25] Although it has been previously argued that Gaelic was retained as the language of the lower classes, the presence of a very humble house in Norse style on marginal land at Doarlish Cashen is the clearest evidence that the Norse settlement was not just an elite movement.[26] This does not negate the survival of Gaelic but does make it likely that Old Norse managed to permeate all classes of people on Man. The dominance of Old Norse can be most clearly seen in the many -by endings to Manx place names, which was a Norse place name element for farm or homestead. There are twenty-three place names recorded before the end of the kingdom of Man and of these only three are of Celtic origin, with the rest being from Old Norse.[27] This would imply that Old Norse was the dominant language during the Viking Age and, though it was later to be replaced by reintroduced Gaelic, it still had an important role to play in the culture and linguistic history of Man.

The destruction of early Christian graves by a Viking Age burial at Balladoole seems to suggest a brutal treatment of the indigenous Christian population by the first Viking settlers, as we have seen. But, if so, this pagan domination did not last. The multicultural and multilingual aspects of life on the Isle of Man, the Western Isles and the Irish Sea region generally, by the twelfth and thirteenth centuries, reveal how Viking settlers there eventually cooperated with other communities to produce a vibrant Christian region with a rich character. In this society one Scandinavian Manx king had a Gaelic court bard, land charters written in Latin, a marriage alliance with rulers in Wales and possibly a Welsh-speaking son.[28] The evidence from the end of the eleventh century shows that although the Manx kings had resolutely clung on to their Scandinavian identity, Gaelic was also understood at the royal court. The survival of the Manx dynasty for almost two centuries is likely to have been due, to a large extent, to successful adaptation to and engagement with indigenous culture while still maintaining traditional aspects of their Hiberno-Norse identity. By doing this, they created a composite kingship that enabled this small kingdom to survive for two centuries. It was an impressive achievement.

THE KINGDOM OF THE ISLES

What became known as the Kingdom of the Isles – comprising the Inner and Outer Hebrides, the islands in the Firth of Clyde and the Isle of Man – lasted from the ninth to the thirteenth century. Called the *Suðreyjar* (southern isles) to differentiate them from the *Norðreyjar* (Northern Isles) of Orkney and Shetland, it was also known as the Kingdom of Man and the Isles. At various times its rulers were independent sea-kings (whose rule rested on their control of the western seaways), and, at other times, it came under overlordship from Norway (either directly or through the

Norwegian vassal the jarl of Orkney), Ireland, England, Scotland and Orkney.

In its earliest period (from the mid-ninth century) the Uí Ímair dynasty of Norse adventurers who, at various times, ruled lands around the Irish Sea region (including in Ireland and York) dominated the region. In this early period their wealth was rooted in the international slave trade which they benefited from, either as slavers or as taxers of the activities of others. While there are debates over the connection of some later rulers to this powerful family, what is clear is that it was never a unified kingdom but was, instead, a collection of lordships ruled by members of the family.

The degree of unity or disunity across this great area depended on changing circumstances. Unlike the other comparative great dynasty, that of Rurik (the Rurikids) in Kiev Rus, their kingdom failed in the long run and disintegrated. Nevertheless, the later Lords of the Isles (who in the form of the Scots MacDonald lords held sway in the Isles until 1493) claimed descent from this great family of Norse/Gaelic rulers. Since the union of Scotland with England in 1707, the title has been one of those carried by the Prince of Wales. In this form, it is a direct link back to the Vikings of the Uí Ímair dynasty who were, at times, perhaps the most powerful royal family in the British Isles.

The Kingdom of the Isles was briefly ruled directly from Norway in the eleventh century after it was seized by the Norwegian ruler Magnus Olafson, also known as Magnus Barelegs. He ruled Norway, as King Magnus III, from 1093 until his death in 1103. On his death a branch of the Uí Ímair family (the Crovan dynasty) regained control and held the Isles until the mid-thirteenth century. In order to survive, at various times they recognized as overlords the kings of Norway, England, and even the pope. The military power of these sea-kings rested on their fleet of galleys powered by sails and oars. In 1156 a coup resulted in the kingdom being seized by Somerled who, via his wife, represented a side-branch of the Crovan dynasty. St Oran's Chapel, the oldest standing building on Iona, may have been built by Somerled. He seems to have hoped to reunify the church in his kingdom with that in Ireland, with Iona as its symbolic centre. He did not succeed. On his death in battle, in 1164, his sea-king empire disintegrated. Eventually, in 1266, the islands became part of the kingdom of Scots by the Treaty of Perth. The independent Viking state had enjoyed a long run but it was finally over.

A Final Thought:
The Viking World
in 1150

By 1150 the Viking Age was effectively over, but it had ended at different times in different parts of the Viking diaspora. It had always been a loose package of raiding mixed with exploration and trading, then settlement; a generally common package of pagan beliefs, the speaking of various forms of the Old Norse language, and membership of small-scale communities that eventually morphed into larger kingdoms.

In 1153, King Eystein of Norway led the last ever recorded Viking raid from Norway against England, when he raided Hartlepool (Durham), Whitby and Scarborough (North Yorkshire), and as far south as the Wash (the bay estuary where Lincolnshire meets Norfolk). His aim was only to seize plunder and there was no strategic ambition.[1] However, lingering echoes of this past culture survived until even later in the twelfth century in the form of the Orkney Viking Svein Asleifarson, who raided twice a year (his "spring trip" and "autumn trip") as far afield as the Scilly Isles, until he was killed, while raiding Dublin in 1171.[2] But this was more the action of a company of Norse pirates than the widespread actions which had been the hallmark of the Viking Age proper.

In Scotland and the Western Isles things were also changing. In 1156 an Argyll chieftain of mixed Norse and Scots ancestry, Somerled, defeated the king of Man, Godred II, in a mid-winter sea-battle, fought by moonlight. Then just two years later, in 1158, he devastated Man while continuing to recognize the overlordship of the Norwegian king. The Isle of Man remained a vassal of Norway until 1266. But then the Norwegian king, Magnus VI, ceded it to Scotland (along with the Hebrides).

In Scandinavia the most precocious kingdom was that of Denmark. By 1150 it had been a united kingdom for over a century and a half. It had been solidly Christian since at least 1050 and a supporter of papal church reforms.[3] Its expanding systems of churches – most notably those at Ribe and Lund – were increasingly stone-built and influenced by the architecture of England, Germany and Italy. It had become a European state, integrated into European cultural influences. The churches were firmly under royal control as a way of resisting German influence and, at times, were allies of the pope in this: he eventually made Lund an archdiocese in 1104.[4]

Denmark's expansionist foreign policy was now refocused on the Baltic. By 1100 it had come under pressure from raids by Wends from the southern Baltic coast, and had struggled to defend its communities, as once others had struggled to fight off Viking attacks. In 1147 the Danes cooperated with the German Saxons against the Wends. However, it was not until the late twelfth century that combined Danish and German campaigns finally neutralized the Wendish raiding threat. In the thirteenth century the Danes allied with the Swedes in crusades against these still-pagan Wends and the Finns, and between 1160 and 1220, the Danes campaigned across the southern Baltic as far east as Estonia. Until 1240 Denmark was the dominant power in the Baltic but then lost out to the Germans, who were also expanding into what they too considered their imperial backyard.

In Norway the strong regionalism that had once characterized the emerging nation was in decline by 1150. Like Denmark, it too was now largely Christian in its practices. However, unlike Denmark it remained strongly connected to the church in the British Isles, and the authority of the archbishop of Nidaros (later Trondheim) stretched as far as Orkney and the Isle of Man. This western connection can also be seen in its twelfth-century church architecture, which was influenced by English styles. However, its rural churches also exhibited a remarkable stave (wooden) construction of tall gables and richly carved wood, with motifs drawn from indigenous Norse art. Most of these were built between 1150 and 1350 and remind us of the combination of Norse and wider European culture that flowed into Scandinavian Christianity. By way of contrast, the medieval stone-built churches of Denmark and Sweden outnumbered those of Norway by a factor of six and three respectively. Norway continued to be focused on the North Atlantic and took control of Greenland in 1261 and Iceland in 1263. Adventures to the south were now restricted to attendance on crusade to the Holy Land, such as that of King Sigurd *Jorsalafari* (Jerusalem-farer) in 1107.

Sweden, by way of contrast, was not thoroughly Christian until 1200, and the northern Sami (not a Norse people) remained pagan until the eighteenth century. Indeed, as late as 1123, King Sigurd of Norway launched a crusade into southern Sweden against recalcitrant pagans in Småland.[5] The twelfth-century church architecture of Sweden reflected that of Germany and was testament to the longevity of the missionary influence of the church of Hamburg-Bremen. Its political unity lagged a long way behind Denmark and Norway. The official union of the *Svear* and *Götar* did not occur until 1172 (a political unity 200 years later than that of Denmark).

As in the past, the newly Christianized Sweden focused its foreign policy onto the eastern Baltic. By 1150 expansion into Finland was well advanced. From 1157 this took on the nature of a crusade – since the Finns were still pagan – and involved cooperation with the Danes. By 1292 Swedish expansion extended as far as Karelia (now in north-west Russia and south-east Finland), until checked by Novgorod. This was ironic, as the power of Novgorod was based on the foundations laid by Swedish Viking expansion to the east over four centuries earlier, with semi-mythical origins. However, the Viking culture there was long subsumed by that of the Slavs. Finally, in 1323, Sweden and Novgorod signed the Treaty of Nöteborg, which established their border for the first time. Similarly, Kiev Rus was now a Slavic state.

In other parts of the Viking diaspora, the Norse culture had long assimilated to the local one, even where it had at first had a significant impact. By 1150 England and Ireland had long absorbed their Norse populations, although these continued to influence the cultural flavour of places as far apart as York and Dublin. But they were no longer distinctive Scandinavian communities.

In contrast, memories of the Viking past still influenced the outlook and culture of Iceland and Greenland and, indeed, there was a resurgence of interest in the Viking past on Iceland in the thirteenth century that led to the compilation of sagas and other collections which preserved and communicated the myths, legends and histories of the Viking past (particularly those connected to Norway). But these were pagan pasts remembered or imagined within the context of Christian communities. Even the transitional conversion of Iceland had now produced a community that was solidly Christian, although its imagination was still affected by pagan dreams. During the thirteenth century, both came increasingly under the influence of Norway, just as life on Greenland was becoming increasingly precarious for its Norse communities.

One legacy of the Viking past in Scandinavia, in the twelfth century, continued to be political instability and infighting leading to civil wars. However, all involved were now Christians. The hammer of Thor had totally succumbed to the victory of the cross of Christ. As this happened, the development of statehood meant that these northern kingdoms now acted within the generally accepted parameters of culture and behaviour of Western Europe as a whole. The Vikings of the diaspora had assimilated and those of Scandinavia were now recognizable states that were integrated into – but no longer as influential on – the states to the south. The Viking Age was truly over and the Christian Scandinavian kingdoms had joined the culture of medieval Europe, even if they were often peripheral members.

About the authors

Martyn Whittock graduated in Politics from Bristol University in 1980. He taught history for thirty-five years and latterly was curriculum leader for Spiritual, Moral, Social and Cultural education at a Wiltshire secondary school. He has acted as an historical consultant to the National Trust and English Heritage. He retired from teaching in July 2016 to devote more time to writing.

He is the author of forty-six books, including school history textbooks and adult history books. The latter include: *A Brief History of Life in the Middle Ages* (2009), *A Brief Guide to Celtic Myths and Legends* (2013), *The Viking Blitzkrieg AD 789–1098* (2013), *The Anglo-Saxon Avon Valley Frontier* (2014), *1016 and 1066: Why The Vikings Caused the Norman Conquest* (2016), and *Norse Myths and Legends* (2017); the last four co-written with Hannah, his elder daughter. Also published by Lion Hudson are *Christ: The First Two Thousand Years* (2016), co-written with his younger daughter, Esther; and *When God Was King* (2018).

Hannah Whittock graduated with a First in Anglo-Saxon, Norse and Celtic (ASNC) from Pembroke College, Cambridge University, in 2011. In 2012 she completed her Master's at Cambridge, researching the relationship of the Bradford on Avon charter of 1001 to the development of the cult of Edward King and Martyr. Her publications include: "Why Does the North-western Boundary of Wiltshire Ignore the River Avon?", in *The Wiltshire Archaeological and Natural History Magazine*, vol. 105 (2012); "The annexation of Bath by Wessex: The evidence of two rare coins of Edward the Elder", in *The British Numismatic Journal*, vol. 82 (2012); and five books co-authored with her father, Martyn. She is a civil servant.

Notes

INTRODUCTION

1. For example, in J. Haslam, "King Alfred, Mercia and London, 874–86: A reassessment", in H. Hamerow (ed.), *Anglo-Saxon Studies in Archaeology and History*, 17, Oxford: Oxford University School of Archaeology, 2011, pp.124–150; R. Ferguson, *The Hammer and The Cross: A New History of the Vikings*, London: Penguin, 2010; S. Brink and N. Price (eds), *The Viking World*, Abingdon: Routledge, 2008; A. Forte, R. Oram and F. Pedersen (eds), *Viking Empires*, Cambridge: Cambridge University Press, 2005; the BBC2 series *Vikings*, broadcast autumn 2012; J. Graham-Campbell, *Viking Art*, London: Thames & Hudson, 2013; J. Carroll, S. H. Harrison and G. Williams, *The Vikings in Britain and Ireland*, London: British Museum Press, 2014.

CHAPTER 1. THE PAGAN VIKINGS

1. Balbirnie, C., "The Vikings at home", *BBC History Magazine*, volume 13, number 9, September 2012, p. 25.

2. For an overview of the use of the term "Viking" and the names used by others to describe them, see M. Arnold, *The Vikings: Culture and Conquest*, London: Hambledon Continuum, 2006, pp. 7–8. See also A. A. Somerville and R. A. McDonald (eds), *The Viking Age: A Reader*, Toronto: University of Toronto Press, 2010, p. xiii.

3. Ekwall, E., *The Concise Oxford Dictionary of English Place-Names*, Oxford: Oxford University Press, 1960.

4. The evidence for different communities in what later became Sweden consists of, for example, the names of different polities (*Svear, Götar*), different archaeological assemblages, different patterns of use of runestones, the lack of a centralized dynasty until late in the Viking Age, and the late stage at which Sweden was unified.

5. For an accessible overview of Viking Age Scandinavia see J. Haywood,

The Penguin Historical Atlas of the Vikings, London: Penguin, 1995, pp. 28–33; A. Forte, R. Oram and F. Pedersen (eds), *Viking Empires*, Cambridge: Cambridge University Press, 2005, pp. 7–53.

6. Forte, A., R. Oram and F. Pedersen (eds), *Viking Empires*, Cambridge: Cambridge University Press, 2005, pp. 51–53.

7. For an expansion of this argument see K. Randsborg, *The Viking Age in Denmark: The Formation of a State*, London: St Martin's Press, 1980.

8. See M. Whittock and H. Whittock, *Norse Myths and Legends: Viking tales of gods and heroes*, London: Little, Brown, 2017.

9. For modern translations of these see A. Faulkes, (ed. and transl.), Snorri Sturluson, *Edda*, London: Everyman 1987 – often known as the *Prose Edda'* – and C. Larrington (trans.), *The Poetic Edda*, Oxford: Oxford University Press, 1996.

10. Skaldic poetry is one of the two main forms of Old Norse poetry and is a highly complicated poetic form, usually reserved for writing historical or praise poems.

11. For an accessible overview see M. L. Colish, *Medieval Foundations of the Western Intellectual Tradition, 400–1400*, New Haven CT & London: Yale University Press, 1997, ch. 8: "Varieties of Germanic Literature: Old Norse, Old High German, and Old English".

12. For an overview of the Norse saga literature see M. Clunies Ross, *The Cambridge Introduction to the Old Norse-Icelandic Saga*, Cambridge: Cambridge University Press, 2010.

13. See J. Lindow, *Handbook of Norse Mythology*, Santa Barbara CA: ABC Clio, 2001, p. 10.

14. Adam of Bremen, *History of the Archbishops of Hamburg-Bremen*, F. J. Tschan (transl.), New York: Columbia University Press, 2002, Book IV, ch. 26, p. 207.

15. Jesch, J., "The Norse gods in England and the Isle of Man", in D. Anlezark (ed.), *Myths, Legends, and Heroes: Essays on Old Norse and Old English Literature in Honour of John McKinnell*, Toronto: University of Toronto Press, 2011, pp. 18–19.

16. Osborn, M., "The Ravens on the Lejre Throne", in M. D. J. Bintley and T. J. T. Williams (eds), *Representing Beasts in Early Medieval England and*

Scandinavia, Woodbridge: Boydell & Brewer, 2015, p. 104; A. Andrén, K. Jennbert and C. Raudvere (eds), *Old Norse Religion in Long-term Perspectives: Origins, Changes, and Interactions: an International Conference in Lund, Sweden, June 3–7, 2004*, Lund: Nordic Academic Press, 2006, p. 128.

17. https://inpress.lib.uiowa.edu/feminae/DetailsPage.aspx?Feminae_ ID=31944 (Accessed June 2017).

18. Parker, P., *The Northmen's Fury: A History of the Viking World*, London: Vintage, 2015, p. 130.

19. See J. D. Richards, "The Scandinavian presence", in J. Hunter and I. Ralston (eds), *The Archaeology of Britain: An Introduction from the Upper Palaeolithic to the Industrial Revolution*, London: Routledge, 1999, p. 200; J. Jesch, "Speaking like a Viking: Language and Cultural Interaction in the Irish Sea Region", in S. E. Harding, D. Griffiths and E. Royles (eds), *In Search of Vikings: Interdisciplinary Approaches to the Scandinavian Heritage of North-West England*, Boca Raton FL: CRC Press, 2015, p. 58.

20. Anglo-Saxon Chronicle annal for 878, in D. Whitelock (ed.), *English Historical Documents, Volume I, c.500–1042*, London: Eyre Methuen, 1979, p. 195. Referring to this event, the later *Annals of St Neots* (early twelfth century) records the tradition that the banner fluttered prior to a victory but hung down before a defeat.

Chapter 2. Storm from the North

1. Whitelock, D. (ed.), *English Historical Documents, Volume I, c. 500–1042*, London: Eyre Methuen, 1979, p. 180.

2. Ibid., p. 842.

3. Jeremiah 1:14, *The Holy Bible, New Revised Standard Version (Anglicised Edition)*, Oxford: Oxford University Press, 1995. All Bible quotes are from this version.

4. Whitelock, D., *English Historical Documents*, p. 843.

5. Ibid., p. 896.

6. Ibid., p. 845.

7. Ibid., p. 845.

8. Ibid., p. 181.

9. Owen-Crocker, G. R., *Dress in Anglo-Saxon England*, Woodbridge: Boydell Press, revised edn, 2004, p. 170.

10. Matthew 24:7.

11. Catling, C., "Raiders and Traders", *Current Archaeology* 245 (August 2010), p. 14.

12. Whittock, H., "The Avon valley as a frontier region from the fourth to the eleventh centuries", unpublished BA dissertation (University of Cambridge, Department of Anglo-Saxon, Norse and Celtic, 2010). For an examination of Malmesbury's location within a disputed frontier zone, see H. Whittock, "Why does the North-western Boundary of Wiltshire Ignore the River Avon?", *The Wiltshire Archaeological and Natural History Magazine* 105, 2012, pp. 96–104.

13. Ó Corráin, D., "Pre-historic and Early Christian Ireland", in R. F. Foster (ed.), *The Oxford Illustrated History of Ireland*, Oxford: Oxford University Press, 1989, p. 33.

14. Hadley, D. M., *The Vikings in England, Settlement, Society and Culture*, Manchester: Manchester University Press, 2006, p. 208.

15. Whitelock, D., *English Historical Documents*, p. 182.

16. Ibid., p. 182, note 2 and p. 830, note 3.

17. Ibid., p.186.

18. Nelson, J. (ed.), *Annales of St Bertin*, Manchester: Manchester University Press, 1991, p. 59.

19. Whitelock, D., *English Historical Documents*, p. 187.

20. Ibid., p. 188.

21. Ibid., pp. 889, 883.

22. Brown, M. P., *Manuscripts from the Anglo-Saxon Age*, London: The British Library, 2007, p. 55 and Plate 41.

23. Forte, A., R. Oram and F. Pedersen (eds), *Viking Empires*, Cambridge: Cambridge University Press, 2005, pp. 68–69.

24. Whitelock, D., *English Historical Documents*, p. 195.

25. Keynes, S. and M. Lapidge (transl.), *Alfred the Great. Asser's Life of King Alfred and Other Contemporary Sources*, Harmondsworth: Penguin, 1983, 27, p.76.

26. Ibid., 49, p. 83.

27. Haywood, J., *The Penguin Historical Atlas of the Vikings*, London: Penguin, 1995, pp. 51–52.

CHAPTER 3. THE VIKING CONVERSION IN ENGLAND

1. Goldberg, E. J., "Popular Revolt, Dynastic Politics, and Aristocratic Factionalism in the Early Middle Ages: The Saxon Stellinga Reconsidered", *Speculum*, Vol. 70, No. 3, July 1995, p. 468.

2. For an archaeological insight into the Viking impact on Repton, see M. Biddle and B. Kjølbye-Biddle, "Repton and the Vikings", *Antiquity* 250, March 1992, pp. 36–51. Also J. Graham-Campbell (ed.), *Cultural Atlas of the Viking World*, New York: Facts On File Inc, 1994, p. 128. Recent work on the evidence, including using stable carbon isotope data along with strontium and oxygen isotope analysis, has confirmed the likelihood that those buried at Repton were indeed members of the Viking Great Army (doubts had previously been raised about earlier conclusions regarding this). See C. Jarman, "Resolving Repton: Has archaeology found the great Viking camp?", *British Archaeology*, March/April, 2018, pp. 28–35.

3. Hamerow, H., *Early Medieval Settlements: The Archaeology of Rural Communities in Northwest Europe, 400–900*, Oxford: Oxford University Press, 2004, p. 151.

4. Brown, M. P., *The Lindisfarne Gospels*, Toronto: University of Toronto Press, 2003, p. 201.

5. Hamerow, H., *Rural Settlements and Society in Anglo-Saxon England*, Oxford: Oxford University Press, 2012, p. 161.

6. See M. Whittock and H. Whittock, *Norse Myths: Viking tales of gods and heroes*, London: Little, Brown, 2017.

7. Ridyard, S., *The Royal Saints of Anglo-Saxon England*, Cambridge: Cambridge University Press, 1988, pp. 61–69.

8. Hart, C., *The Danelaw*, London: Hambledon, 1992, p. 46. See also P. Grierson and M. Blackburn, *Medieval European Coinage 1. The Early Middle Ages (5th–10th centuries)*, Cambridge: Cambridge University Press, 1986, pp. 319–320.

9. Blackburn, M. and H. Pagan, "The St Edmund coinage in the light of a parcel from a hoard of St Edmund pennies", *British Numismatic Journal*, 72, 2002, p. 1.

10. North, J. J., *English Hammered Coinage, Volume 1: Early Anglo-Saxon to Henry III, c. 600–1272*, London: Spink & Son Ltd, 1994, p. 109.

11. Blackburn, M. and H. Pagan, "The St Edmund coinage", p. 2.

12. Ibid.

13. Ibid.

14. Logan, F. D., *A History of the Church in the Middle Ages*, London: Routledge, 2002, pp. 83–84.

15. A point examined in detail in A. Redmond, *Viking Burial in the North of England: a Study of Contact, Interaction and Reaction between Scandinavian Migrants with Resident Groups, and the Effect of Immigration on Aspects of Cultural Continuity*, BAR, British Series 429, Oxford: John and Erica Hedges Ltd, 2007.

16. Sandred, K. I., "East Anglian place-names", in J. Fisiak and P. Trudgill (eds), *East Anglian English*, Woodbridge: Boydell & Brewer, 2001, pp. 45–52.

17. Richards, J. D., "Pagans and Christians at a Frontier: Viking burial in the Danelaw", in M. Carver (ed.), *The Cross Goes North: Processes of Conversion in Northern Europe, AD 300–1300*, Woodbridge: Boydell & Brewer, 2006, pp. 390–391.

18. Richards, J. D., *Viking Age England*, London: English Heritage/ Batsford, 1991, p. 104.

19. Ibid.

20. See K. Holman, *The Northern Conquest: Vikings in Britain and Ireland*, Oxford: Signal Books, 2007.

21. Abrams, L., "The Conversion of the Danelaw", in J. Graham-Campbell, R. Hall, J. Jesch, and D. N. Parsons (eds), *Vikings and the Danelaw*, Oxford: Oxbow Books, 2001, p. 40.

CHAPTER 4. THE CROSS AND THE HAMMER: CHRISTIANS AND PAGANS IN THE NORTH OF ENGLAND

1. Whitelock, D. (ed.), *English Historical Documents, Volume I, c. 500–1042*, London: Eyre Methuen, 1979, p. 282.

2. Ibid, p. 277.

3. Frank, R., "Viking atrocity and Skaldic verse: the rite of the blood-eagle", *ASE Review* 99, 1984, pp. 340–341.

4. Whitelock, D., *English Historical Documents*, pp. 286–287.

5. Aird, W. M., *St Cuthbert and the Normans: the Church of Durham, 1071–1153*, Woodbridge: Boydell Press, 1998, pp. 30–31.

6. Extracts from the anonymous *Life of St Cuthbert*, in Whitelock, D., *English Historical Documents*, pp. 286–288.

7. Jupp, P. C., and C. Gittings, *Death in England: An Illustrated History*, Manchester: Manchester University Press, 1999, p. 72.

8. Richards, J. D., *Viking Age England*, London: English Heritage/Batsford, 1991, p. 116.

9. Ibid., p. 118

10. Ibid., p. 119.

11. See Carver, M., "Why that? Why there? Why then? The politics of early medieval monumentality", in H. Hamerow and A. MacGregor (eds), *Image and Power in the Archaeology of Early Medieval Britain*, Oxford: Oxford University Press, 2001, pp. 1–22.

12. All the runic inscriptions from the Isle of Man (along with a huge collection of other runic inscriptions) can be found at the University of Uppsala runic database: http://www.nordiska.uu.se/forskn/samnord.htm (Accessed July 2017).

13. Griffiths, D., *Vikings of the Irish Sea*, Stroud: History Press, 2010, p. 146.

14. Richards, J. D., "The Scandinavian Presence", in J. Hunter and I. Ralston (eds), *The Archaeology of Britain*, London: Routledge, 1999, p. 200.

15. Griffiths, D., *Vikings of the Irish Sea*, p. 146; J. D. Richards, *Viking Age England*, p. 124.

16. Jupp, P. C. and C. Gittings, *Death in England*, p. 74.

17. North, J. J., *English Hammered Coinage, Volume 1, Early Anglo-Saxon to Henry III, c.600–1272*, London: Spink and Son, 1994, pp. 113–116.

18. Blackburn, M. and H. Pagan, "The St Edmund coinage in the light of a parcel from a hoard of St Edmund pennies", *British Numismatic Journal*, 72, 2002, p. 2.

19. Abram, C., *Myths of the Pagan North: The gods of the Norsemen*, London: Hambledon Continuum, 2011, p. 98.

20. Somerville, A. A. and R. A. McDonald, *The Viking Age: A Reader*, Toronto: University of Toronto Press, 2010, p. 96.

CHAPTER 5. THE OTHER ISLAND...

1. The St Gall Priscian manuscript (St Gall, Stiftsbibliothek, ms 904).

2. A translation by K. Meyer, http://irisharchaeology.ie/2015/01/tonight-i-fear-not-the-vikings-an-early-irish-poem (Accessed September 2017). It might be more freely translated as: "Bitter is the wind this night/White the tresses of the seas/I do not think that Viking hoards/Will come on such nights as these."

3. In Thurneysen, R., *Old Irish Reader*, Dublin: The Dublin Institute for Advanced Studies, 1981, p. 39. Hear it recited at: https://www.asnc.cam.ac.uk/spokenword/i_isacher.php?d=tt (Accessed September 2017).

4. Ibid.

5. https://www.asnc.cam.ac.uk/spokenword/i_isacher.php?d=tt (Accessed September 2017).

6. Ferguson, R., *The Hammer and the Cross*, London: Penguin, 2010, p. 77.

7. Smyth, A. P., "The Black Foreigners of York and the White Foreigners of Dublin", *Saga-book of the Viking Society*, 19, 1974, pp. 101–117.

8. Downham, C., *Viking Kings of Britain and Ireland: The Dynasty of Ívarr to AD 1014*, Edinburgh: Dunedin, 2007, pp. 36–37, note 141.

9. Hayward, J., *The Penguin Historical Atlas of the Vikings*, London: Penguin, 1995, p. 72.

10. http://irisharchaeology.ie/2014/11/ranvaiks-casket-an-ornate-shrine-stolen-during-viking-raids-on-ireland/ (Accessed September 2017).

11. Ferguson, R., *The Hammer and the Cross*, pp. 72–73.

12. Ibid.

13. Ó Corráin, D., "Ireland, Wales, Man, and the Hebrides", in P. Sawyer (ed.), *The Oxford Illustrated History of the Vikings*, Oxford: Oxford University Press, 1997, pp. 95–96.

14. Ferguson, R., *The Hammer and the Cross*, p. 76.

15. He was king in York from 941 to 944, and in Dublin from 945 to 947.

16. All the church was subject to Rome (in Western Europe) but divided into archdioceses for administrative purposes. These were often associated with particular kingdoms or geographical areas.

17. Forte, A., R. Oram and F. Pedersen (eds), *Viking Empires*, Cambridge: Cambridge University Press, 2005, p. 226.

18. Quoted in D. Ó Corráin, "Ireland, Wales, Man, and the Hebrides", in P. Sawyer (ed.), *The Oxford Illustrated History of the Vikings*, p. 108.

19. Trinity College Dublin: https://dh.tcd.ie/clontarf/Religion%3A%20 Heathens%2C%20 Christians%20or%20 Something%20in%20 Between%3F (Assessed September 2017).

20. Ó Cróinín, D., *Early Medieval Ireland 400–1200*, London: Pearson Education, 1995, p. 262.

21. Ó Corráin, D., "Ireland, Wales, Man, and the Hebrides", in P. Sawyer (ed.), *The Oxford Illustrated History of the Vikings*, p. 101.

22. Forte, A., R. Oram and F. Pedersen (eds), *Viking Empires*, p. 225.

CHAPTER 6. THE DUCHY OF THE NORTHMEN

1. Graham-Campbell, J. (ed.), *The Viking World*. London: Frances Lincoln, 2001, p. 32.

2. Dudo of St Quentin says it was spoken there until at least the 930s and implies that Richard I, the Fearless, was a fluent speaker. See E. Christiansen (transl.), *Dudo of St Quentin, History of the Normans*, Woodbridge: Boydell & Brewer, 1998, pp. xvii-xviii.

3. Nelson, J. L., "The Frankish Empire", in P. Sawyer (ed.), *The Oxford Illustrated History of the Vikings*, Oxford: Oxford University Press, 1997, p. 31.

4. Graham-Campbell, J. (ed.), *The Viking World*, p. 32.

5. Szabo, J. F. and N. E. Kuefler, *The Bayeux Tapestry: A Critically Annotated Bibliography*, Lanham MD: Rowman & Littlefield, 2015, p. 493; see also E. Carson Pastan, S. D. White and K. Gilbert, *The Bayeux Tapestry and Its Contexts: A Reassessment*, Woodbridge: Boydell & Brewer, 2014, p. 242.

6. Harper-Bill, C. and E. Van Houts (eds), *A Companion to the Anglo-Norman World*, Woodbridge: Boydell & Brewer, 2007, p. 262.

7. Morris, M., *The Norman Conquest*, London: Windmill Books, 2013, pp. 48–49.

8. Bates, D., "In search of the Normans", *BBC History Magazine*, volume 13, number 8, August 2012, p. 33.

9. Hargreaves, C., *Normandy*, London: New Holland Publishers, 2007, p. 29.

10. In 1066, Duke William outlined his claim to the English throne to the pope. Unfortunately, this document has not survived but the case seems to have rested on a promise of the crown made by Edward the Confessor and an oath to support this claim (later broken) by Harold Godwinson, the earl of Wessex. It also probably contained accusations of laxness in the Anglo-Saxon church that needed rectifying. See M. Morris, *The Norman Conquest*, pp. 142–143.

11. Ibid., p. 201.

12. Williams, A., A. P. Smyth and D. P. Kirby, *A Biographical Dictionary of Dark Age Britain: England, Scotland, and Wales, c. 500–c. 1050*, London: B. A. Seaby, 1991, p. 28.

13. Morris, M., *The Norman Conquest*, pp. 16–17.

14. John, E., *Reassessing Anglo-Saxon England*, Manchester: Manchester University Press, 1996, p. 180.

CHAPTER 7. THE CHRISTIAN VIKINGS OF DENMARK

1. http://www.medievalhistories.com/harold-bluetooth-coins-hoard-vendsyssel/ (Accessed November 2017).

2. http://en.natmus.dk/historical-knowledge/denmark/prehistoric-period-until-1050–ad/the-viking-age/the-monuments-at-jelling/the-jelling-stone/ (Accessed November 2017).

3. Graham-Campbell, J., *The Viking World*, London: Frances Lincoln, 2001, 3rd edn, p. 147.

4. Lund, N., "Scandinavia c. 700–1066", in R. Mckitterick, *The New Cambridge Medieval History II, c. 700–900*, Cambridge: Cambridge University Press, 1995, p. 216.

5. Ibid.

6. Ibid.

7. Ibid., p. 209.

8. Ibid.

9. Sawyer, P., "The process of Scandinavian Christianization in the tenth and eleventh centuries", in B. Sawyer, P. Sawyer and I. Wood (eds), *The Christianization of Scandinavia*, Alingas: Viktoria Bokförlag, 1987, p. 68.

10. Ibid.

11. Ibid.

12. Ibid, p. 69.

13. Ibid.

14. Ibid., p. 70.

15. Ibid., p. 80.

16. Roesdahl, E., *Viking Age Denmark*, London: British Museum Press, 1982, p. 177.

17. Sawyer, P., "The process of Scandinavian Christianization", p. 80.

18. Ibid., p. 80.

19. Whitelock, D. (ed.), *English Historical Documents, Volume I, c. 500–1042*, London: Eyre Methuen, 1979, p. 347.

20. Campbell, A. (ed. and transl.), *Encomium Emmae reginae*, Camden third series 72, London: Camden Classic Reprints, 1949, pp. 6–15.

21. Adam of Bremen, *History of the Archbishops of Hamburg-Bremen*, F. J. Tschan (transl.), Records of Civilization: Sources and Studies 53, New York: Columbia University Press, 1959, ii. 30.

22. Sawyer, P. H., "Swein Forkbeard and the historians", in I. Wood and

G. A. Loud (eds), *Church and Chronicle in the Middle Ages: Essays Presented to John Taylor*, London: Continuum, 1990, p. 37.

23. Ibid., p. 38.

24. Lawson, M. K., *Cnut: the Danes in England*, Harlow: Longman, 1993, pp. 93–94.

25. Ibid., p. 94.

26. Ibid., p. 96.

27. Saxo Grammaticus, *Danorum Regum* X. 16, E. Christensen (ed. and transl.), BAR International Series, 84, Oxford: BAR, 1980, pp. 31–34.

28. Lund, N., "Cnut's Danish Empire", in A. R. Rumble (ed.), *The Reign of Cnut: The King of England, Denmark and Norway*, London: Leicester University Press, 1994, p. 38.

29. Whitelock, D., *English Historical Documents*, pp. 476–477.

30. Sawyer, P. H., "Cnut's Scandinavian Empire", in A. R. Rumble (ed.), *The reign of Cnut: King of England, Denmark and Norway*, London: Leicester University Press, 1994, p. 19.

31. Ibid., p. 20.

32. Vollsnes, A. O. and B. Foster (transl.), *Ludvig Irgens-Jensen: The Life and Music of a Norwegian Composer*, London: Toccata Press, 2014, p. 153.

33. Campbell, W. M., "Queen Emma and Ælfgifu of Northampton: Canute the Great's women", *Mediaeval Scandinavia* 4, 1971, pp. 3–4.

34. Ibid., p. 75.

35. Wicker, N. L., "The Scandinavian Animal Styles in Response to Mediterranean and Christian Narrative Art", in M. Carver (ed.), *The Cross Goes North: Processes of Conversion in Northern Europe AD 300–1300*, Woodbridge: Boydell Press, 2005, p. 542.

36. Other examples of the cross alone (without a figure) have been found on other sites: some fifty miniature silver crosses and four hundred iron ones have so far been discovered from the Scandinavian Viking Age. See A. Winroth, *The Conversion of Scandinavia*, New Haven CT & London: Yale University Press, 2012, p. 134.

37. http://en.vikingemuseetladby.dk/about-the-museum/news/extraordinary-find-denmarks-oldest-crucifix (Accessed February 2017).

38. Ibid.

39. Fuglesang, S. H., "Crucifixion iconography in Viking Scandinavia", *Proceedings of the Eighth Viking Congress, Arhus 24–31 Aug. 1977,* 1981, p. 81.

40. Ibid., pp. 87–88.

41. Ibid., p. 88.

42. Ibid., p. 89.

CHAPTER 8. THE CHRISTIAN VIKINGS OF NORWAY

1. The date of the start of Harald Finehair's reign is uncertain. Various dates between 860 and 880 have been suggested. Even his death (though usually dated as 930) has, by some historians, been placed as late as 940. The most detailed account of his life is found in the much later account written by Snorri Sturluson, *Heimskringla*, although he also features in a number of other Icelandic sagas. See A. A. Somerville and R. A. McDonald (eds), *The Viking Age: A Reader,* Toronto: University of Toronto Press, 2010, pp. 434–439.

2. Strom, F., "Poetry as an instrument of propaganda", in U. Dronke et al (eds), *Speculum Norroenum: Norse studies in memory of Gabriel Turville-Petre,* Odense: Odense University Press, 1981, p. 442.

3. Williams, G., "Hákon Aðalsteins fóstri: aspects of Anglo-Saxon kingship in tenth century Norway", in L. E. M. Walker and T. R. Liska (eds), *The North Sea World in the Middle Ages. Studies in the Cultural History of North-western Europe,* Dublin: Four Courts Press, 2001, p. 119.

4. Ibid., p. 115.

5. Ibid.

6. Ibid.

7. Krag, C., "The early unification of Norway", in K. Helle (ed.), *The Cambridge History of Scandinavia Vol 1: Prehistory to 1520,* Cambridge: Cambridge University Press, 2003, p. 190

8. See O. Snorrason, and T. M. Andersson (transl.), *The Saga of Olaf Tryggvason,* Ithaca NY: Cornell University Press, 2003.

9. Nordeided, S. W., "Urbanism and Christianity in Norway", in

J. Sheehan and D. Ó Corráin (eds), *The Viking Age: Ireland and the West. Papers from the Proceedings of the Fifteenth Viking Congress, Cork, 18–27 August 2005*, Dublin: Four Courts Press, 2010, p. 253.

10. Birkeli, F., *Earliest Missionary Activities from England to Norway*, Nottingham: University of Nottingham Press, 1971, p. 27.

11. Sawyer, B. and P. Sawyer, "Scandinavia enters Christian Europe", in K. Helle (ed.), *The Cambridge History of Scandinavia, Volume I, Prehistory to 1520*, Cambridge: Cambridge University Press, 2003, p. 153.

12. Skre, D., "Missionary Activity in Early Medieval Norway", *Scandinavian Journal of History*, 23, 1998, p.18.

13. Bagge, S. and S. W. Nordeide, "The Kingdom of Norway", in N. Berend (ed.), *Christianization and the Rise of Christian Monarchy: Scandinavia, Central Europe and Rus' c. 900–1200*, Cambridge: Cambridge University Press, 2007, p. 131.

14. Nordeide, S. W., "Urbanism and Christianity in Norway", p. 251.

15. Bagge, S. and S. W. Nordeide, "The Kingdom of Norway", p. 133.

16. Birkeli, F., *Earliest Missionary Activities from England to Norway*, pp. 31–33.

17. Bagge, S. and S. W. Nordeide, "The Kingdom of Norway", p. 130.

18. Birkeli, F., *Earliest Missionary Activities from England to Norway*, p. 35.

19. Skre, D., "Missionary Activity in Early Medieval Norway", p. 18.

20. Toy, J., "St Botolph: An English Saint in Scandinavia", in M. Carver, *The Cross Goes North: Processes of Conversion in Northern Europe AD 300–1300*, Woodbridge: Boydell Press, 2005, pp. 567–570.

21. Sawyer, B. and P. Sawyer, "Scandinavia enters Christian Europe", p. 152.

22. Birkeli, F., *Earliest Missionary Activities from England to Norway*, p. 28.

23. Somerville, A. A. and R. A. McDonald (eds), *The Viking Age: A Reader*, Toronto: University of Toronto Press, 2014, 2nd edn, p. 408.

24. Edgington, S., "Siward – Sigurd – Sigfrid? The Career of an English Missionary in Scandinavia", *Northern Studies 26*, 1989, pp. 56–57.

25. Skre, D., "Missionary Activity in Early Medieval Norway", p. 10.

26. Bagge, S. and S. W. Nordeide, "The Kingdom of Norway", p. 135.

27. Hagland, J. R., "The Christianization of Norway and possible influences from the eastern churches", *Palaeobulgarica* 20:3, 1996, p. 11.

28. Bagge, S. and S. W. Nordeide, "The Kingdom of Norway", p. 136.

29. Ibid., p. 139.

CHAPTER 9. THE CHRISTIAN VIKINGS OF SWEDEN

1. The poem called *Ynglingatal* (composed sometime between c.900 and 1100), the *Västgötalagen* or *Westrogothic law* (compiled in the early thirteenth century) and the *Gutasaga*, which recounts the history of Gotland before the conversion to Christianity (again thirteenth century).

2. For a succinct overview of Viking Age Scandinavia see J. Haywood, *The Penguin Historical Atlas of the Vikings*, London: Penguin, 1995, pp. 28–33; see also A. Forte, R. Oram and F. Pedersen (eds), *Viking Empires*, Cambridge: Cambridge University Press, 2005, pp. 7–53.

3. Haywood, J., *The Penguin Historical Atlas of the Vikings*, p. 32.

4. Ibid., p. 116.

5. Sawyer, P., "The Viking Legacy", in P. Sawyer (ed.), *The Oxford Illustrated History of the Vikings*, Oxford: Oxford University Press, 1997, p. 258.

6. Quoted in E. Orrman, "Church and society", in K. Helle (ed.), *The Cambridge History of Scandinavia, volume I*, Cambridge: Cambridge University Press, 2003, p. 421.

7. Ibid., p. 422.

8. Ibid., pp. 422–425.

9. Lager, L., "Art as a medium in defining 'us' and 'them'", in J. Staeker (ed.), *The European Frontier*, Symposium Lund 2000, CCC-papers, Lund: Lund Studies in Medieval Archaeology, 2000, p. 154.

10. Wicker, N. L., "The Scandinavian Animal Styles in Response to Mediterranean and Christian Narrative Art", in M. Carver (ed.), *The Cross Goes North: Processes of Conversion in Northern Europe AD 300–1300*, Woodbridge: Boydell Press, 2005, p. 544.

11. Nylen, E. and J. P. Lamm, *Stones, Ships, Symbols: The Picture Stones of Gotland from the Viking Age and Before*, Möklinta: Gidlunds, 1988, p. 76.

12. Gräslund, A. S., "Pagan and Christian in the Age of Conversion", in J. E. Knirk and C. Blindheim (eds), *Proceedings of the Tenth Viking Congress, Larkollen, Norway 1985*, Oslo: Universitetets oldsaksamling, 1987, p. 86.

13. Sawyer, B., "Viking-Age rune-stones as a crisis symptom", *Norwegian Archaeological Review* 24.2, 1991, p. 101.

14. Ibid.

15. Ibid.

16. Herschend, F., *The Recasting of Symbolic Value: Three Case Studies on Rune Stones*, Uppsala: Societas Archaeologica Upsaliensis, 1994, p. 26.

17. Ibid, p. 27.

18. Sawyer, B., "Viking-Age rune-stones as a crisis symptom", p. 102.

19. Ibid.

20. Ibid., p. 103.

21. Lager, L., "Runestones and the Conversion of Sweden", in M. Carver (ed.), *The Cross Goes North: Processes of Conversion in Northern Europe AD 300–1300*, Woodbridge: Boydell Press, 2005, p. 500.

22. Ibid.

23. Sawyer, B., "Viking-Age rune-stones as a crisis symptom", p. 102.

24. Ibid.

25. Lager, L., "Runestones and the Conversion of Sweden", p. 504.

26. Ibid., p. 505.

27. Sawyer, B., *The Viking-Age Rune-Stones: Custom and Commemoration in Early Medieval Scandinavia*, Oxford: Oxford University Press, 2000, p. 140.

28. Ibid.

29. Gräslund, A. S., "Pagan and Christian in the Age of Conversion", p. 92.

30. Ibid.

31. Gräslund, A. S., "The Role of Scandinavian Women in Christianisation: The Neglected Evidence", in M. Carver (ed.), *The Cross Goes North: Processes of Conversion in Northern Europe AD 300–1300*, Woodbridge: Boydell Press, 2005, p. 492.

32. Sawyer, B., *The Viking-Age Rune-Stones*, p. 140.

33. Gräslund, A. S., "The Role of Scandinavian Women in Christianisation", p. 494.

34. Ibid.

35. Sawyer, B., *The Viking-Age Rune-Stones*, p.128.

36. Ibid.

37. Ibid.

CHAPTER 10. VIKINGS IN THE EAST: CHRISTIAN VIKINGS IN RUSSIA AND THE BYZANTINE EMPIRE

1. Somerville, A. A. and R. A. McDonald (eds), *The Viking Age: A Reader*, Toronto: University of Toronto Press, 2014, p. 290.

2. Ibid.

3. Ibid

4. Peterson, G. D., *Vikings and Goths: A History of Ancient and Medieval Sweden*, Jefferson NC: McFarland, 2016, p. 230.

5. For a succinct overview of the expedition see K. Hjardar and V. Vike, *Vikings at War*, Oxford: Casemate, 2016, p. 367.

6. See J. Hayward, *The Penguin Historical Atlas of the Vikings*, London: Penguin, 1995, p. 100, for a brief outline of the roots of these terms.

7. Unlike the city, this Russian region never changed its name back to St Petersburg.

8. Blanchard, I., *Mining, Metallurgy and Minting in the Middle Ages*, Stuttgart: Franz Steiner Verlag, 2001, p. 562.

9. http://islamicceramics.ashmolean.org/Samanids/shortage.htm (Accessed August 2017).

10. Ferguson, R., *The Hammer and the Cross*, London: Penguin, 2010, pp. 129–131, gives a good account of the events in one of the well-known traditions.

11. Ibid, p. 131.

12. Colucci, M., "The Image of Western Christianity in the Culture of Kievan Rus", *Harvard Ukrainian Studies*, 12/13, 1989, pp. 576–586.

13. Page, R. I., *Chronicles of the Vikings*, London: British Museum Press, 1995, p. 84.

14. Noonan, T. S., "Scandinavians in European Russia", in P. Sawyer (ed.), *The Oxford Illustrated History of the Vikings*, Oxford: Oxford University Press, 1997, p. 151.

15. Ibid.

16. Page, R. I., *Chronicles of the Vikings*, p. 101.

17. Holman, K., *The A to Z of the Vikings*, Lanham MD, Plymouth: Scarecrow Press, 2003, p. 196.

18. The following quotes from the thirteenth-century account are from R. I. Page, *Chronicles of the Vikings*, pp. 101–104.

19. Ibid., p. 84.

20. Ibid., p. 87.

21. Gräslund, A. S. and L. Lager, "Runestones and Christianity", in S. Brink and N. Price (eds), *The Viking World*, Abingdon: Routledge, 2008, p. 634.

22. Page, R. I., *Chronicles of the Vikings*, p. 85.

CHAPTER 11. CHRISTIAN VIKINGS OF THE NORTH ATLANTIC

1. Miller, W. I., *Bloodtaking and Peacemaking: Feud, Law, and Society in Saga Iceland*, Chicago IL: University of Chicago Press, 1990, p. 14.

2. Miller, W. I., *Bloodtaking and Peacemaking* (Laxdæla saga, 2:4–5).

3. Ibid., p. 15.

4. Ibid.

5. Ibid., p. 171.

6. Byock, J., *Viking Age Iceland*, London: Penguin, 2001, p. 9.

7. Vésteinsson, O., "Patterns of Settlement in Iceland: A Study in Prehistory", *Saga-Book* 25.1, 1998, p. 20.

8. Vésteinsson, O., "The Archaeology of *Landnám*", in W. W. Fitzhugh and E. War (eds), *Vikings. The North Atlantic Saga*, Washington DC: Smithsonian Institute Press, 2000, pp. 172–73.

9. Ibid., p. 26.

10. Þorláksson, H., "The Icelandic Commonwealth Period: Building a New Society", in W. W. Fitzhugh and E. War (eds), *Vikings: The North Atlantic Saga*, Washington DC: Smithsonian Institute Press, 2000, p. 181.

11. Byock, J., *Viking Age Iceland*, p. 1.

12. Vésteinsson, O., "A Divided Society: Peasants and the Aristocracy in Medieval Iceland", *Viking and Medieval Scandinavia*, volume 3, 2007, p. 117.

13. Ibid., p. 131.

14. Ferguson, R., *The Hammer and the Cross*, London: Penguin, 2010, pp. 300–301.

15. Fidjestøl, B., "Pagan beliefs and Christian impact: The Contribution of Scaldic Studies", in A. Faulkes and R. Perkins (eds), *Viking Revaluations: Viking Society Centenary Symposium 14–15 May 1992*, London: Viking Society for Northern Research, 1993, p. 102.

16. Attwood, A., "Christian poetry", in R. McTurk (ed.), *A Companion to Old Norse-Icelandic Literature and Culture*, Oxford: Wiley-Blackwell, 2010, p. 48.

17. http://skaldic.abdn.ac.uk/m.php?p=verse&v=t&i=2509 (Accessed November 2017).

18. Rafnsson, S., "The Atlantic Islands", in P. Sawyer (ed.), *The Oxford Illustrated History of the Vikings*, Oxford: Oxford University Press, 1997, p. 117.

19. Lousdal Jensen, T., "New signs of pre-Viking life on the Faroe Islands", *Science Nordic*, 28 January 2013, http://sciencenordic.com/new-signs-pre-viking-life-faroe-islands (Accessed November 2017).

20. Rafnsson, S., "The Atlantic Islands", p. 117.

21. Stefansson, M., "The Norse island communities of the western ocean", in K. Helle (ed.), *The Cambridge History of Scandinavia, Volume I, Prehistory to 1520*, Cambridge: Cambridge University Press, 2003, p. 213.

22. See Abrams, L., "Early Religious Practice in the Greenland Settlement", *Journal of the North Atlantic*, 2009–2010, pp. 52–65.

CHAPTER 12. THE FIRST AMERICAN CHRISTIANS

1. Ingstad, H. and A. Stine Ingstad, *The Viking Discovery of America: The Excavation of a Norse Settlement at L'Anse aux Meadows, Newfoundland*, St John's, Newfoundland: Breakwater Books, 2000, p. 141. (Previously published in F. Hødnebø and J. Kristjánsson (eds), *The Viking Discovery of America*, Oslo: J. M. Stenersens, 1991.)

2. See H. Ingstad and A. Stine Ingstad, *The Viking Discovery of America*.

3. http://whc.unesco.org/en/list/4/ (Accessed September 2017).

4. Kolodny, A., *In Search of First Contact: The Vikings of Vinland, the Peoples of the Dawnland, and the Anglo-American Anxiety of Discovery*, Durham NC: Duke University Press, 2012, p. 95.

5. http://whc.unesco.org/en/list/4/ (Accessed September 2017).

6. Kunz, K., "The Saga of the Greenlanders", in Ö. Thorsson, *The Sagas of Icelanders*, London: Penguin Books, 2001, p. 640, footnote.

7. For an accessible account of this discovery see H. Ingstad and A. Stine Ingstad, *The Viking Discovery of America*.

8. Taylor, P. B., "The Hønen runes: A survey", *Neophilologus*, volume 60, issue 1, January 1976, pp. 1–7. See also C. Cavaleri, "The Vínland Sagas as Propaganda for the Christian Church: Freydís and Gudríd as Paradigms for Eve and the Virgin Mary", Master's thesis, University of Oslo, 2008.

9. See I. Hahn, "Linguistic Research on the Kensington Runestone", *Arctic Studies Centre Newsletter*, Smithsonian Institution, National Museum of Natural History, December 2003, Number 11, pp. 12–15, https://naturalhistory.si.edu/arctic/html/pdf/news03.pdf (Accessed September 2017).

10. The outline of the accounts in the two sagas, that follows, is indebted to the excellent overview provided by K. Kunz, "The Vinland Sagas", in Ö. Thorsson (ed.), *The Sagas of Icelanders*, London: Penguin Books, 2001, pp. 632–635.

11. Kunz, K., "The Saga of the Greenlanders", in Ö. Thorsson (ed.), *The Sagas of Icelanders*, London: Penguin Books, 2001, p. 636.

12. Ibid., p. 643.

13. Kunz, K., "Eirik the Red's Saga", in Ö. Thorsson (ed.), *The Sagas of Icelanders*, London: Penguin Books, 2001, p. 653.

14. Ibid., p. 658.

15. Ibid., p. 660.

16. Ibid., p. 663.

17. Ibid., p. 668.

CHAPTER 13. A CHRISTIAN VIKING KING
OF ENGLAND

1. See M. Whittock and H. Whittock,*1016 and 1066: Why the Vikings Caused the Norman Conquest*, Ramsbury: Robert Hale, 2016.

2. See Rex, P., *Edgar: King of the English 959–75*, Stroud: Tempus, 2007.

3. For accessible overviews of his reign see A. Williams, *Æthelred the Unready: The Ill-Counselled King*, London: Hambledon Continuum, 2003; and R. Lavelle, *Aethelred II, King of the English*, Stroud: The History Press, 2008.

4. Roach, L., *Æthelred the Unready*, New Haven & London: Yale University Press, 2017, pp. 279–283.

5. Ibid., p. 246; and he provides a fascinating examination of these apocalyptic views generally, in: "Apocalypse and Invasion 1002–9", pp. 186–251.

6. Haywood, J., *The Penguin Historical Atlas of the Vikings*, London: Penguin Books, 1995, p. 108.

7. For a detailed exploration of the use of silver in the Viking Age see G. Williams and J. Graham-Campbell (eds) *Silver Economy in the Viking Age*, Walnut Creek, CA: Left Coast Press Inc., 2007.

8. Page, R. I., *Reading the Past: Runes*, London: British Museum Publications, 1987, p. 46. The reference to *danegeld* is a little puzzling as this term was not used in England until after 1066. Perhaps this particular runestone was a later memorial to a much earlier event.

9. Graham-Campbell, J., *The Viking World*, London: Frances Lincoln Limited, 2001, p. 164.

10. Hunter Blair, P. and S. Keynes, *An Introduction to Anglo-Saxon England*, Cambridge: Cambridge University Press, 3rd edn, 2003, pp. 96–97.

11. Whitelock, D. (ed.), *English Historical Documents, Volume I, c. 500–1042,* London: Eyre Methuen, 1979, p. 239.

12. Boyle, A., "Death on the Ridgeway. The Excavation of a Viking Mass Burial", Danes in Wessex conference, Wessex Centre of History and Archaeology, University of Winchester, September 2011; L. Loe, "Death on Ridgeway Hill: How Science unlocked the secrets of a mass grave", *Current Archaeology*, February 2015, issue 299, pp. 38–43.

13. *British Archaeology*, July/August 2012, Number 125, p. 8.

14. An accessible overview of this event and the start of the cult of St Ælfheah can be found in S. Foot, "Canterbury's other martyr", *BBC History Magazine*, volume 13, number 4, April 2012, pp. 30–31. Foot suggests that the traditional account of his death may have a basis in reality. This seems a reasonable conclusion, since the event was recounted in near-contemporary accounts.

15. Whitelock, D., *English Historical Documents*, p. 245.

16. Cusack, C. M., *The Rise of Christianity in Northern Europe, 300–1000,* London: Cassell, 1999, pp. 147–148.

17. Giandrea, M. F., *Episcopal Culture in Late Anglo-Saxon England,* Woodbridge: Boydell Press, 2007, p. 58.

18. Lawson, M. K., *Cnut: England's Viking King,* Stroud: History Press, 2011, p. 90.

19. We should really refer to these territories in Central Europe as "the Empire" or "the Roman Empire". After the crowning of Charlemagne, by Pope Leo III in 800, the Roman title of emperor in Western Europe was revived and then gained a long-lasting foundation on the crowning of Otto I as emperor in 962. After 1157 the term "holy" was used and, after 1254, the form "Holy Roman Empire" came into use. However, there is some justification in using the term before these dates, to avoid confusion with the earlier Roman Empire and the Eastern Roman Empire (the Byzantine).

20. http://blogs.bl.uk/digitisedmanuscripts/2011/06/the-new-minster-liber-vitae.html (Accessed October 2017).

21. Henry of Huntingdon, *The Chronicle of Henry of Huntingdon, comprising The History of England, From the Invasion of Julius Caesar to the accession of Henry II*, T. A. M. Forester (ed. and transl.), London: Henry, G. Bohn, 1853, p. 199.

22. Trow, M. J., *Cnut: Emperor of the North*, Stroud: The History Press, 2005, p. 125.

23. See: http://www.bbc.co.uk/news/magazine-13524677, "Is King Canute Misunderstood?", 26 May 2011, for the way the tradition has been misunderstood by some in the press and politics (Accessed March 2018).

24. Trow, M. J., *Cnut: Emperor of the North*, p. 125.

25. Translated by Elisabeth Okasha, in L. Watts, et al, "Kirkdale – The Inscriptions", *Medieval Archaeology* 41 (1997), p. 81.

26. See J. Blair, "The Kirkdale Dedication Inscription and its Latin Models: *Romanitas* in Late Anglo-Saxon Yorkshire", in A. Hall, O. Timofeeva and A. Kiricsi (eds), *Interfaces Between Language and Culture in Medieval England: A Festschrift for Matti Kilpio*, Leiden: Brill, 2010, pp. 139–145.

27. Bolton, T., *The Empire of Cnut the Great: Conquest and the Consolidation of Power in Northern Europe in the Early Eleventh Century*, Leiden: Brill, 2009, pp. 209–211.

28. Jesch, J., "Scandinavians and cultural Paganism in Late Anglo-Saxon England", in P. Cavill (ed.), *The Christian Tradition in Anglo-Saxon England*, Cambridge: D. S. Brewer, 2004, pp. 58–60.

29. Ferguson, R., *The Hammer and the Cross*, London: Penguin, 2010, p. 341.

30. Jesch, J., "Scandinavians and cultural Paganism in Late Anglo-Saxon England", p. 61.

31. Ibid., p. 67.

Chapter 14. Christian Jarls of the Northern and Western Isles

1. Sveinsson, E. O., "Orkney-Shetland-Iceland", *The Viking Congress Lerwick, July 1950,* (1954), Aberdeen University Studies, 132, p. 271.

2. Thompson, W. P. L., *History of Orkney*, Edinburgh: The Mercat Press, 1987, p. 54.

3. Ferguson, R., *The Hammer and the Cross*, London: Penguin, 2010, p. 69.

4. Barrett, J. H., "Christian and Pagan Practice during the Conversion of Viking Age Orkney and Shetland", in M. Carver (ed.), *The Cross Goes North: Processes of Conversion in Northern Europe, AD 300–1300*, Woodbridge: Boydell & Brewer, 2005, p. 211.

5. Morris, C. D., "Viking Orkney: A Survey", in C. Renfrew (ed.), *The Prehistory of Orkney*, Edinburgh: Edinburgh University Press, 1985, p. 212.

6. Woolf, A., *From Pictland to Alba, 789–1070*, Edinburgh: Edinburgh University Press, 2007, p. 307.

7. Stefansson, M., "The Norse island communities of the western ocean", in K. Helle (ed.), *The Cambridge History of Scandinavia, Vol.1: Prehistory to 1520*, 2003, p. 206.

8. Sveinsson, E. O., "Orkney-Shetland-Iceland", p. 274.

9. Thompson, W. P. L., *History of Orkney*, p. 46.

10. Ibid., p. 39.

11. Ibid., p. 63.

12. Ibid., p. 55.

13. Forte, A., R. Oram and F. Pedersen, *Viking Empires*, Cambridge: Cambridge University Press, 2005, p. 275 and note 37.

14. For an overview of the debate see J. H. Barrett, "Christian and Pagan Practice during the Conversion of Viking Age Orkney and Shetland", pp. 219–221.

15. Sawyer, P., *Kings and Vikings: Scandinavia and Europe AD 700–1100*, London: Methuen, 1982, p. 39.

16. Stefansson, M., "The Norse island communities of the western ocean", p. 205.

17. Sawyer, P., *Kings and Vikings*, p. 34.

18. Thompson, W. P. L., *History of Orkney*, p. 52.

19. Ibid., *History of Orkney*, p. 57.

20. Haywood, J., *The Penguin Historical Atlas of the Vikings*, London: Penguin, 1995, p. 76.

21. Ibid.

22. Woolf, A., *From Pictland to Alba*, p. 276.

23. Gammeltoft, P., "Scandinavian Naming-systems in the Hebrides", in G. Williams (ed.), *West over Sea: Studies in Scandinavian Sea-Borne Expansion and Settlement Before 1300*, Leiden: Brill, 2007, p. 480.

24. Liestøl, A., "An Iona rune stone and the world of Man and the Isles", in C. Fell et al (eds), *The Viking Age in the Isle of Man*, London: Viking Society for Northern Research, 1983, p. 87.

25. Megaw, B. R. S., "Norsemen and native in the Kingdom of the Isles. A re-assessment of the Manx evidence", *Scottish Studies*, 20, 1976, p. 5.

26. Gelling, P. S., "Celtic Continuity in the Isle of Man", in L. Laing (ed.), *Studies in Celtic Survival*, BAR British Series 37, Oxford: British Archaeological Reports, 1977, p. 79.

27. Kinvig, R. H., *The Isle of Man: A Social, Cultural and Political History*, Liverpool: Liverpool University Press, 1975, p. 68.

28. McDonald, R. A., *Manx Kingship in its Irish Sea Setting, 1187–1229: King Rǫgnvaldr and the Crovan dynasty*, Dublin: Four Courts Press, 2007, p. 40.

A FINAL THOUGHT:
THE VIKING WORLD IN 1150

1. Forte, A., R. Oram and F. Pedersen, *Viking Empires*, Cambridge: Cambridge University Press, 2005, p. 288.

2. Haywood, J., *The Penguin Historical Atlas of the Vikings*, London: Penguin, 1995, p. 130.

3. Including introduction of tithes and monastic reform.

4. It was the first Scandinavian one and this promotion secured its independence from Hamburg-Bremen.

5. Murray, A. V., *The Crusades: An Encyclopedia, Volume 4*, Santa Barbara CA: ABC-CLIO, 2006, p. 1126; see also L. B. Orfield, *The Growth of Scandinavian Law*, Philadelphia PA: University of Pennsylvania Press, 1953, p. 230.

Bibliography

Abram, C., *Myths of the Pagan North: The gods of the Norsemen*, London: Hambledon Continuum, 2011

Birkeli, F., *Earliest Missionary Activities from England to Norway*, Nottingham: University of Nottingham Press, 1971

Bolton, T., *The Empire of Cnut the Great: Conquest and the Consolidation of Power in Northern Europe in the Early Eleventh Century*, Leiden: Brill, 2009

Brink, S. and N. Price (eds), *The Viking World*, Abingdon: Routledge, 2008

Byock, J., *Viking Age Iceland*, London: Penguin, 2001

Carroll, J., S. H. Harrison and G. Williams, *The Vikings in Britain and Ireland*, London: British Museum Press, 2014

Carver, M. (ed.), *The Cross Goes North: Processes of Conversion in Northern Europe, AD 300–1300*, Woodbridge: Boydell & Brewer, 2005

Cusack, C. M., *The Rise of Christianity in Northern Europe, 300–1000*, London: Cassell, 1999

Ferguson, R., *The Hammer and The Cross: A New History of the Vikings*, London: Penguin, 2010

Fitzhugh, W. W. and E. War (eds), *Vikings. The North Atlantic Saga*, Washington DC: Smithsonian Institute Press, 2000

Forte, A., R. Oram and F. Pedersen (eds), *Viking Empires*, Cambridge: Cambridge University Press, 2005

Graham-Campbell, J., *Viking Art*, London: Thames & Hudson, 2013

Griffiths, D., *Vikings of the Irish Sea*, Stroud: History Press, 2010

Hart, C., *The Danelaw*, London: Hambledon, 1992

Haywood, J., *The Penguin Historical Atlas of the Vikings*, London: Penguin, 1995

Helle, K. (ed.), *The Cambridge History of Scandinavia, Volume I, Prehistory to 1520*, Cambridge: Cambridge University Press, 2003

Hjardar, K. and V. Vike, *Vikings at War*, Oxford: Casemate, 2016

Holman, K., *The Northern Conquest: Vikings in Britain and Ireland*, Oxford: Signal Books, 2007

Ingstad, H. and A. Stine Ingstad, *The Viking Discovery of America: The Excavation of a Norse Settlement at L'Anse aux Meadows, Newfoundland*, St John's, Newfoundland: Breakwater Books, 2000

Lawson, M. K., *Cnut: the Danes in England*, Harlow: Longman, 1993

McDonald, R. A., *Manx Kingship in its Irish Sea Setting, 1187–1229: King Rǫgnvaldr and the Crovan dynasty*, Dublin: Four Courts Press, 2007

Morris, M., *The Norman Conquest*, London: Windmill Books, 2013

Page, R. I., *Reading the Past: Runes*, London: British Museum Publications, 1987

Page, R. I., *Chronicles of the Vikings*, London: British Museum Press, 1995

Parker, P., *The Northmen's Fury: A History of the Viking World*, London: Vintage, 2015

Peterson, G. D., *Vikings and Goths: A History of Ancient and Medieval Sweden*, Jefferson NC: McFarland, 2016

Richards, J. D., *Viking Age England*, London: English Heritage/ Batsford, 1991

Roesdahl, E., *Viking Age Denmark*, London: British Museum Press, 1982

Rumble, A. R. (ed.), *The Reign of Cnut: King of England, Denmark and Norway*, London: Leicester University Press, 1994

Sawyer, B., P. Sawyer and I. Wood (eds), *The Christianization of*

Scandinavia, Alingas: Viktoria Bokförlag, 1987

Sawyer, B., *The Viking-Age Rune-Stones: Custom and Commemoration in Early Medieval Scandinavia*, Oxford: Oxford University Press, 2000

Sawyer, P., *Kings and Vikings: Scandinavia and Europe AD 700–1100*, London: Methuen, 1982

Sawyer, P. (ed.), *The Oxford Illustrated History of the Vikings*, Oxford: Oxford University Press, 1997

Somerville, A. A. and R. A. McDonald (eds), *The Viking Age: A Reader*, Toronto: University of Toronto Press, 2014

Thompson, W. P. L., *History of Orkney*, Edinburgh: The Mercat Press, 1987

Thorsson, Ö. (ed.), *The Sagas of Icelanders*, London: Penguin Books, 2001

Trow, M. J., *Cnut: Emperor of the North*, Stroud: The History Press, 2005

Whitelock, D. (ed.), *English Historical Documents*, Volume I, c. 500–1042, London: Eyre Methuen, 1979

Whittock, M. and H. Whittock, *1016 and 1066: Why the Vikings Caused the Norman Conquest*, Ramsbury: Robert Hale, 2016

Whittock, M. and H. Whittock, *Norse Myths and Legends: Viking tales of gods and heroes*, London: Little, Brown, 2017

Woolf, A., *From Pictland to Alba, 789–1070*, Edinburgh: Edinburgh University Press, 2007

Index